Against All Odds:
Aiding Political Parties in Georgia and Ukraine

Cover design: René Staelenberg, Amsterdam

ISBN 978 90 5629 631 5
NUR 697

© Max Bader / Vossiuspers UvA – Amsterdam University Press, 2010

Against All Odds:
Aiding Political Parties in Georgia and Ukraine

ACADEMISCH PROEFSCHRIFT

ter verkrijging van de graad van doctor
aan de Universiteit van Amsterdam
op gezag van de Rector Magnificus
prof. dr. D.C. van der Boom
ten overstaan van een door het college voor promoties
ingestelde commissie,
in het openbaar te verdedigen in de Agnietenkapel
op donderdag 3 juni 2010, te 12:00 uur

door

Max Bader

geboren te Breda

Promotiecommissie:

Promotor:	Prof. dr. A.W.M. Gerrits
Co-promotor:	P. Burnell, Phd., DLitt.
Overige leden:	Prof. dr. I.C. van Biezen
	Dr. A. Freyberg-Inan
	Dr. M. de Goede
	Prof. dr. M. Kemper
	Prof. dr. J.A. Verbeek

Faculteit der Geesteswetenschappen

TABLE OF CONTENTS

ACKNOWLEDGEMENTS

Many thanks to my supervisor André Gerrits and my co-supervisor Peter Burnell for the great support, inspiring discussions, and valuable comments over the past three years.

My gratitude also extends to Annette Freyberg-Inan, Marieke de Goede, Maja Nenadović, and Marlene Spoerri for reading and commenting on the manuscript.

I gratefully acknowledge funding for this research by the Netherlands Organization for Scientific Research (NWO) within the framework of the project *International intervention, democracy and political parties: the external dimension of democratization processes in the Balkans and the former Soviet Union*.

Max Bader
Amsterdam, November 2009

LIST OF FIGURES AND TABLES

LIST OF ABBREVIATIONS

AMS	Alfred Mozer Stichting
BMZ	Bundesministerium für wirtschaftliche Zusammenarbeit und Entwicklung (Federal Ministry for Economic Cooperation and Development)
BYuT	Yulia Tymoshenko Bloc (Blok Yulii Tymoshenko)
CDS	Christian-Democratic Union (Ukraine) (Khristian'sko-Demokratichnyi Soiuz)
CDUG	Christian-Democratic Union of Georgia
CEE	Central and Eastern Europe
CEPPS	Consortium for Elections and Political Process Strengthening
CIPDD	Caucasus Institute for Peace Democracy and Development
CP	Conservative Party (Georgia)
CVU	Committee of Voters of Ukraine
CUG	Citizens' Union of Georgia
DG	Democracy and Governance
EFS	Eduardo Frei Stichting
ENP	Effective Number of Parties
ENP	European Neighborhood Policy
ENPI	European Neighborhood and Partnership Instrument
EU	European Union
FES	Friedrich Ebert Stiftung
FNG	For a New Georgia
FNS	Friedrich Naumann Stiftung für die Freiheit
FOIA	Freedom of Information Act
FSU	Former Soviet Union
IDEA	Institute for Democracy and Electoral Assistance
IFES	International Foundation for Electoral Systems
IGO	Intergovernmental organization
IRI	International Republican Institute
IWSG	Industry Will Save Georgia
KAS	Konrad Adenauer Stiftung
KPU	Communist Party of Ukraine (Kommunistichna Partiia Ukrainy)
KUN	Congress of Ukrainian Nationalists (Kongres Ukrainskykh Natsionalistov)
LP	Labor Party
MP	Member of Parliament
MR	Young Rukh (Molodyi Rukh)
NATO	North Atlantic Treaty Organization
NDI	National Democratic Institute for International Affairs
NDP	National-Democratic Party (Georgia)
NDP	People's Democratic Party (Ukraine) (Narodno-Demokratichna Partiia)
NGNI	New Georgia New Initiative
NIMD	Netherlands Institute for Multi-party Democracy
NIS	Newly Independent States

NRP	New Rights Party
NRU	People's Movement of Ukraine (Narodnyi Rukh Ukrainy)
NSNU	People's Union Our Ukraine (Narodnyi Soiuz Ukrainy)
NU	Our Ukraine (bloc) (Nasha Ukraina)
NUNS	Our Ukraine - People's Self-Defense (Nasha Ukraine – Narodnaia Samooborona)
ODIHR	Office for Democratic Institutions and Human Rights
OSCE	Organization for Security and Cooperation in Europe
PP	People's Party (Georgia)
PPPU	Party of Industrials and Entrepreneurs of Ukraine (Partiia Promyslovtsiv i Pidpryiemtsev Ukrainy)
PR	proportional representation
PRP	Party for Reform and Order (Partiia Reformy i Poriadok)
PRU	Party of the Regions (Partiia Regionov Ukrainy)
RPG	Republican Party of Georgia
SDPU	Social Democratic Party of Ukraine (Sotsial-Demokratichna Partiia Ukrainy)
SDPU (o)	Social Democratic Party of Ukraine (united) (Sotsial-Demokratichna Partiia Ukrainy) (ob'iednana)
SI	Socialist International
SMD	single-member district
SPU	Socialist Party of Ukraine (Sotialistichna Partiia Ukrainy)
TACIS	Technical Assistance to the Commonwealth of Independent States
ToT	training-of-trainers
UNM	United National Movement
U.S	United States
USAID	United States Agency for International Development
USDP	Ukrainian Social-Democratic Party
USG	United States Government
VVD	Volkspartij voor Vrijheid en Democratie (People's Party for Freedom and Democracy)
ZYeU	For a United Ukraine (Za Yedinu Ukrainu)

Let me now take a more comprehensive view, and warn you in the most solemn manner against the baneful effects of the Spirit of Party, generally.

This Spirit, unfortunately, is inseparable from our nature, having its root in the strongest passions of the human Mind. It exists under different shapes in all Governments, more or less stifled, controuled, or repressed; but in those of the popular form it is seen in its greatest rankness and is truly their worst enemy.

The alternate domination of one faction over another, sharpened by the spirit of revenge natural to party dissention, which in different ages and countries has perpetrated the most horrid enormities, is itself a frightful despotism. But this leads at length to a more formal and permanent despotism.

-George Washington

Under democracy one party always devotes its chief energies to trying to prove that the other party is unfit to rule - and both commonly succeed, and are right.

-H.L. Mencken

Хотели как лучше, а получилось как всегда (they wanted do as good as possible, but it turned out like always)

-В.С. Черномырдин

If you think there's a solution, you're part of the problem.

-George Carlin

INTRODUCTION

Following the demise of communist regimes in Eastern Europe, international actors moved into the region to help the post-communist states and their societies break away from the legacy of authoritarian rule and let democracy take root. In nearly all post-communist states, political parties were among the recipients of the new wave of democracy assistance by international actors. Assistance to political parties, naturally, has been guided by the expectation that the assistance was indeed well-positioned to generate real effects on political parties. While parties, individual or several, were the immediate targets of assistance programs, the ultimate objective of assistance was to contribute to the emergence of party systems characterized by a degree of stability and adherence to democratic standards by all significant parties. Consistent with the failure of democratic transitions in most of the former Soviet Union (FSU), however, democratic party systems in that region did not crystallize, and assistance to political parties was unable to contribute to the accumulation of a mass of viable, democratic, and representative parties. This thesis is concerned with the question why party assistance over the course of the second decade of multi-party politics in Georgia and Ukraine failed to have a substantial positive impact.

Due to a high degree of party turnover in both Georgia and Ukraine, much assistance, in practical terms, throughout the years has been rendered futile. Of the five forces[1] that were elected to the current convocation of the Verkhovna Rada of Ukraine, only one - the Communist Party of Ukraine - was also present ten years ago, and ironically, this party has barely received assistance from Western organizations. In Georgia, none of the forces present in the 2008 parliament was in parliament ten years earlier. Georgian parties which have survived as well as new parties are said to suffer from largely the same flaws that parties suffered from in the 1990s (Dolidze 2005). In 2009, a well-known Georgian political scientist termed the political party system 'embryonic at best' (Nodia 2009). The weakness of parties in Georgia has also been noted by donors and providers of political party assistance. An evaluation of USAID-funded Democracy and Governance programs in Georgia in 2002 noted that 'Georgia's party system remains weak, inchoate and unstable. Parties and parliamentary factions form, transform, and quickly disintegrate [...]' (ARD, Inc. 2002: v). A 2006 evaluation of party assistance by Dutch party institutes commented: 'Political parties actually hardly exist in Georgia. Political movements are in fact more or less loyal clans around individididuals' (Verheije et al. 2006: 59).[2]

In Ukraine, a modicum of continuity in political party development has become discernable in the new century, especially since the orange Revolution (Wilson and Birch 2007). Still, a noted expert on Ukraine in 2007 speaks of 'the incredible weakness of political parties in Ukraine' (D'Anieri 2007: 43), and in a 2008 scholarly article it is argued that 'Ukraine's party system is undeveloped and fluid' (Slomczynski et al. 2008: 93). In 2009, Our Ukraine, the political force that initially as an electoral bloc, and later as a party had been the biggest recipient of party assistance since the beginning of the decade, was on the brink of disintegration (Topolianskiy 2009). The negative assessment of Ukrainian parties is echoed in writings by the donors and providers of political party assistance. A work plan for 2006 of the International Republican Institute remarks: 'Though almost 100 political parties are registered in Ukraine, few are anything more than personality-driven organizations' (IRI 2005d: 4) and '[...]few political parties have developed into well-defined ideological forces that could guide the country's path' (idem: 2). A 2008 publication by the Konrad Adenauer Stiftung argued that, prior the Orange Revolution, parties in Ukraine had only 'peripheral significance'. Moreover, 'The parties of Ukraine still contain many features of projects. They are first and foremost personality-centered networks, which are strongly interwoven with the economic interests of their leaders' (KAS 2008a: 32).[3]

These assessments of the state of party development in Georgia and Ukraine suggest that party assistance has been ineffectual in engendering durable change in Georgian and Ukrainian parties. In a most general formulation, party assistance seeks to contribute to the development of stable, democratic, and representative parties. Accordingly, the effectiveness of assistance is measured by the degree to which recipient parties become more stable, democratic, and representative. The limited effectiveness of party assistance in Georgia and Ukraine confirms rather than disconfirms the observations of those who have written about party assistance. Carothers (2006a: 162) finds that assistance to parties 'rarely has transformative impact, despite the hopes and sometimes beliefs of its providers' and 'is unlikely [...] to produce decisive changes in the basic organization and operation of parties (idem: 218). Gero Erdmann (2006: 1) similarly notes that 'transformative effects' from political party assistance have hitherto been seldom observed, while Peter Burnell (2000: i) argues about political party assistance that 'the effects are likely to be modest, the consequences marginal to political development'. The donor community, by contrast, does report success stories of party assistance.[4] In light of the paucity of detailed case studies of party assistance, little can be said with certainty about the mean impact of assistance programs (Burnell 2000c: 20).

The failure of party assistance to generate transformative effects is problematic for two reasons. First, after impressive growth in the 1990s, party assistance is now carried out in around 75 countries at a considerable financial cost.[5] The fact that these resources are allocated for an effort that, outside the donor community, is widely believed to be ineffectual, invites serious thinking about whether the effort is still worthwhile and whether its providers are sufficiently held accountable. Second, parties remain crucial institutions in political processes, both in democracies where they fulfill indispensable procedural functions such as organizing government and recruiting candidates for elections (Lipset 2000; Schattschneider 1942), or as 'agents of change' in authoritarian settings. The low degree of institutionalization of party systems in many target countries of party assistance is believed to depress the quality of democratic governance (Tóka, 1997). If parties are weak in settings with an uneven electoral playing field, moreover, they are unable to mount an effective challenge to incumbent forces. The poor state of political parties outside most Western democracies suggests that, in theory, they could benefit massively from assistance; in practice, however, parties are rarely transformed as a consequence of party assistance.

Since they are often vehicles of personal ambitions and products of deep-reaching legacies of political culture, parties are infamous for being resistant to reform. In new democracies, undemocratic attitudes are still widely found within parties. For these and related reasons, parties are sometimes depicted as the 'weakest link' in democratization (Carothers 2006a: Randall 2007: 642). Party assistance, accordingly, is riven with difficulties. While rather tangible results are achieved in different areas of democracy assistance - aimed at, for instance, reform of the judiciary or the electoral system - party assistance is less likely to produce quick results. Altogether, party assistance is 'one of the most controversial and vexing policy areas in democracy promotion' (Melia 2005: 24). It targets a type of actor that is a participant and a stakeholder of domestic political processes and that is typically on the forefront of political change. The perception that party assistance is not very effective combined with its enhanced sensitivity raises important (political) questions about the assistance effort. The following chapters are concerned with the question why party assistance in Georgia and Ukraine, despite a sustained effort of many years, has not been capable of helping parties to become viable and democratic organizations. Logically, the degree of effectiveness of party assistance programs is a function of the adequacy of the input of assistance on the supply-side plus the permissiveness of conditions on the recipient-side of assistance. An answer to the question about the ineffectiveness of party assistance in Georgia and Ukraine therefore is sought both in the nature of the assistance effort and in domestic determinants of party (system) development in

11

Georgia and Ukraine. The weight of domestic factors has been identified before as a brake on the effectiveness of party assistance programs. Carothers (2006a: 162) explains the absence of a 'transformative effect' from party assistance from 'the difficulty of the task and the inadequacies of much of the assistance', where the difficulty of the task is largely determined by constraining factors over which providers of assistance have little control. Elsewhere he argues that 'party aid tends to have only rather limited effects not only because parties are hard organizations to try to help but also because parties are shaped by a whole set of underlying conditions and structures upon which party aid usually has no bearing' (Carothers 2006a: 182). A study of party assistance in Eastern Europe and Eurasia commissioned by USAID in a similar vein contends that the success of party assistance hinges on a number of (domestic) structural variables which are outside the control of providers of assistance and therefore 'may impede the success of even the most expertly designed party assistance programs' (USAID 2007: 9).

The main argument which is unfolded in the following chapters is that domestic constraints on the development of stable and democratic parties in Georgia and Ukraine have practically presented a sufficient condition for the failure of party assistance. Assistance has been unable to outweigh these domestic constraints, which include foremost the impact on party politics of a less-than-democratic regime context and a high degree of volatility in party politics. This conclusion is alarming because the domestic constraints on party development in Georgia and Ukraine are also observed, in varying degrees, in many other countries where assistance is provided. The supply-side of assistance is investigated by conceptualizing party assistance as a type of norm promotion. As will be demonstrated, conditions that are often seen as conducive to norm diffusion are largely absent in the diffusion in Georgia and Ukraine of what will be referred to as the 'party assistance norm'. The effectiveness of party assistance in Georgia and Ukraine is further undermined by the requirement to adhere to standards of good practice, obliging the providers of assistance, among others, to work with an inclusive, non-partisan selection of parties. The discussion of the input of assistance is supported by data that were collected by the author over the course of nearly one hundred interviews with both recipients and providers of assistance.

Significance of the study
Roughly until the early 1990s, scholarly publications on Third Wave democratization tended to downplay the weight of external factors on domestic political processes. In the introduction to a path-breaking volume on democratic transitions, Schmitter (1986: 5), for instance, noted: '[O]ne of the firmest conclusions that emerged...was

that transitions from authoritarian rule and immediate prospects for political democracy were largely to be explained in terms of national forces and calculations. External actors tended to play an indirect and usually marginal role... '. Despite the fact that the external dimension can no longer be said to be a 'forgotten dimension of democratization' (Pridham 1991: 18), as, indeed, 'our appreciation of the international dimensions of democratization has grown' (McFaul et al. 2008: 6), 'our understanding of the causal impact of international instruments on domestic outcomes is still underdeveloped and unsystematic' (ibid). Schmitz (2004: 409) similarly notes that 'even though a consensus is emerging on the significance of international influences on regime change (...), surprisingly little systematic work has explored the exact mechanisms linking international norms and domestic political change'. Rather than uncovering the 'exact mechanisms' of effects from international factors on political processes, a few studies have attempted to measure the aggregate effect of foreign aid on democratization, finding no evidence of a relation between aid levels and democratization (Knack 2004), and a 'significant, albeit modest, impact on democratic outcomes' from USAID democracy assistance programs on democratization (Finkel et al. 2007: 435). The conclusion of Schmitter and his collaborators about the relative insignificance of external factors in democratization is reflected in literature on political parties. Since party politics is regarded as being overwhelmingly shaped by domestic factors, authors in studies of party politics rarely involve international factors, with probably the biggest share of the studies that do involve international factors focusing on the effects of Europeanization on national political parties (e.g. Ladrech 2002; Lewis and Mansfeldová 2007). Notwithstanding the typically much larger role of domestic factors in party development than of international factors, as Burnell (2000b: 3) argues, 'the study of party politics in new democracies must be alert to the role of international factors including international party support'.

Knack (2004: 262) notes that quantitative studies such as his 'must be complemented by case study evidence that more closely examines the effectiveness of particular democracy-promoting programs'. This thesis is concerned with the effectiveness of one type of democracy-promoting program - political party assistance. In the sole book-length investigation of the topic, Carothers argues credibly that party assistance 'rarely has transformative impact' (Carothers 2006a: 162) and 'is unlikely [...] to produce decisive changes in the basic organization and operation of parties (idem: 218). Assistance is also frequently looked upon as an ineffectual undertaking by recipients.[6]

According to Burnell (2000c: 20), however, 'at present we simply do not know enough about the consequences, intended and unintended, to reach such conclusions [about the alleged limited impact of party assistance]. Large-scale empirical research by area specialists and comparativists is needed first'. Erdmann (2006: 1) similarly observes that, in the absence of detailed case-oriented studies, it is as yet too early to pass a verdict on the effects of party assistance. This thesis contributes to filling the void of empirical scholarly research on party assistance. Starting from the observation that parties in Georgia and Ukraine during the time that they have participated in assistance programs generally have remained weak and unreformed organizations, the thesis asks why party assistance has not been able to make inroads in (contributing to) the reform of parties.

The thesis purports to remedy crucial shortcomings of existing research on external influences in political processes (McFaul et al. 2008). First, contra the tendency of studies on democracy promotion to focus overwhelmingly on the input of the outside factor, 'isolating the effects of outside factors requires an assessment of domestic factors in the process of democratic change. The study of international democracy promotion, in other words, necessitates breaking the domestic-international barrier' (idem: 7). Jacoby (2006: 625) similarly argues that 'a focus on external influences is a growth area only if it addresses the union of foreign and domestic influences'. Instead of jumping immediately to a discussion of party assistance, this study first investigates the domestic variables which have shaped party development in Georgia and Ukraine in order to understand why party assistance has not been able to generate more effect. As will be argued, domestic constraints on the development of stable and democratic parties have invalidated the assistance effort to such an extent that the assistance has become highly ineffectual. The discussion of the domestic variables is not just an upbeat to the case studies of party assistance, but itself contains innovative perspectives on the nature of party development in (semi-)authoritarian states, in particular those of the FSU, with fluid party politics. Through a synthesis in the overall argument of the domestic and international dimensions of party development, this study weaves together insights from two subfields of political science. The discussion of domestic variables is informed by insights into areas of investigation that are traditionally situated within Comparative Politics - party politics, constitutional design, electoral legislation, etc. The body of literature on norm diffusion which provides insights for the discussion of party assistance, on the other hand, is embedded in International Relations. Integrating the two subfields of political science is increasingly acknowledged as a productive approach (Schmitz 2004). Indeed, in a discussion of transnational diffusion, Bloom and Orenstein (2005: 4-5) concurrently note that 'following developments in international relations theory and sociological institutionalism (...) Comparative Politics scholars have begun to collapse boundaries between International Relations and Comparative Politics'.

A second shortcoming that this study addresses is that 'existing analyses on international democracy promotion focus on the democracy promotion efforts (the "supply side") of individual countries' (McFaul et al. 2008: 6-7). The case studies in this thesis, by contrast, look at the entire range of significant actors in party assistance in Georgia and Ukraine. The distinction between U.S. and European providers of assistance masks striking similarities in approaches and conceptual underpinnings. As will be argued throughout the pages of this thesis, party assistance programs, whether by U.S. or by European actors, are shaped by a shared underlying norm about the type of organization that recipient parties transform into.

The third shortcoming of existing research that this study helps to correct is that 'to date, studies of democracy promotion have tended to follow "successful" cases of democratization' (McFaul et al. 2008: 9), a point reiterated by a string of authors. 'There has been a bias to focus on successful cases of diffusion' (Checkel 1999b: 86), and 'efforts to explore norms suffer from a bias toward the norm that worked' (Legro 1997: 34). Since 'scholars [...] have a tendency to select for study a subset of events that actually occur and to neglect events that do not occur', 'very few studies have looked at failed campaigns' (Levy 2007: 201). However, 'serious analysis of the external influences on internal change cannot focus only on cases of successful democratic breakthroughs, but must heed equal attention to cases where either significant external efforts to encourage transition to democracy produced little effects, or where successful transition to democracy has apparently taken place with virtually no external role' (Magen 2009: 17). Despite the call to study negative cases, few have taken up the task.[7]

This thesis further contributes to existing scholarly work by explicitly conceptualizing party assistance as a type of norm promotion. Doing so, the thesis draws on insights from social constructivist literature on the transnational diffusion of norms, rules, and policies. Rather than operationalizing a theoretical framework of norm diffusion throughout, the thesis turns to insights from social constructivism to gain a complementary perspective on the failure of the party assistance as norm promotion. Providers of political party assistance have previously been identified as 'norm entrepreneurs' (Brucker 2007; Dakowska 2005: 155), and party assistance has been associated with norm promotion (Carothers 2006a: 188-9), but a systematic treatment of party assistance as a type of norm promotion has not been performed before. Viewing party assistance as norm promotion in line with constructivist literature is done on the premise that the approach is instrumental in explaining the failure of assistance to effectively pass over a set of standards of behavior regarding party operation that collectively constitutes a norm. The discussion of norm diffusion in this study diverges from most other discussions of norm diffusion in two respects: first, as noted above, scholars tend to look at 'successful' norms that *do* travel across borders. Here, by contrast, the focus is on cases of failed norm promotion despite concerted efforts. Second, while in most studies the norm recipients are states, represented by government bureaucracies, this study descends to a lower level of analysis at which the recipients are non-state organizations. Although there are no restrictions to studying norm diffusion to actors below the level of states, this is done relatively rarely.

Georgia and Ukraine are expressly understood as negative cases of norm diffusion. Studying negative cases of norm diffusion in party assistance is particularly relevant because the non-occurrence of diffusion is believed to be more common in party assistance than instances of successful diffusion. Georgia and Ukraine present poignant cases for the examination of failed party assistance. They have been among the biggest recipients per capita of democracy assistance, both in the FSU and worldwide, and party assistance programs in the two states have been bigger than in most surrounding states. Furthermore, Georgia and Ukraine have experienced dramatic instances of regime change in the form of 'electoral revolutions' which have raised important questions, both scholarly and political, about the role and impact of Western democracy promotion. Besides these factors, Georgia and Ukraine have not been unlike other FSU states (with the exception of the Baltic states) in terms of political trajectory and party (system) development. As these other states, Ukraine and Georgia have not gone through a transition to liberal democracy. The persistence of (semi-)authoritarianism in Ukraine (until 2005) and Georgia, like elsewhere in the FSU, has had a profound impact on party politics. In FSU states such as Georgia and Ukraine, where some degree of political pluralism was preserved, party politics has been characterized by a large degree of volatility and weak party institutionalization. Given that Georgia and Ukraine are rather typical cases within the FSU, the findings from the two case studies of this thesis are expected to prove generalizable to other FSU states to at least some degree. Moreover, it is expected that the main argument developed throughout this study, concerning the centrality of domestic constraints on party development in explaining the relative failure of party assistance, holds up for other cases which contain the first, and at least one of the second and third of the following conditions: the presence of party assistance programs; a less-than-democratic political setting; and a high degree of volatility in party politics. In-depth investigations of cases, naturally, would have to demonstrate whether the findings from this study indeed hold up in different locations with analogous conditions.

Plan of the thesis

After this introduction, the thesis proceeds as follows. Chapters one, two and three lay the ground for the case-study based chapters four, five, and six. Chapter one addresses key questions related to empirical research on political party assistance. Its first section provides a working definition of party assistance and explains the relation of party assistance to adjacent concepts such as democracy assistance and democracy promotion. Section two specifies the type of case study research conducted for this study. In relation to the case-studies, section three makes explicit five paramaters that are relevant to any research design in the social sciences. In the process, this section delineates the subject of inquiry and sets its temporal and spatial boundaries. Finally, the chapter discusses data-gathering and the use of sources, in particular with respect to interviewing.

Chapter two offers an introduction to political party assistance and identifies the elements of what will be referred to as the 'party assistance norm'. The first section introduces general features of party assistance to the extent that they apply to party assistance in Georgia and Ukraine. The next section discusses two principal standards of good practice which play an important role in party assistance and, as will be demonstrated later in chapters five and six, bear consequences for the effectiveness of assistance. In section three, party assistance is conceptualized as a form of norm promotion in line with other phenomena that are similarly conceptualized as norms. From a collection of publications by the donors and providers of party assistance, the key elements of the 'party assistance norm' are deduced. Drawing extensively on insights from social constructivist literature into the diffusion of norms, section four, finally, presents a number of tentative explanations for the failure of party assistance that subsequently will be revisited in the course of chapter six.

Political party assistance has a bearing on party development in recipient countries and by extension on political change. Besides, it is only one type in a broader effort of democracy assistance and only form of external influence on political parties. Chapter three discusses several of the layers of the context of political party assistance in Georgia and Ukraine. The first section notes where Georgia and Ukraine have been situated in regime classifications. Section two discusses the foremost explanations for why Georgia and Ukraine, unlike a range of other post-communist states, have not become liberal democracies after 1991. Section three pauses on the sources of the Rose and Orange Revolutions, probably the most significant political events in Georgia and Ukraine since the early 1990s. Together, sections one, two, and three deal with political change. Section four looks at other forms of democracy assistance than assistance to parties, and section five, finally, gives an overview of other elements in the 'international dimension' of political party development than party assistance.

To understand why party assistance has not been able to generate more effect, it is imperative to consider which domestic factors have blocked the development of stable and democratic parties in Georgia and Ukraine. Chapter four provides an extensive discussion of these factors. Section one argues what has been distinctive about party politics in Georgia and Ukraine, particularly relative to party politics in Central and Eastern Europe. Section two notes the pitfalls of studying party politics that are as volatile as they have been in Georgia and Ukraine for most of the post-communist period. Sections three, four, and five in turn discuss three of the major constraints on party development in Georgia and Ukraine - the elite-driven nature of party development, the limited overall leverage of parties, and the impact on party politics of the less-than-democratic political context. Section six demonstrates how these constraints have translated into the incentives that have driven party creation and operation. Section seven traces trends in party development during the years that the research comprises. Section eight argues on the basis of which criteria parties in Georgia and Ukraine should be classified in order to capture the dynamics of party politics in these countries. Section nine, finally, summarizes the main implications flowing from the discussion in this chapter, for party assistance.

Chapters five and six present the findings from the two case studies of political party assistance in Georgia and Ukraine from 1999-2000 until 2007-2008. The first two sections of chapter five consist of a raw overview of party assistance programs in Georgia and Ukraine, respectively. Sections three and four assess to what extent providers of assistance have complied with the two core standards of good practice that were identified in chapter two. Chapter six is specifically concerned with the failure of party assistance in Georgia and Ukraine. Its opening section explores what effects there have been from party assistance in the two recipient countries. The second, most crucial section assesses how party assistance has related to the domestic constraints on party development that were highlighted in chapter four. Section three shifts focus to the recipients of assistance, listing the main reasons why these have failed to comply with the party assistance norm. Finally, the chapter takes a quick tour of the main shortcomings in the input of political party assistance, which in varying degrees have contributed to invalidate the effort.

18

The conclusion summarizes the core arguments put forward in preceding chapters regarding the failure of party assistance in Georgia and Ukraine, and in addition reflects on the implications of the findings from this research for the future of party assistance.

CHAPTER ONE: RESEARCHING PARTY ASSISTANCE

Due to the paucity of existing research, there is no common wisdom, let alone established standards, on how to study political party assistance. This chapter addresses a number of questions which pertain to the scholarly investigation of party assistance. The first section explains how political party assistance is conceptualized in this research by highlighting its relation to adjacent phenomena - foremost democracy assistance and democracy promotion. The next two sections identify the type of case study research undertaken in this thesis and then reveal the key parameters - variables, time-frame, level of analysis, and population - of this case study research. The final section discusses the sources - interviews and 'gray literature' - from which data have been collected for the case studies (chapters five and six). This section particularly reflects on the pitfalls associated with interviewing as a method of data-gathering and on how these pitfalls have been dealt with.

1.1. THE INTERNATIONAL DIMENSION OF DEMOCRATIZATION

In a strict sense, democratization is never fully endogenous. Around two thirds of current democracies are said to be products of foreign imposition or intervention (Whitehead 1996: 252), and of the ones that are not, few, most of them found in the West, can credibly boast to be home-grown. The 'international dimension', then, is almost always at play in democratization in some form and to some degree. A telling example is that in Africa former British colonies have almost without exception adopted a Westminster-type parliamentary system, while a majority of former French colonies are now in majority semi-presidential after the French example (Van Cranenburgh 2008: 954). The international dimension of democratization encompasses different types of mechanisms and processes, only one of which is the targeted promotion of democracy abroad. Democracy promotion, in turn, involves many different possible policies (Schraeder 2003: 26), distinguished, among other things, by the degree of consent to the policy on the part of the target state, and ranging from approaches in which democratic institutions and procedures are directly targeted, to approaches in which the promotion of democracy is achieved through activity in areas which indirectly affect democracy. A democracy promotion policy that has a direct bearing on democratic institutions, and that is executed with the consent of recipients, is democracy assistance (or aid). Alongside governing institutions, the judiciary, parliament, civil society actors and others, political parties feature as common recipients of democracy assistance. In sum, as table one illustrates, political party assistance is a subtype of democracy assistance, which itself is a subtype of democracy promotion, which in turn is one element in the overall international dimension of democratization.

	international dimension of democratization	democracy promotion	democracy assistance	political party assistance
external influences on domestic political processes	√	√	√	√
targeted effort to promote democracy		√	√	√
non-coercive and provided by specialized actors			√	√
political parties as exclusive recipients				√

Table 1. Defining attributes of the international dimension of democratization, democracy promotion, democracy assistance, and political party assistance

Democracy promotion is different from other elements in the international dimension of democratization in that it is a policy which purposefully seeks to foster democratization, while other elements in the international dimension are either uncontrolled or merely contribute to democratization by way of a side-effect of other policies. In addition to purposeful democracy promotion, democratization is influenced from the outside by diffuse 'contagion' effects and by socialization resulting from linkage to democracies. Contagion, or 'inspiration', takes place mainly in the form a demonstration effect, which leads state actors to want to imitate or emulate foreign examples (Jacoby 2006). Socialization, understood here simply as 'a process of learning in which norms and ideals are transmitted from one party to another' (Checkel 1999a) familiarizes actors in non-democracies with democratic values and practices, for instance through integration into international organizations, thereby increasing the likelihood that these actors will accept and adopt these values and practices. Contagion and socialization effects are enhanced by linkage through interstate relations between non-democracies and democracies, through transnational civil society, trade agreements, and more. The spatial clustering of democracies and autocracies suggests that distance of non-democracies to democracies is an important predictor of democratization or the failure thereof (Gleditsch and Ward 2006: Wejnert 2005).

Following Schmitter and Brouwer (1999: 13), democracy promotion is defined here as consisting 'of all overt and voluntary activities adopted, supported, and (directly or indirectly) implemented by (public or private) foreign actors explicitly designed to contribute to the political liberalization of autocratic regimes and the subsequent democratization of autocratic regimes in specific recipient countries'. Inherent in this definition is that the promotion of democracy is always an explicit purpose of these activities. Democracy promotion includes 'hard' coercive policies, with military intervention on the extreme end, and 'soft' non-coercive policies, epitomized by democracy assistance. Furthermore, promoting democracy can be done either by directly seeking to affect the functioning of political institutions, as in democracy assistance, or indirectly, while remaining mindful of the objective of promoting democracy.

Next to democracy assistance, the following democracy promotion policies can be distinguished: First, (armed) intervention aimed at enforcing the removal of an authoritarian regime to be supplanted by a more democratic one is the most coercive democracy promotion strategy. As such, armed intervention has been found to be relatively ineffectual (Pickering and Peceny 2006). Second, diplomacy in state-to-state relations has the potential to lead undemocratic leaders to abandon undemocratic practices (Adesnik and McFaul 2006). With rhetorical action as its principal instrument, diplomacy can convey the message to undemocratic leaders that their policies and type of government are inappropriate or illegitimate. When elections are looming in less-than-democratic states, democratic governments and intergovernmental organizations often seek to convince undemocratic leaders of the importance of free and fair elections. The diplomatic effort of Western actors during the Orange Revolution in Ukraine counts as an instance of particularly effective democracy promotion (Pifer 2007). Third, conditionality policies, including sanctions as a response to non-compliance with rules or norms, have on several occasions turned out to be an effective instrument of democracy promotion, especially when linked with a strong external incentive such as accession to the European Union (Grabbe 2006; Schimmelfennig 2007). Finally, naming and shaming of governments raises the cost of undemocratic practices. When the failure to adhere to democratic norms is credibly exposed, undemocratic leaders face dilemmas in legitimating their rule, both domestically and in their international relations. Opposite the promotion of democracy, authoritarianism is sometimes also bolstered, and democratization undermined from the outside, mainly by propping up incumbent authoritarian leaders in friendly states (e.g. Ambrosio 2007). Efforts to 'promote democracy backwards' (Burnell 2006) in the early twenty-first century have been pursued by China and Russia among others. In part, these efforts are a reaction against the perceived threat of democracy promotion to regime continuity domestically and in neighboring states. In the former Soviet

Union, an informal 'authoritarian international' (Silitski 2007) is said to have been established of leaders who support each other in their efforts to pre-empt an electoral revolution of the type that has occurred in Georgia, Ukraine, and Kyrgyzstan.

Democracy promotion, including democracy assistance, has expanded considerably over the last two decades. More countries are now engaged in promoting democracy, and they spend a larger percentage of foreign aid on promoting democracy than before. According to one calculation, the share of democracy assistance in official development assistance grew from 0,5% to 5% between 1991 and 2000 (World Bank 2004: 211). Increasingly, promoting democracy has been recognized as an appropriate thing for states and other actors to do. The establishment of democracy promotion as a 'world value' (McFaul 2004) is reflected by, among others, the creation of the Community of Democracies, the members of which have committed themselves to promoting democracy, and the signing of international declarations such as the Warsaw Declaration, which initiated the Community of Democracies, and the The Hague Statement on Enhancing the European Profile in Democracy Assistance.

Three factors do most to explain the increase of democracy promotion in recent decades. First, as a result of the collapse of communist regimes during 1989-1991 and a range of political openings around the same time in other parts of the world, a larger number of countries than before became natural targets of democracy promotion and recipients of assistance. Second, the end of the Cold War invalidated the argument, widely popular during the Cold War, that authoritarian regimes should be supported if they are on the same side in the stand-off against the socialist bloc. Third, the idea that liberal democracy is the most legitimate form of government, both normatively and because of the desirable consequences that democracy breeds, became more widely accepted (Fukuyama 1992). Domestically, democracy protects citizens from arbitrary rule, grants personal freedoms, political liberties and the right to self-determination, and enables human development, among other things (Dahl 1998: 45). Though the exact relationship between democracy and development remains disputed, there has also been an increasing recognition that, against earlier beliefs, democracy does not stand in the way of economic growth and may even provide better conditions for economic growth in poor countries than autocratic rule (Siegle et al. 2004). Indeed, 'the idea that many countries face a cruel choice between development and democracy has been supplanted by a growing appreciation that these two desirable goals are related in complex ways' (Burnell 2000a: 43). In the international domain, democracies are believed to be more prone to peace, at least in relation to each other (Owen 1994), harboring the promise of a more secure, less conflict-ridden world.

Democracies moreover make more reliable economic trading partners (Perlin 2003: 6-7).

Being not as visible and not as contested, democracy assistance is on 'the quiet side' of the spectrum of democracy promotion strategies (Carothers 2007: 10). It is distinct in at least two respects: first, it is invariably implemented with the consent of its recipients (Burnell 2000b: 4) and second, it is implemented by specialized actors, for whom democracy assistance is a prominent area of activity or an exclusive area of activity. These specialized actors include intergovernmental organizations, government agencies and nongovernmental organizations, of which many are at arm's length of a government bureaucracy. Typically, not necessarily, the assistance is not-for-profit and supported by grants. Most democracy assistance is directed at one of three comprehensive areas: the electoral process, state institutions, and civil society (Carothers 1999: 88). Assistance to the electoral process can be divided into two types of assistance: assistance aimed at the conduct of free and fair elections, and assistance to political parties. As democracy assistance *tout court*, party assistance is implemented by specialized actors, which, in the case of party assistance, receive the bulk of their funding from the government while being formally autonomous. In contrast to some other forms of democracy assistance, party assistance is supposed to be only technical: providers of assistance are not allowed to hand out direct financial donations. Party assistance is related to, but separate from other types of democracy assistance, including electoral assistance and legislative strengthening, which are termed 'indirect party aid' by Carothers (2006a: 90-2). Party assistance in the strict definition applied in this thesis is aimed at improving the performance of the primary representative and procedural functions of parties (cf. Bartolini and Mair 2001) and at creating a viable party system by working with several parties simultaneously. In addition to being distinct from other types of democracy assistance, it is also distinct from other forms of external influence on parties, such as for-profit consultancy and the inclusion in party internationals.

1.2. CASE STUDY RESEARCH

This research project comprises case studies of assistance to political parties in two countries over a certain period of time. According to Gerring (2004: 341), a case study is best defined as 'an in-depth study of a single unit (a relatively bounded phenomenon) where the scholar's aim is to elucidate features of a larger class of similar phenomena'. The relevance of a single case study for cases that are not investigated is also featured in George and Bennett's (2005: 5) definition of a case study as 'the detailed examination of an aspect of a historical episode to develop or test historical explanations that may be generalizable to other events'. In his influential classification of case study types, Lijphart (1971: 691) distinguishes between six types - atheoretical, interpretative, hypothesis-generating, theory-confirming, theory-infirming, and deviant case studies. The type of case studies conducted in this thesis is identified as being of the hypothesis-generating genus, touted by Sartori (1991: 252) as the most valuable type in comparative political research. Since hardly any theoretical claims on party assistance have been formulated as yet, the case studies conducted here could not be theory-confirming, theory-infirming, or deviant. Neither, however, are the case studies atheoretical or interpretative, since there is an explicit interest in formulating generalizable propositions beyond the singular findings from the two cases under investigation.

If the variables that have the biggest weight in explaining the outcome are present in other cases in equal weight, then the findings from the two case studies in this thesis can be assumed to be replicable to those other cases. The main argument that is unfolded in the following chapters is that domestic determinants of party development in Georgia and Ukraine have practically presented a sufficient condition for the failure of party assistance. The foremost of these domestic determinants - a less-than-democratic political context and a high degree of volatility in party politics - are found widely. Of the roughly one hundred countries that have entered a 'transition' in recent decades, a small minority has consolidated liberal democracy (Carothers 2002: 9). Today, most political regimes in the world are neither liberal democracies nor closed autocracies (Diamond 2002; Roessler and Howard 2007). At the same time, a high degree of volatility in party politics, mostly referred to as 'weak party system institutionalization', is a common diagnosis for party systems, whether in Latin America (Mainwaring and Scully 1995; Sanchez 2008b), Africa (Basedau and Stroh 2008; Kuenzi and Lambright 2005), South East Asia (Stockton 2001; Ufen 2007) or the post-communist world (Casal Bertoa 2008; Meleshevich 2007).[8] Weak party system institutionalization and defective democracy are often found together in countries since the two phenomena are known to reinforce each other (Thames and Robbins 2007; Tóka 1997). A cursory overview of the approximately seventy-five countries where party assistance is provided today (Carothers 2006a: 86) teaches that the combination of weak party system institutionalization and a less-than-democratic political context are typical for a majority of these countries.[9] In sum, in the large number of states where three conditions are present - the provision of party assistance, a high degree of volatility in party politics, and a less-than-democratic

26

political context - are the findings from the two case studies of this thesis expected to be replicable to at least some degree.

Since it is believed that party assistance generally does not produce significant effects (see page 11), the two case studies of this thesis are presumed to be typical with respect to the outcome value. More often than not, indeed, party assistance has not been able to make inroads in helping to transform parties and party systems. As noted earlier, case-oriented research in which an outcome does not occur is relatively uncommon. The selection of cases with a negative outcome is warranted here because a positive outcome of the dependent variable, though rare, *is* possible (Mahoney and Goertz 2004). The two case studies are conducted parallel to each other; the analysis is carried out diachronically within the boundaries of the individual cases. Depending on the way the term is understood, the research method applied in the case studies may be associated with 'process-tracing'. Since the outcome value in this study is negative, process-tracing here cannot be understood as establishing a causal mechanism in the sense of dividing that causal mechanism into smaller steps to examine exactly how causes have led to an observed outcome (e.g. Van Evera 1997: 64). The aim is rather to put forward propositions about how the outcome of interest (the failure of political party assistance) relates to its explanatory variables. The evidence to support these propositions is disparate and often inconclusive. In the words of Gerring (2007: 171), most distinctive about process-tracing is indeed 'the noncomparability of adjacent pieces of evidence. All pieces of evidence are relevant to the central argument (they are not 'random' but they do not comprise observations in a larger sample).'

Although case studies deal with historical episodes, the case studies conducted here do not amount to merely a historical account of the phenomenon of party assistance in Georgia and Ukraine during a given period of time: 'systematic process analysis is a very different project from the one in which most historians engage. It demands examination of the histories behind outcomes but one guided more extensively by theory than are most of those undertaken by historians' (Hall 2003: 395).[10] Different bodies of theory guide the investigation of the explanations for the failure of party assistance in Georgia and Ukraine. Where the focus is on the external dimension, theories of norm diffusion, developed mainly by social constructivist scholars working in the field of International Relations, assume central position. Where the focus is on the internal dimension, on the other hand, the rich literature on party politics from the field of Comparative Politics is key. Four topics from this literature have particular relevance in this research: types of parties and party systems, party politics in post-communist societies, party politics in undemocratic settings, and party system institutionalization.

1.3. RESEARCH PARAMETERS

Any theoretical model in the social sciences contains at least the following five parameters: 'First, every model pertains to a certain level of analysis - individual, group, national, world-systemic, or some intermediate gradation. Second, it has one or more dependent variables. Third, it has one or more explanatory variables. Fourth, it applies to a certain relevant universe of cases. And fifth, it applies to events or processes that take place during a certain period of time' (Coppedge 1999: 466). In this section these five parameters are made explicit. In the process, the scope and boundaries of the investigation are laid bare.

The level of analysis to which this investigation pertains is neither a micro-level of individuals nor a macro-level of states or the global systemic level, but an intermediate level of organizations, groups. Since the question of interest concerns the possible effect of party assistance programs on political parties, the units of analysis are the recipients of political party assistance - political parties - rather than its providers. The dependent variable in this investigation is the effect from party assistance programs on political parties. For both cases, the outcome of the dependent variable has a negative value: party assistance has generated very limited positive effect on relevant parties in Georgia and Ukraine over the course of the period under investigation. The task at hand is to explain this negative outcome: why have providers of assistance not succeeded in transferring the gist of assistance programs to parties? Since the limited effect of party assistance programs finds expression in the persistent weakness of political parties, an equally crucial question is why parties have remained so poorly institutionalized. While the first question asks about the adequacy of the party assistance programs crafted by foreign actors, the second question is concerned with domestic constraints on the development of stable parties. The range of explanatory variables involved in this investigation, accordingly, is divided between variables which relate to domestic factors ('the internal dimension') and variables which relate to outside factors (the 'external', or 'international' dimension). The explanatory variable representing the external dimension is the input of political party assistance by foreign actors. Different domestic constraints on stable and democratic party development in Georgia and Ukraine collectively constitute the explanatory variable of the internal dimension. As chapter four will argue, the domestic constraints on party development are primarily divided into two outcomes of party politics in Georgia and Ukraine, which in turn have been conditioned by three key explanatory variables.

The universe of cases consists of all countries in which political parties receive, or in the recent past have received party assistance. The two U.S.-based providers of assistance, the National Democratic Institute for International Affairs (NDI) and the International Republican Institute (IRI) have programs in about sixty countries, while the main German political foundations Konrad Adenauer Stiftung (KAS) and Friedrich Ebert Stiftung (FES) are active in over eighty countries and engage in party assistance in most of these. Most other providers of party assistance have no offices in recipient countries and work in fewer of those. As noted, the cases of Georgia and Ukraine are presumed to be most-similar to cases where the same domestic constraints on stable party development are observed, and where providers of assistance have executed noteworthy programs. Adding geography and political legacy to the equation, replication of the findings from the two cases of this thesis appears most promising in such states as Armenia, Kazakhstan, Moldova, and Kyrgyzstan. The likelihood of analogous findings for the failure of assistance elsewhere, then, is highest in countries which share the basic conditions of the failure of assistance plus contingent factors such as geography and legacy, followed by states which merely share the basic conditions.

The period of time during which the events and processes that are studied here unfolded is a roughly equal number of years before and after the 'electoral revolutions' which ushered in regime change in Georgia and Ukraine. For both Georgia and Ukraine, this boils down to two legislative elections (and between-election periods) before, and two legislative elections after the Rose and Orange Revolutions, respectively. A few simple factors inform and justify the choice to somewhat narrow the time frame to 1999-2008 for Georgia and 1998-2007 for Ukraine: first, the time periods are sufficiently protracted to track possible alterations of strategy and change within parties and the elusive party systems of Georgia and Ukraine. Second, only a few providers of assistance were active in Georgia and Ukraine during the 1990s. Party assistance in those years was limited in scope, and obtaining reliable data from these initial years is even more cumbersome than it is for more recent years. Third, the occurrence of the Revolutions has raised expectations about the role and the effect of the assistance. In the case of both the Rose and Orange Revolutions, democracy assistance efforts, including assistance to political parties, have been ascribed much weight in explanations of why the regime change occurred. Concerning the post-Revolution period, much optimism has existed (initially) regarding the chances of successful democratization and the role Western actors could play in helping to enforce durable political change in both countries. In light of this, the inability of party assistance to have an impact on parties is a salient given.

1.4. SOURCES AND DATA

The principal sources of information used for the case studies of political party assistance in Georgia and Ukraine have been, first, a large number of interviews with persons involved in party assistance either as recipients or as providers, and second, various types of documents composed and archived by the providers of assistance and the funding institutions of party assistance. These are primary sources; secondary sources about party assistance are rare.

Close to one hundred interviews have been conducted for this research. Most interviewees fall under one of the following categories: staff, including policy offers, at the central offices (locations: Washington D.C., Berlin, The Hague) of providers of assistance dealing with the design and implementation of party assistance programs; leading and supporting staff, both Western expatriate and local, at the country offices (Kyiv and Tbilisi) of providers of assistance; political party representatives formerly or currently dealing with the international relations of their parties (often called 'international secretaries'); and representatives of political parties who have participated or otherwise been involved in assistance programs. In addition, a number of academics, journalists and NGO representatives have been interviewed in both Georgia and Ukraine, mainly in order to receive alternative assessments of the state of political party (system) development and of the (perceived) impact of party assistance programs.

Since the subject of inquiry in this research is well-defined, a sample of possible informants could be constructed prior to the process of interviewing, The initial selection of informants, in other words, involved non-probability sampling in which informants were selected on the basis of positional criteria (Tansey 2007: 770). Typically, several persons in each country office of the providers of assistance and from each relevant political party, who were directly involved in party assistance, have been interviewed. From other categories, at least one person per party or provider of assistance was singled out prior to the actual interviewing process. After the start of the interviewing process, more informants were found through chain-referral or 'snowballing' (Burnham et al. 2004: 207; Richards 1996). In practical terms, each informant was requested to provide names of further possible informants, who in turn could point to others. In this stage of the interviewing process, informants were selected on the basis of a combination of positional and reputational criteria (Tansey 2007: 770). Probability sampling has not been applied in any stage of the interviewing process.

Because of the politically sensitive nature of the subject of party assistance, there has been a risk of missing crucial information in interviews. To minimize this risk, informants have been assured that they would remain anonymous. An overview of the interviews that have been held, including names and positions of informants, as well as the time and location of the interviews, can be provided to anyone interested on a condition of confidentiality. Interviews have not been recorded; instead, detailed notes were made which can be consulted by anyone interested, again, on a condition of confidentiality. To obtain as much valuable information as possible, finally, it has been stressed during interviews that the data would be used for scholarly purposes only.[11] The form of interviews has invariably been semi-structured. In semi-structured interviews, the 'main questions and script are fixed, but interviewers are able to improvise follow-up questions and to explore meanings and areas of interest that emerge' (Arksey and Knight 1999: 7). Per category of informants, a set of similar questions was asked: party representatives, for instance, was always asked how they assess the impact of assistance programs; practitioners, for instance, was always asked after their relationship with the central offices of their organizations. In addition to these fixed questions, informants were given the opportunity to emphasize issues which they deemed particularly relevant. With few exceptions, interviews have been conducted in languages that were either native or near-native to interviewees.

Interviewing as a method of data-collection comes with a number of pitfalls. A first problem is that, due to the substantial turnover in the organizations providing assistance and in parties, informants may not produce much reliable information about assistance of several years earlier. Moreover, particularly representatives of political parties tend to want to look forward and not recall past events and actions. The high rate of party turnover in both Georgia and Ukraine means that many parties that have received assistance during the time period under research no longer exist and that some of those that do, have been around for only a few years. Taken together, institutional memory within parties and providers of assistance is often limited. The way to counteract this dilemma has been to take interviews, whenever possible, from former employees of the providers of assistance, from former representatives of still existing parties, and from representatives of now defunct parties. Nonetheless, significantly more information has been retrieved about recent assistance than about assistance of several years ago.

31

Second, non-probability sampling of informants from political parties of informants may instigate considerable bias (Tansey 2007 : 769). Informants from parties probably are not representative of their parties, especially because they are generally more experienced in speaking with outsiders. The problem of selection bias is aggravated by the chain-referral mechanism of obtaining new informants, as informants are likely to refer to like-minded persons. Given that sampling criteria could not have been different than positional for some important categories of informants, non-probability sampling in this research has been imperative.

Third, informants sometimes make claims contradictory to claims of other informants. In some cases this may be because informants, many of which are directly involved in the assistance effort, have an interest in presenting a skewed account of the assistance. A general strategy to counter the pitfalls outlined above, and one that particularly addresses the last-mentioned pitfall, has been 'triangulation' of sources. According to Arksey and Knight (1999: 21), 'the basic idea of triangulation is that data are obtained from a wide range of different and multiple sources'. Triangulation is advisable not only to adjudicate between contradictory claims, but also to verify and corroborate any significant data point obtained through interviews. Multiplication of data points has been achieved by consulting documents, whenever available, to back up claims by informants, and by speaking with several persons about the same subject. In addition, it has been found to be informative to speak with former staff of the providers of assistance, and with former party members. Within parties, interviews have been conducted with a range of persons from party leaders to rank-and-file activists. At the providers of assistance and their funding institutions, interviews have been conducted with persons ranging from high-ranking officials and policy-makers to junior policy staff.

A second main type of sources consulted for this research are documents compiled by the providers and funders of party assistance. These are, first, publicly available strategy documents, evaluations, policy guidelines etc., which in most cases are available from the websites of the concerned organizations. These documents do not discuss party assistance in Georgia and Ukraine specifically, with the exception of a handful of quarterly reports of NDI and IRI that are available from USAID's Development Experience Clearinghouse website.[12] Instead, many of these documents take on either party assistance overall, or democracy assistance and promotion in Georgia and Ukraine. A second type of documents, sometimes referred to as 'gray literature', that have been consulted is not publicly available. These documents comprise work plans and reports on concluded activities. On occasion, these documents have been received directly from informants. Besides, a request has been filed to USAID, with a reference to the Freedom of Information Act (FOIA), to obtain all work plans of NDI and IRI concerning their activities in Georgia and Ukraine since 1999. USAID has been unable, or unwilling, to provide most requested documents. All work plans of NDI in Ukraine and IRI in Georgia remained missing. In addition, work plans of NDI in Georgia for 2003 and of IRI in Ukraine for 2001 were not provided. NDI and IRI work plans and other written documentation have been used mainly to corroborate data from interviews. Since a considerable share of NDI and IRI documentation has been missing, and there is no publicly available equivalent to NDI and IRI work plans and quarterly reports with regard to the *Stiftungen*, interview data have been handled with reserve.

Chapter Two: Party Assistance and Norm Promotion

There is a remarkable degree of similarity in party assistance by different actors. This concerns the types of activities that are common in party assistance – training seminars, consultations, study trips - (section 2.1); a number of 'standards of good practice' consisting of formal and informal constraints which guide party assistance by all major actors (section 2.2); and a shared 'party assistance norm' which conveys a conception of how parties are supposed to operate in a democracy (section 2.3). In this chapter, these different elements are presented in subsequent sections. Finally, drawing on the academic literature on norm diffusion, the chapter sums up insights which have relevance in explanations of the compliance or the lack of compliance of parties with the 'party assistance norm'.

As the assistance providers themselves confirm, the bulk of party assistance in Georgia and Ukraine has not been unlike party assistance in many other places, especially elsewhere in the post-communist world. A sound understanding of what conventional party assistance is, then, is imperative to explain why party assistance overall in Georgia and Ukraine has been inadequate in its opposition to domestic constraints on party development. Viewing party assistance as a type of norm promotion provides the opportunity to connect with theoretical and empirical literature on norm diffusion, which has been investigated in relation to a wide variety of phenomena of which some share characteristics with party assistance, but not to party assistance itself. The wealth of insights accumulated in this literature, which is mainly associated with the international relations theory of social constructivism, helps explain the failure of providers of assistance to transmit the gist of their programs to political parties in the case studies in chapters five and six.

2.1. Introduction to party assistance

The range of providers of political party assistance comprises party-related actors, international organizations, and party internationals (Carothers 2006a: 78-83). In Georgia and Ukraine, international organizations and party internationals have not been involved in noteworthy assistance efforts as direct providers, leaving only the party-related actors. Rough calculations have put the amount of overall aid to political parties around the mid-2000s at 139 million euro (Catón 2007: 12) and 200 million dollar (Carothers 2006a: 86). Of the party-related actors, by far the largest are the two U.S party institutes National Democratic Institute for International Affairs (NDI) and International Republican Institute (IRI), and two German political party foundations, the Konrad Adenauer Stiftung (KAS) and the Friedrich Ebert Stiftung (FES), affiliated with the Christian Democratic Union (CDU) and Social-Democratic Party of Germany (SPD), respectively. Party-related actors from other countries are considerably smaller, and typically have no permanent offices in recipient countries. NDI and IRI have been present for a relatively long time in both Georgia and Ukraine. FES has a considerable party assistance program in Ukraine, but not in Georgia. KAS equally has a large program in Ukraine, and started working with parties in Georgia only in 2007. A third German political party foundation, the Friedrich Naumann Stiftung für die Freiheit (FNS), affiliated with the Free Democratic Party (FDP), works with parties in Georgia and Ukraine, albeit on a modest scale. In Georgia, finally, the Netherlands Institute for Multiparty Democracy (NIMD), in close cooperation with a local NGO, implemented an assistance program from 2005 until 2008. Party assistance efforts by other actors in Georgia and Ukraine, most notably party-related actors from European democracies, are substantially more limited.

The principal actors in party assistance in Georgia and Ukraine, then, are NDI, IRI, KAS, FES, FNS, and NIMD. These six organizations probably account for over ninety per cent of expenditures on party assistance worldwide.[13] On a considerable more limited scale, the Dutch party institutes Eduardo Frei Stichting (EFS), Alfred Mozer Stichting (AMS) and the international bureau of VVD are also involved in party assistance in Georgia and Ukraine. The identity of these organizations is shaped by their relationships with political parties and with the state. The U.S. party institutes are only loosely affiliated with the Democratic and Republican Parties. The exact relationship of the party institutes' work with U.S. foreign policy is disputed: while the institutes prefer to view themselves as independently acting NGOs, the fact that they are funded largely by the U.S. government implies that their work is part of official foreign policy in a broad sense (Carothers 2006a: 146). The *Stiftungen* are deemed to be close to their mother parties (*parteinah*), but they are autonomous in formal terms (Egger 2007: 41-3). As organizations that complement German foreign policy and advise the German Ministry of Foreign Affairs (Pogorelskaja 2002: 33), the *Stiftungen* are also closer to the state than the U.S. party institutes are. NIMD, while enjoying considerable autonomy, is steered collectively by seven political parties that have representation in the Dutch parliament.

The mandate for party assistance by the U.S. party institutes is put down in several USAID documents. Among USAID's four overarching goals is 'building sustainable democracies'. The Center for Democracy and Governance, responsible for implementing this goal, in turn, is organized in line with four democracy-related objectives, one of which is 'more genuine and competitive political processes', comprising, among other things, assistance to political parties (USAID 2006b: 25). 'Strengthen democratic political parties' is also mentioned explicitly as one of eleven program components related to democracy and governance from a total of forty USAID program components (USAID 2006a). Government-funded German democracy promotion is said to have three objectives: to contribute to peaceful relations between states, to create and stabilize regime types with which the West can effectively cooperate, and to help create market economies which can become reliable economic partner of the West (Lapins 2007: 15-6). The German Federal Ministry for Economic Cooperation and Development (BMZ), the principal funder of party assistance by the *Stiftungen*, is careful to note that promoting democracy coheres with other goals of foreign aid and that the German government with regard to its democracy promotion 'is not limited to a specific form of democracy' (BMZ 2005: 5). No mention is made in government documents of party assistance by the *Stiftungen*. A KAS report (2007a: 375) merely notes that 'German law does not prohibit cooperating with and/or promoting political parties'. NIMD, established in 2000 by seven of the biggest Dutch political parties, and funded primarily by the Ministry of Foreign Affairs within the framework of development cooperation policy, [14] is the only one among the organizations discussed here for which party assistance is an exclusive focus of activity. Besides party assistance, the U.S. party institutes are engaged in, among others, civil society assistance, election monitoring, civic education and governance reform. The international work of the *Stiftungen* includes assistance to civil society, support for scholarly research, organization of discussions and debates, and counsel to governments and parliaments (Egger 2007: 45)

Funding for assistance by the U.S. party institutes comes mostly from the United States Agency for International Development (USAID), with a much smaller portion from the National Endowment for Democracy (NED). With IFES, NDI and IRI are part of the Consortium for Elections and Political Process Strengthening (CEPPS), which is primarily a funding mechanism designed to streamline procedures of application for funding. By virtue of their inclusion in the CEPPS, NDI and IRI enjoy a privileged status as recipients of USAID funds. Party assistance by the U.S. party institutes is in most cases carried out under cooperative agreements, granting the party institutes a considerable degree of autonomy. IRI and NDI reportedly spend 43 and 35 per cent of their budgets on party assistance, amounting to an estimated combined sum of $68 million in 2005 (Carothers 2006a: 85). Total U.S. expenditures on party assistance are still modest: in 1999, only three per cent of USAID Democracy and Governance funds were directed at party assistance (USAID 1999b: 4).[15] In Georgia, NDI and IRI have worked with budgets of between half a million and one million dollar annually.[16] In interviews, representatives from NDI and IRI in Georgia have chosen not to disclose what part of these budgets was used for party assistance specifically. NDI and IRI budgets in Ukraine were larger than in Georgia, but exact information on funding has not been disclosed in interviews. Funding for party assistance in Ukraine by the *Stiftungen* comes from the German Ministry for Economic Cooperation (BMZ). Estimates of the percentage of funds (for international activities) spent on party assistance vary from 5%-10%[17] to 10-30% (Carothers (2006a: 85) and 20-30% (Erdmann 2006: 3), amounting to a combined party assistance budget in the tens of millions of euros. Representatives of KAS, FES and FNS have not revealed in interviews how much their organizations spend on party assistance in Ukraine. The NIMD program in Georgia, finally, was funded by the Office for Democratic Institutions and Human Rights (ODIHR) of the OSCE at a cost of around two hundred thousand euro per year.[18]

There are several ways to discern between different forms of party assistance programs, mostly on the basis of what element of the party's functioning is targeted. A distinction that is often made regarding assistance to individual parties, whether provided to only one party or several indvidual parties simultaneously, is between 'operational and structural development' programs and 'election-related' programs (Doherty 2002: 6; USAID 1999b: 12; USAID 2007: ii). The former category of programs addresses, among other things, membership recruitment, message development, the organization of regional and local branches, outreach, financial management, and inclusion of women and youth; programs of the latter category are often about campaign strategy, mobilizing party members, message development (again), and campaign finance. The distinction also concerns the timing of the programs, with election-related programs typically executed in the run-up to parliamentary elections. Election-related programs are not primarily interested in longer-term, structural development of parties. Publications issued by the donors and providers of assistance, however, reveal that the development of stable, representative, and responsive parties is the overriding objective for all actors involved in party assistance (see section three in this chapter). In this sense, structural-operational development in party assistance takes precedence over election-related activities.

A different area of parties' functioning, in the legislature, is the target of a third type of assistance programs, which variably are seen as part of party assistance or as a separate type of assistance. Here, this type of assistance is not understood as party assistance for two reasons. First, parties and parliamentary factions are often far from congruent in the Georgian and Ukrainian parliaments, signifying a shortage of party cohesiveness. Therefore, it is often factions rather than parties which are recipients of this type of assistance, sometimes called 'legislative strengthening'. Second, actors in party assistance in Georgia and Ukraine distinguish between assistance to the legislature and assistance to parties organizationally. In Georgia since the Rose Revolution, for example, NDI works in parliament, while IRI assists parties, whether represented in parliament or not, with regard to their operation outside parliament.

Party assistance in a broad sense, it has been argued, also encompasses 'party system assistance', and 'indirect party assistance' (Carothers 2006a: chapter four). Party system assistance comprises the promotion of interparty relations (a major focus of NIMD's multi-party approach) and amending the institutional framework under which parties operate. Given the impact of institutional design on party development and operation, amending legislation on political parties and the conduct of elections can help create more favorable conditions for stable and democratic party development. Promoting interparty relations often takes the form of 'coalition-building' among parties, with coalitions being either temporary electoral coalitions or formal mergers of several parties. Since coalition-building has been an important element in assistance programs in both Georgia and Ukraine, it is understood as an inherent element of the party assistance effort for the purposes of this research. Assistance targeted at legislative reform, on the other hand, is not included conceptually here as party assistance. Finally, 'indirect party aid' concerns other types of democracy assistance than party assistance, which indirectly have an impact on the functioning of parties (outside parliament), such as electoral assistance, aid to civil society, and legislative strengthening (Carothers 2006a: 90-1).

The quintessential activity in direct party assistance are educational training seminars (Carothers 2006a: 113). Party assistance training can be classified according to the number of parties participating in the seminars, the audience present at the seminars, the type of instructor(s), and whether the topic has been selected by the recipient party, or has been proposed by the provider of assistance, alternatively. First, seminars are held either for an individual party or for several parties at once. If providers of assistance organize seminars for individual parties, they often also organize seminars for other parties, unless they maintain a strictly fraternal, party-to-party approach with only one party. Multi-party seminars can be for parties from the same part of the political spectrum or to a range of parties which represent a cross-section of the party universe of a country. Second, factors which mark the type of audience present at party assistance programs are the hierarchical position of participants (from party leaders to rank-and-file activists and party members), whether participants are from the capital or from regions outside the capital, gender distribution, and age. Providers of assistance are often keen on having ordinary party activists, party representatives from the regions, women, and young people participate in seminars. Third, particularly seminars at an early stage of assistance programs are often conducted by Western experts. As programs evolve, the training is sometimes delegated to local instructors. Training of trainers (ToT), who pass on their acquired knowledge and skills to people from their party, is viewed as a desirable aim of assistance programs. Finally, topics of seminars are sometimes proposed by the provider of assistance, and in other instances picked by the parties themselves. Since it is generally agreed that assistance should be carried out in accordance with parties' particular needs, this latter variant is regarded as the more desirable one.

Next to seminars, two standard elements in party assistance in Georgia and Ukraine and elsewhere, but not necessarily everywhere, are political counsel, mostly to party leaders, and study trips (Carothers 2006a: 113). Counsel is typically offered to parties during 'consultations' of the heads of the local offices of the providers of assistance with the leaders of individual parties. For providers of assistance, these consultations also serve the goal of maintaining contact with party leaders and getting updated on party development and inter-party relations. The main purpose of study trips is to familiarize political party representatives, most of whom are from the party leadership, with political processes in the donor countries of political party assistance, and to contribute to the integration of recipient parties into international networks. In addition to these standards elements of party assistance, some providers of assistance include different types of activities that may be rubricated under party assistance. European providers of assistance which maintain fraternal relations with parties in recipient countries, for instance, sometimes lobby for their parties to receive membership in transnational parties. IRI organizes public opinion polling, the findings of which are communicated to parties. NIMD organizes round tables for party representatives with the explicit aim to foster interparty dialogue. There is considerable variation in the leeway providers of assistance on the ground have in designing and implementing assistance programs. To varying degrees, NDI, IRI, KAS, FES, and FNS receive orders from the central offices and have to report to embassies and, in the case of NDI and IRI, to USAID. In Georgia and Ukraine at least, the country offices of the main providers of assistance all say to enjoy a large degree of autonomy vis-à-vis the central offices of their organizations.[19]

2.2. STANDARDS OF GOOD PRACTICE

The implementation of party assistance is constrained by a number of formal requirements and informal norms, to which the providers of assistance are kept in part by legal obligation and in part by voluntary adherence. These 'standards of good practice' are extensively put down in policy documents and strategy papers of the funders and providers of assistance. The standards of good practice in party assistance are driven by two overriding motives. First, the assistance should not interfere too directly in the internal political affairs of recipient countries or be perceived as doing this. USAID even states that, because of 'the need to avoid interference in the domestic affairs of sovereign states' (1999: 2) the assistance it funds by law 'may not be used to influence the outcome of any election' (1999: 20). FES (Saxer 2006a: 7) acknowledges that party assistance is not neutral, but assistance providers should avoid creating the impression that they interfere in internal affairs. Second, aiding parties should ultimately be aimed at promoting democracy in recipient countries. Party assistance, in other words, is always at the service of the superior objective of democracy promotion. The first motive instructs assistance to avoid favoring certain political forces over others by working with parties across the political spectrum, while the second motive imposes seemingly strict criteria regarding the selection of recipient parties. As will be demonstrated in chapter five, the extent to which providers of assistance comply with these standards has important implications for the effectiveness of the party assistance effort.

The requirement of non-partisanship compels providers of assistance to work with a set of political forces which collectively are representative of the democratic part of the party universe in a given country (USAID1999b: 20; Doherty 2002: 4). USAID (2003b: 1) prescribes that USAID-funded assistance must make 'a good faith effort to assist all democratic parties with equitable levels of assistance'. Since it is difficult for individual providers to cover a wide range of forces, inclusiveness is often expected to be achieved by the cumulative efforts of assistance providers from the same country. Having agreed on how to divide the party universe, the two U.S. party institutes may thus each work with a different set of parties. The traditional focus of the *Stiftungen* on only one party or one part of the political spectrum is defended by pointing to the alleged situation that, by granting assistance simultaneously to different parts of the political spectrum, the work of the *Stiftungen* collectively does ensure inclusiveness.[20] The argument is untenable because the *Stiftungen* are in fact unevenly represented and involved in party assistance in many countries (Carothers 2006a: 149-50; Erdmann 2006: 6-7). Until 2007 in Georgia, for instance, of the *Stiftungen* only FNS was involved in party assistance, while FES had a considerable presence but chose not to engage in party assistance, and KAS had only one representative. USAID and the U.S. party institutes argue that the requirement of inclusiveness may be loosened in conditions with an uneven electoral playing field (Doherty 2002: 5; USAID 2003b: 10). When democratic parties are put at a disadvantage by a 'strict authoritarian system', providers of assistance may opt to engage in coalition-building of democratic forces or even work with only one party. Two other admonitions for assistance providers aimed at avoiding direct interference in domestic politics are to conclude programs one month before elections (USAID 1999b: 2) and not to make financial contributions to parties (BMZ 2002: §§ I to III ; USAID 2000: 15).

A second key standard of good practice in party assistance concerns the selection of parties that receive assistance. Two criteria of eligibility stand out: parties need to be democratic and they need to be 'viable' or 'significant'. For the *Stiftungen*, to the extent that these hold on to the traditional fraternal approach, do these criteria come on top of the obvious criterion of ideological or programmatic kinship. Parties need to be democratic both in terms of attitude and of actual behavior, and both with respect to their internal operation and with respect to their operation in the party system and in society. Attitudinally, parties are deemed democratic when they, among other things, embrace political and civil liberties and accept the holding of elections as the sole legitimate means of obtaining power (USAID 2003b: 9). Behaviorally, recipient parties, especially when they are in power, should respect competing parties (USAID 1999b: 1) and act responsibly and constructively in government and in parliament. Furthermore, parties, in their internal functioning, should maintain 'an acceptable level of internal democracy or a stated aspiration to achieve this' (Doherty 2002: 4; see also KAS 2008a: 76). Due to the typically large numbers of parties in environments where multipartism is a relatively new phenomenon, assistance providers are rarely able to offer assistance to all available democratic parties. Next to the core criterion of democratic attitudes and behavior, a second criterion of eligibility therefore is 'viability', or 'significance' of parties. Viability is almost invariably mentioned as a core criterion for eligibility to receive assistance (e.g. Doherty 2002: 4; USAID 2006b: 27). A party is considered viable either when it has a relatively large base of support and has been successful in previous elections (USAID 2003b: 10), when it has representation in parliament, [21] when it is seen as having chances to win representation in parliament,[22] or simply assessed qualitatively.

42

2.3. THE PARTY ASSISTANCE NORM

Over the past decade and a half there has been an upswing in research that studies how norms travel across borders. Much of this research draws on insights from social constructivism, emphasizing ideational rather than merely rationalist sources of behavior. A substantial portion of the literature on transnational diffusion is concerned with how international norms acquire widespread acceptance (Finnemore and Sikkink 1998), for instance with regard to grand issues such as democracy (Carothers 1992; McFaul 2004) and human rights (Risse-Kappen et al. 1999) and more specific issues such as the international monitoring of elections (Hyde 2007; Kelley 2008), whaling (Peterson 1992) or landmines (Price 1998). Whereas the unit of analysis in a majority of these studies is at the macro-level (nation-states), the approach can equally be applied to the sub-national level of organizations or institutions, such as political parties, or even to individuals.

As an increasing number of studies have demonstrated how norms shape behavior, it has become accepted that norms present an important object of study. Social constructivist accounts of norm diffusion have shed light on how norms are crafted, promoted, framed, and internalized in different contexts. The 'mainstream' constructivism that is a source of insights in this study for explanations of the non-compliance of recipient parties with the party assistance norm, is often contrasted with a different strand of constructivism that is sometimes called 'critical' or 'radical' and that is associated with postmodernism (Hopf 1998; Price and Reus-Smit 1998). Although mainstream constructivists are skeptical of exclusively rationalist accounts of norm diffusion, they do not, as critical constructivists do, reject a positivist research agenda and methodology (Checkel 1998: 327). Of great influence in theorizing about norm diffusion are two ideal-type 'logics' (Magen 2006; March and Olsen 1989). When norm diffusion follows a 'logic of consequences', the recipients adopt the norm because they assume that adoption brings in benefits which outweigh possible costs. When, on the other hand, norm diffusion follows a 'logic of appropriateness', the recipients have come to view compliance as intrinsically appropriate behavior, and are not necessarily driven by a cost-benefit analysis. Mechanisms and instruments which are employed by norm 'entrepreneurs' to induce recipients into complying with a certain norm include the provision of external incentives (e.g. Schimmelfennig and Sedelmeier 2004), mostly in the form of conditionality; persuasion (Checkel 2002) and arguing (Risse 2003); and 'social influence', exerted by the norm entrepreneurs upon the recipient through 'the distribution of social rewards and punishments' (Johnston 2001).

It is argued here that the promotion of democratic, stable, and representative parties by international actors amounts to norm promotion. Providers of party assistance, correspondingly, are 'norm entrepreneurs' or 'agents of change', and political parties are 'norm recipients' or 'norm-takers'. A norm is understood in this context as 'a standard of appropriate behavior for actors with a given identity' (Finnemore and Sikkink 1998: 891). The assumption throughout the following chapters is that, underlying political party assistance, a norm is implicit in party assistance that conveys a comprehensive idea of how parties should operate in the electorate, as organizations, and in government, and what functions they should fulfill. Although there is 'no initial formalized process of norm setting' in the case of party assistance, 'international aid actors with similar points of view on the core issues all work to spread the core values and over time the values start to gain some traction as norms' (Carothers 2006a: 188-9). In other words, despite the fact that party assistance is a multi-faceted effort involving a variety of actors and approaches, there is a remarkable degree of consensus among providers of party assistance on which issues are central in the assistance to political parties - reflecting the current flaws of parties and an idea of how they in fact should operate - such that we can speak of a shared norm. Naturally, it is persons rather than parties who are the actual recipients of the party assistance norm. Persons who are in the position to enact change within Georgian and Ukrainian parties typically are only in the higher echelons of their parties. When, in the following, reference is made to political parties as recipients, the implication is that it is really party representatives with leverage over their parties who are the direct recipients.

From strategy papers, statements of intentions, reports and evaluations,[23] issued on an irregular basis by the funding and implementing organizations of party assistance, the core elements of the party assistance norm can be deduced.[24] Three elements which feature in virtually every standard-setting document by NDI, IRI, USAID, KAS, FES, and NIMD on party assistance, stand out. First, instead of being the political vehicle for a narrow leadership, parties should be broad-based and have solid organizational structures. Most crucially, parties should strive to attract a considerable and active membership (e.g. NDI 2003, ch.V; Saxer 2006a: 7; USAID 1999b; 17), with, ideally, a strong role for women and youth, and have organizational capacity at the regional and local levels (e.g. NIMD 2004: 22; Saxer 2006b: 11; USAID 1999b: 12). In a 2008 publication, NDI even argues that 'In all sustainable democracies, the party system must be deeply and durably entrenched in the fabric of society' (NDI 2008b: ii). Second, instead of serving primarily the interests of the leadership, parties should be representative of the interests of identifiable societal groups (e.g. USAID

2003b: 1; USAID 2006d: 27). To this end, parties should advocate a coherent program, whether inspired by a traditional political ideology or not (e.g. NIMD 2004: 22; Saxer 2006b: 11; USAID 1999b: 8). Electoral competition, correspondingly, should be issue-based rather than revolve about personal reputation or clientelist linkage. Programmatic positioning by parties should decrease the impact of personalism in elections, provide voters with the opportunity to make informed choices, and enhance vertical accountability. Third, instead of being entirely at the discretion of the party leader(s), parties should uphold the principle of internal democracy, on different levels of the party, and in different areas of decision-making (e.g. NIMD 2004: 22; Saxer 2006b: 11; USAID 1999b: 37). For most donors, internal democracy within parties is a requisite to be eligible for assistance (Doherty 2002: 4; KAS 2007a: 374).

These three elements constitute the core of the party assistance norm. Not surprisingly, they are highly related: the absence of thick organizational structures often goes together with programmatic vagueness and a lack of internal democracy. Strong with regard to all three elements is especially the 'mass integration' party type which emerged in Western Europe before the Second World War and which is said to provide the blueprint for the party assistance norm (Carothers, 2006: 124; Erdmann, 2006: 6). Most educational party assistance seminars that are not election-related focus on one or several elements of the norm. In addition to the three core elements of the norm, a number of secondary elements of the norm that feature in most, but not all standard-setting documents by the funders and providers of assistance, can be identified. The importance of financial accountability and transparency is frequently emphasized (e.g. Doherty 2002: 7; Saxer 2006b: 7). On a party-systemic level, the party assistance norm wants parties to seek constructive relations with each other (e.g. NDI 2008b: 3; NIMD 2004: 21) and to act responsibly in parliament and government (e.g. Saxer 2006b: 11; USAID 1999b: 38). In its 1999 strategy paper on party assistance, USAID (1999: 30) captures almost all elements of what is understood here as the party assistance norm in one sentence:

> "Implicit in this [NDI and IRI political party development programs] is the belief that parties should be broad-based and internally democratic and have the skills and organizational capacity to compete in elections, recruit and maintain members, communicate effectively, govern effectively, and serve as loyal opposition. In addition, they believe that party systems need to strike a balance between the need for representation of all major sectors [...]"

The party assistance norm relates to an image of political parties which is in decline in many Western democracies, and which is certainly absent in the United States. Far from all parties in the West are 'internally democratic, financially transparent, managed in a rational, nonpersonalistic fashion, highly inclusive of women at all levels, ideologically coherent, committed to issue-based, grassroots work (rather than negative, personality-oriented television campaigning), and driven by ethical and policy principles rather than opportunism', as Carothers (2006a: 123) summarizes what he calls the 'mythic model' of parties that informs the design of many party assistance programs. While U.S providers of assistance promote a model of parties that is not found at home, the *Stiftungen* implicitly, sometimes explicitly (KAS 2007a: 378) hold up the example of the post-war German political party system in their work. At the same time, German donors insist that they are not after 'exporting' one specific type of party organization (BMZ 2005: 5; KAS 2007a: 380).

Not all activities that are undertaken as an element in party assistance programs are exclusively informed by the party assistance norm. This applies particularly to most election-related training seminars that seek to teach campaign skills to parties, and that are not so much concerned with the long-term structural development of parties. Judging from the documents that are issued by the funding and implementing organizations of party assistance, however, these election-related seminars are secondary in importance to seminars on 'operational and structural development', as the overarching objective of party assistance is to contribute to the development of stable and democratic parties.

2.4. PROMOTION OF THE PARTY ASSISTANCE NORM

Considering the state of parties in Georgia and Ukraine, they have yet to start internalizing (elements of) the party assistance norm. This section provides an outline of tentative explanations of the limited extent of compliance with the party assistance norm by recipient parties in Georgia and Ukraine. The explanations draw on insights from literature on norm diffusion that have particular relevance to party assistance. The outline of these tentative explanations provides some hints regarding the inadequacy of party assistance in countries like Georgia and Ukraine with volatile party politics and an ambiguous or less-than-democratic political setting. The two case studies in chapters five and six subsequently provide empirical information that helps to assess the relative weight of these explanations for the cases of Georgia and Ukraine. Section 6.3 particularly will revisit the arguments made in the current section. Most of the literature on norm diffusion is influenced by social constructivist insights, placing emphasis on explanations of norm diffusion that are non-rationalist. Much literature on norm diffusion, however, is also sensitive to more goal-oriented considerations by actors, and so is the discussion here, especially where the discussion looks at the incentives for compliance of norm recipients.

Theory and case-study work on norm diffusion posit that the likelihood of compliance increases, first, as the norm is more robust, with norm robustness hinging on intrinsic features of the norm (e.g. Finnemore and Sikkink 1998: 906-8; Legro 1997: 34); second, as the 'fit' between the international norm and existing local norms is bigger, as well as the relation between the 'norm entrepreneurs' and norm recipients more empathic (e.g. Cortell and Davis 2000; Risse 1999: 534); and third, as the incentive structures of norm recipients, whether material or immaterial, are more reconcilable with adoption of the norm (e.g. Kelley 2006; Schimmelfennig and Sedelmeier 2004: 663-7). Stated simply, the first explanation points attention to the input of the norm promotion; the third explanation, by contrast, looks exclusively at the recipient-side of the diffusion process; and the second explanation studies the specific interaction between the supply-side and the recipient-side in the process of norm diffusion. As should be expected for a complex phenomenon such as norm diffusion, the three strands of explanation, which are consecutively discussed below, are interrelated: only a combination of the different explanations can present a comprehensive explanation of why a given norm does or does not travel.

Norm robustness

Norm robustness refers to intrinsic features of the norm. Two such intrinsic features in particular contribute to undercut the robustness of the party assistance norm: its lack of determinacy and the absence of a clear moral dimension. Determinacy of a norm has an informational value in relation to recipients: without a clear understanding of what is expected of them, recipients may construe their own interpretation of the norm which diverges from the original norm (Schimmelfennig and Sedelmeier 2004: 664). Notwithstanding a remarkable degree of correspondence between documents on party assistance by different funders and providers, and also between the actual strategies that are pursued in party assistance, there are few explicit references to the existence of a single norm that is advocated by providers of assistance. The attributes of the norm can be derived from documents without too much difficulty, but the sum of these attributes has not been recognized by practitioners as amounting to a uniform norm. Moreover, there are no joint statements, of the sort of the Paris Declaration on Aid Effectiveness, which spells out standards and principles regarding development aid, or the standard-setting Declaration of Principles for International Election

Observation, by providers of assistance from different countries on how party assistance should be conducted and what elements it should contain.

The party assistance norm lacks a particularly compelling ethical dimension, unlike, for instance, norms which advocate a ban on torture or landmines. Providers of party assistance do not so much make a moral appeal to party representatives to change their ways, as they seek to convince them of the instrumental value of reform. The norm fails to inspire a sense of moral 'oughtness' (Florini 1996) on parties, decreasing the odds that norm recipients will internalize the norm out of 'a logic of appropriateness'. An important role is played here by group dynamic: parties are less embarrassed by their failure to comply with the norm as long as most other parties equally fail to comply. Another problem is the realization that compliance with elements of the party assistance is limited and possibly dwindling among political parties in the countries from which assistance is funded. In recent decades, parties in Western democracies have become more embedded in state structures at the expense of being representative of groups in society (Katz and Mair 2002; Van Biezen 2004); they have seen their membership figures drop (Mair and Van Biezen 2001); and they are not as programmatically distinct as before while having a stronger focus on elections (Scarrow et al. 2000). The parties with which the core providers of party assistance are associated, therefore, present questionable examples for emulation.

Not only is the norm not robust, implementation of the promotion of the norm also falls short of intensity. The major providers opt to work in a large number of countries. Standards of good practice in party assistance moreover prescribe that providers of assistance work with a representative, inclusive set of parties, so that the amount of assistance per party is further decreased. The amount of assistance individual parties receive, consequently, is small, and the relation between recipients and providers of assistance is a relatively loose one.

Normative fit and cultural match

Related to this last point, the second explanation of the ineffectiveness of party assistance that draws on insights from literature on norm diffusion suggests a limited 'normative fit' or 'cultural match' linking the supply-side and the recipient-side of the party assistance norm. Normative fit (e.g. Schimmelfennig 2005: 7) refers to the relation between the international norm and local norms, traditions, and practices. The degree of normative fit in party assistance is primarily compromised by the idealistic nature of the party assistance norm. The norm harks back to a 'mythic model' of parties that hardly exist, if they have ever existed at all, in Western democracies. On the recipient-side, the local norm on party operation generally does not strongly condemn the absence of thick organizational structures, internal democracy, and a distinct and consistent program. The relatively young political parties in countries where party assistance is provided tend to be different types of organizations, driven by different incentive structures and 'models of behavior' (Strom 1990) than their older Western counterparts which have gone through consecutive stages of development. There is, in brief, a vast and seemingly insurmountable distance between on the one hand the realities of party development in countries where parties receive assistance, and on the other hand the image of parties that is conveyed by the party assistance norm.

Risse (2003: 10) finds that norm diffusion is more forthcoming when norm entrepreneurs and recipients can mutually empathize, which in turn is only possible when they to some degree share a 'gemeinsame Lebenswelt' (common lifeworld). Given that political cultures of recipients vis-à-vis providers are so different, understanding between the two sides is limited. Not only are recipients strange to the political culture of advanced democracies which underpins the party assistance norm, providers of assistance often also lack essential insight into the nature of party politics in the countries in which they work. In keeping with the widespread realization that democracy assistance suffers from a lack of insight into local conditions (e.g Carothers 1999: 261), it has been frequently argued that party assistance programs should be informed by more thorough analysis of local conditions (CMI 2007: 15; Kumar 2005: 514).

Incentives

Considering the arguments above, it seems unlikely that norm compliance is achieved in party assistance merely through a logic of appropriateness. To make compliance feasible, norm recipients need some sort of incentive (cf. McDonagh 2008). The third explanation for the general ineffectiveness of party assistance points to incentives of political party actors. Literature on norm diffusion offers clues on why incentives, whether provided by party assistance or existing independent from party assistance, are unlikely to induce party actors into compliance with the party assistance norm.

The two incentives that can be expected to induce compliance are, first, the anticipation of electoral gain, and second, the elevation of social status. While the first incentive is tangible and only has domestic relevance, the second is immaterial and has relevance both domestically and in the interaction with the providers of assistance. If getting more votes would follow from adoption of the party assistance

49

norm, then this would be the most compelling argument for parties to comply with the norm. Diamond (2003: 45) argues that one incentive for parties to reform is that 'parties that do modernize and reform themselves may gradually develop wider appeals and competitive advantages over those that do not'. An NDI publication (2008b: 4) says that the 'overall goal [of party assistance] is to demonstrate that grassroots outreach, open accountability, and greater representation of the public – in short, democratic practice – have themselves given parties a competitive edge in countries around the world'. In most countries where party assistance is provided, however, it is far from evident that shedding off established practices will bring in electoral benefits. Party-citizen linkages based on personal reputation and clientelism, which are more common than programmatic linkage in many countries, can be as effective for winning votes. Likewise, limited organizational density does not preclude electoral success.

The elevation of social status for parties concerns their relationship with the providers of assistance as well as the way in which the parties are viewed domestically by other parties and by the public at large. Since full compliance with the party assistance norm is so rare, it is difficult to say whether there really is a relation with elevated social status. There is strong anecdotal evidence at least that participation in party assistance programs and having ties with providers of assistance are considered a feat of prestige for parties.[25] It is not obvious that the possible additional social rewards which follow compliance with the party assistance norm, however, are a strong enough incentive for parties to be induced into compliance.

The principal mechanism through which providers of assistance can offer incentives for compliance is conditionality. The provision of external incentives through conditionality can be an important driver in domestic reforms, as especially the example of European Union enlargement demonstrates (Schimmelfennig and Sedelmeier 2004). There is little, however, that norm entrepreneurs in party assistance can put on the table by way of 'carrots'. One potential 'carrot' is assistance with the integration of parties into transnational party organizations, which is widely considered as prestigious by recipient parties. There hardly appears to exist a relation, though, between the degree of compliance with the norm and the chances of being integrated into transnational parties. The 'party of power' United National Movement in Georgia, for instance, has received observer status in the European People's Party, despite its association with undemocratic practices (Mitchell 2008: 94).

Just as 'carrots', 'sticks' are not used credibly and consistently in party assistance. Exclusion from assistance programs, public shaming, or any other form of social punishment is rarely taken as a measure by providers of assistance to discourage non-compliance. This helps create a situation in which '[t]he assistance goes on and on, uninformed by any strategic conception about how to produce change in the other party, as the counterpart party gradually learns that it can basically do anything it wants and still have access to the study tours, exchange visits, material aid, conferences, and all the rest (Carothers 2006a: 130). Overall, the impression emerges that political party assistance, in part also due to the limited intensity of the assistance effort, is rather toothless.

Positive incentives for compliance are partially offset by competing 'negative' incentives. Party leaders, for instance, may actively oppose the establishment of procedures of internal democracy because they are interested in maintaining their control over the party. Adoption costs indeed are in particular excessively high for leaders, who often 'own' their parties and would under no condition voluntarily cede control, something that is mostly well understood by the party's supporters. Also, parties in many countries are intently set up as projects designed to fulfill only short-term objectives, and therefore do not take an interest in developing into stable, representative forces. The fact that providers of assistance have often been 'naïve about the incentive structures that shaped political activity' is seen as part of the explanation of the limited effectiveness of previous party assistance programs (Power 2008: i). Recent documents by the funders and providers of assistance implicitly acknowledge the failure to take parties' incentives and interests into account. A USAID report (2007: iv) argues that providers of assistance should understand 'the real incentives of parties and politicians', while a NDI report (2008b: 3) acknowledges that 'parties have a fundamental interest in winning or maintaining political power' and that NDI should 'build the incentives for internal reform by shaping its programs around these interests'.

CHAPTER THREE: THE CONTEXT OF PARTY ASSISTANCE IN GEORGIA AND UKRAINE

Party assistance, when it works, has a positive impact on how parties develop. As party (system) development is one element in processes of political change, so is party assistance one type of intervention in the broad palette of democracy assistance, with other types of assistance aiming at different aspects of politics and government, such as elections, legislative functioning, or an independent judiciary. Party development is affected foremost by domestic factors, but external, international factors can have a noticeable impact. With all other possible international factors in party development, party assistance constitutes the international dimension of party development. The context of party assistance, then, is shaped by the following four areas: party development, the area that party assistance seeks to have a direct impact on; democracy assistance, in which party assistance is embedded organizationally and conceptually; political change; and elements in the 'international dimension' of party development other than party assistance. In a graphical illustration, the relationship between party assistance and the context of party assistance looks like this:

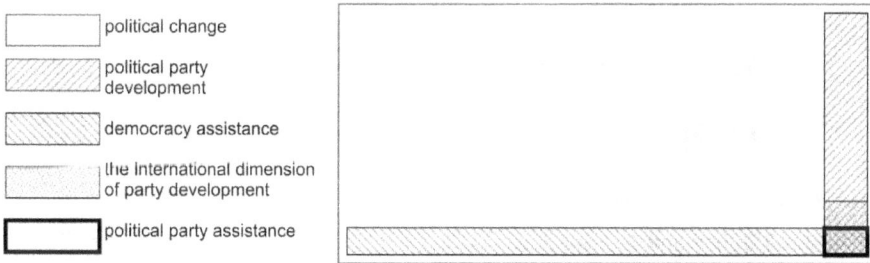

Figure 1. The context of political party assistance

As figure one demonstrates, party assistance is a subset both of party development and of democracy assistance. Party development and democracy assistance in turn are subsets of political change. Party assistance is also one element in the international dimension of party development. The international dimension of party development by default is a subset of overall party development.

The effectiveness of party assistance hinges on well crafted programs and on the permissiveness of domestic factors in party development. The party assistance programs that have been operated in Georgia and Ukraine will be assessed in chapters five and six. The next chapter pinpoints the outcomes of party development in Georgia and Ukraine throughout the post-communist period, and identifies which factors have blocked the development of a stable and democratic party system. The current chapter reviews the remaining areas which shape the context of party assistance with relation to Georgia and Ukraine - political change (sections one to three), democracy assistance (section four), and the international dimension of party development (section five). This review provides some insight into the rationale which underlies party assistance, and into the factors which constrain and facilitate its implementation.

The opening section discusses how the post-communist political regimes of Georgia and Ukraine have been looked upon and where they have been situated in regime classifications. Second, a number of the foremost explanations - the impact of the 'leninist' legacy, ill-suited political culture and popular values, problems with state-building and internal diversity, economic issues, inadequate institutional design, limited linkage and leverage to and from the West, and agency - for the failure of comprehensive democratization during most of the post-communist period are outlined. Concluding the discussion of political change, the causes of the Rose and Orange Revolutions, as well as the role of the West in these arguably most defining political events of the period since 1991 in Georgia and Ukraine, are set forth. Next, the chapter provides some evidence of the extent and form of Western democracy assistance in Georgia and Ukraine both before and after the Revolutions. Finally, international factors other than party assistance that have an impact on party development in Georgia and Ukraine are briefly discussed.

3.1. IN THE GRAY ZONE

Ukraine (until 2005) and Georgia have been among the large majority of 'transitional' states which in the years after the initial move away from (politically closed) autocracy did not consolidate to become liberal democratic regimes (Carothers 2002: 9). Both states have for the most time lingered in the 'partly free' category of the both widely used and heavily criticized Freedom House Freedom in the World comparative assessment of political and civil rights.[26] Georgia scored 5 in the first years under Shevardnadze, before improving to 3.5 in the late 1990s and regressing to 4 in the years immediately preceding the Rose Revolution. After the Revolution, Georgia's rating improved to 3-3.5, and then fell back to 4 in 2007 and 2008. Ukraine scored 3.5 in most years until 2003, then slipped to 4 in 2003 and 2004, before improving markedly to 2.5 in the years since the Revolution.[27] The literature on regime classifications has termed regimes like those in Georgia and Ukraine competitive authoritarian (Levitsky and Way 2002), semi-liberal authoritarian (Siaroff 2005), electoral authoritarian (Schedler 2006) where the emphasis is on the authoritarian practices inherent in these regimes; and illiberal democratic (Merkel 2004: 49), delegative democratic (O'Donnell 1994) and other democratic-with-adjective designations (Collier and Levitsky 1997) where the emphasis is rather on the procedural and institutional elements of the political systems.

Manifestations of the less-than-democratic nature of Georgia and Ukraine (until 2005) include, as in many other places, an uneven political playing field, inadequate safeguards of civil and political rights, and weak horizontal accountability due to a concentration of power in the executive. In assessments of Ukraine under Kuchma, the focus is most often on the corruptive entanglement of the political and economic domains, and on the frequent prevalence of informal practices over formal institutions (neopatrimonialism). Way (2005: 4) contends that Kuchma's 'competitive authoritarian' regime rested on the two pillars: 'first, an extensive set of largely informal authoritarian institutions and processes that served to harass oppositionists and to falsify election results; and second, a coalition of oligarchic forces in parliament and in the administration that organized support for Kuchma, competing for his patronage'. D'Anieri (2007: 69) similarly argues that 'machine politics' under Kuchma was characterized by a combination of patronage, selective law enforcement, and control over the economy and law enforcement. Since the Revolution, abuse of power by the executive and the leverage of oligarchs over politics have decreased. Much analysis of the 'façade democracy' (Devdariani 2004) or 'Potemkin democracy' (King 2001) of Shevardnadze-era Georgia stresses the impact of all-pervasive corruption and weak state capacity on how the country was governed. Wheatley (2005: 218) argues that Georgia essentially was a 'contested oligarchy', where a number of influential groups vied for political and economic power, while the state was largely incapable of providing for the common good. According to King (2001: 100), 'Georgia is a chronically weak state. In a region of only minimally successful countries, however, the Georgian case is particularly dire [...] Indeed, it is worth asking whether a state called "Georgia" even exists today in any meaningful sense'. Since the Revolution, corruption is no longer all-pervasive and government has become more effective, while political competition is as circumscribed as before the Revolution.

3.2. CONSTRAINTS ON DEMOCRATIZATION

Among the factors that are most commonly believed to have constrained democratization in the former Soviet Union and elsewhere in the post-communist world are, in random order, 'the leninist legacy', elite political culture and popular values, problems with state-building and nation-building, constitutional design and electoral legislation, economic problems, weak linkage and leverage to and from the West, and finally agency. These factors are discussed here in turn. Adjudicating the relative weight of the factors which contribute to constrain democratization is beyond the scope of this chapter. The implications of a number of the factors discussed here for party (system) development specifically are discussed in the next chapter.

Legacies

Defined as 'the structural, cultural, and institutional starting points of ex-communist countries at the outset of the transition' (Pop-Eleches 2007: 910), legacies are widely believed to cast a long shadow over the political trajectories of post-socialist states. Hanson (1997) argues that the 'leninist legacy' (Jowitt 1992) is made up of distinct ideological, political, socioeconomic, and cultural legacies. Ruling forces in Georgia and Ukraine have quickly, and without too much opposition, rejected the ideological legacy of marxism-leninism. The Communist Party of Ukraine remained widely popular throughout the 1990s but was kept continuously out of power. Elements of the political legacy have left deeper traces. The type of communist rule - patrimonial communsim - that Kitschelt et al. (1999) argue was prevalent in the Soviet Union, helps to explain the adoption of strong presidential rule in Georgia and Ukraine as well as the ubiquity of patronage and neopatrimonialism (March 2006: 343). Regarding the institutional legacy, D'Anieri (2007: 81) notes that institutional continuity and little turnover in elites have inhibited a more decisive break with the past. Georgia and Ukraine, moreover, ratified their post-communist constitutions only in 1995 and 1996, respectively. The systematic corruption, rule-breaking, and clientelism that were rife in the governance of Soviet Georgia, finally, are found to have been continued after 1991 (Wheatley 2005: 24). The socioeconomic legacy of the Soviet Union necessitated drastic economic reforms in the early post-communist years. These reforms were poorly managed (Ukraine) or hardly managed at all (Georgia) and were complicated by far-reaching economic retraction. Ramifications of the cultural legacy of leninism are discussed separately below.

Political culture and value systems

Popular values and political and civic culture have for long been seen as important variables in political regime outcomes (Almond and Verba 1963; Inglehart 1990; Putnam 1993), though the weight of values is also contested (Jackman and Miller 1996; Muller and Seligson 1994). The relationship between values and regime outcome is a chicken-and-egg question: do the right values produce democracy

(Inglehart and Welzel 2005) or does democracy produce values that help sustain democracies (Muller and Seligson 1994)? Political culture, a poorly defined concept (Formisano 2000; Johnson 2003), is shaped by, among other things, interpersonal trust, popular trust in political and administrative institutions, belief in democracy, and civic participation. When societies display low scores on these variables, they are thought to be less likely to be or to become democracies. According to Jowitt (1991: 13), the leninist legacy includes 'a ghetto political culture that views the state with deep-seated suspicion; a distrustful society where people habitually hoard information, goods, and goodwill, and share them with only a few intimates; a widespread penchant for rumormongering that undercuts sober public discourse; and an untried, often apolitical leadership, barely familiar with and often disdainful of the politician's vocation'. Hanson (1997: 232) similarly refers to a 'distinctive late Leninist culture of cynicism and alienation from the public sphere'. The actuality of these observations is confirmed by value surveys. Georgians and Ukrainians tend to trust only a narrow circle of relatives and acquaintances while distrusting fellow citizens (Panina 2005: 40-1; Sapsford and Abbott 2006: 63). Especially before the Revolutions, trust in political institutions (the president, government, parliament, etc.) was abysmally low (CEORG 2004; Gutbrod 2006: 43). At the same time, Georgians and Ukrainians do support the principles of democracy and increasingly reject authoritarian rule (Haerpfer 2008; IRI et al. 2007: 48). Finally, civic participation, including membership of political parties, by international comparison, is low (Carson 2000; Howard 2003).

Nation-building and state-building

The 'transition' to democracy has often been cast as a dual process of political reforms and economic reforms. A number of states in the post-communist world, especially in the Western Balkans and the former Soviet Union, for the first time experienced modern statehood and had to cope with questions that flowed from this. For these states, coming to terms with their newfound stateness constituted the third element in what has been termed their 'triple transition' (Offe 2004). State-building requires first and foremost that the legal borders of the state are not disputed by any large domestic grouping. This requirement has not been met by Georgia, which as a newly independent state lost control over two of its regions, Abkhazia and South Ossetia. Furthermore, for a number of years until 2004 the region of Adjara was ruled as a de facto independent state, albeit one that did not seek formal independence. At least partly responsible for Georgia's woes was the territorial-administrative structure that was inherited from Soviet Georgia (Duffy Toft 2000). While the loss of two regions has not necessarily been a constraint on democratization, restoring 'territorial integrity' has been a major political issue throughout the post-communist years.

In addition to establishing fixed and undisputed borders, some authors contend that nation-building is an equally important task for new states. In a seminal article, Rustow (1970) noted that some degree of national integration has to be accomplished for democracy to be consolidated. Nation-building should limit cultural diversity, which is often seen as being an obstacle to democratization, especially when diversity stems from ethnic differences (Horowitz 1985; Roeder 1999). Diversity in Ukraine is manifested in an ethnic cleavage (through a large Russian minority), a linguistic cleavage (Russian and Ukrainian), different cultural and ideological outlooks ('Eastern Slavic' against ethnic Ukrainian) and, most crucially, regional differences in voting patterns, with the greatest distinction between the eastern and Western *oblasti*.[28] Sasse (2001) argues that regional diversity not only causes trouble, but as well has contributed to political stability by balancing opposing political interests. From the conviction that its diversity nonetheless presents a constraint on Ukraine's development, Kuzio (2001) has intimated that active nation-building should be undertaken as a fourth task of Ukraine's transition. By contrast, other authors advocate the promotion of a state-nation rather than a nation-state model, along the lines of equally diverse states such as Canada, Belgium, and Switzerland (Stepan 2005) and the promotion of an inclusive, civic national identity rather than an ethnic national identity (Szporluk 2000; Wilson 2002a).

Constitutional design and electoral legislation
Georgia was a presidential republic until the Rose Revolution, after which, through the introduction of the post of prime-minister, executive-legislative relations formally became semi-presidential. Ukraine has had semi-presidential government all along since 1991. Until 2006, when constitutional amendments entered into force that had been agreed upon during the Orange Revolution, most power was concentrated in the presidency, while afterwards powers between the president and the prime minister were more balanced. In terms of the actual distribution of power, Georgia throughout the post-communist period and Ukraine until 2006 have been 'superpresidential' (Fish 2005: 224-44; Ishiyama and Kennedy 2001), meaning simply that the presidency was by far the most powerful institution.

It is widely argued that political arrangements with a strong legislature fare better at consolidating democracy and accommodating conflict than presidential regimes (Bunce 2000; Foweraker and Landman 2002; Norris 2008). Presidential regimes can excessively concentrate power in the presidency, provide disincentives for stable party development, have a tendency to personalize politics, and are prone to incite conflict due to the winner-take-all nature of the presidential contest and the fact that the presidential term is fixed (Linz 1990; Fish 2006). Against these arguments, some authors maintain that presidentialism does not necessarily bode ill for democratization (Horowitz 1990; Mainwaring and Shugart 1997). The perils associated with strong presidential rule have been clearly discernable in Georgia and Ukraine. In Ukraine specifically, long-lasting clashes between president and parliament have been common. In both states, presidents have abused executive power and evoked irreconcilable opposition. Also, as the next chapter will discuss in detail, the weakness of party development in Georgia and Ukraine is partly explained by strong presidentialism. Considering the drawbacks of presidentialism, Ukraine has been wise to cut the powers of the president after the Revolution, resulting in a more balanced distribution of powers between president and the prime minister, and a stronger legislature. One of the first measures in Georgia after Saakashvili assumed the presidency was to install a prime minister, but at the same to further enhance presidential power, so that Georgia is now even more 'superpresidential' than before the Revolution (Fairbanks 2004: 118).

All elections in Georgia since 1992 and two parliamentary elections in Ukraine before the Orange Revolution have been conducted according to a mixed system, combining national party list voting and single member districts (SMDs). As with the perils of strong presidential rule, a majority of scholarly research finds that a large degree of proportionality is better suited for states moving away from authoritarianism, especially in 'plural societies' (Hoffman 2005; Lijphart 1995; Norris 2008). Among other things, the first-past-the-post principle in SMD races tends to personalize electoral campaigns. Moreover, SMD elections are more likely to be fraudulent than MMD elections (Birch 2007). Most negative consequences flowing from a mixed electoral system, as the next chapter will argue, are related to weak party development. While the electoral system remained unchanged in Georgia after the Rose Revolution, SMD voting has been abandoned in Ukraine in favor of party list voting for all seats in the legislature.

The economy
A further explanation for why Georgia and Ukraine did not complete a transition to democracy is found in economic factors. Severe economic contraction in the first years of independence led to a marked decrease in per capita income and GDP, rendering Georgia and Ukraine poor countries in comparison with most democracies, as well as in comparison with Russia. In 1999, Ukrainian GDP stood at 37% of the 1989 level (Prizel 2002: 365). From that moment, the economy recovered fast, with GDP growing at an average annual rate of 7% between 2000 and 2007 (Pleines 2008: 1179). The

Georgian economy was hit even harder. Reportedly, during the turmoil of 1992-1993 GDP decreased by eighty per cent (Papava and Tokmazishvili: 27). From the mid-1990s, subsequently, the Georgian economy began to grow at a fast rate. Still, in 2005 52% of Georgians were reported to live below the poverty line (Jones 2006: 35), against 29% of Ukrainians in 2008 (Gorobets 2008: 95).

The once widespread belief that a certain level of economic development is a prerequisite for democratization has been replaced by a more nuanced view on the relation between economic development and democracy. At a minimum, it is now accepted that high per capita income increases the likelihood that democracy is sustained (Bunce 2000: 707). Considering the low per capita income of Georgia and Ukraine, their chance to sustain democracy from this perspective seems small in comparison. Two related phenomena which have had an adverse effect on democratization are corruption and the interwovenness of state governance and the economy. These phenomena can be seen both as obstacles to democratization and as a consequence of the shortage of democratization. Georgia in 1999 was ranked eigty-fourth in a sample of ninety-nine states by Transparency International in its annual Corruption Perceptions Index (McFaul 2006: 171). Ukraine took the eighty-third position out of ninety-one in 2001 in the same index (Birch 2003: 525). Under Shevardnadze, four groups were seen as controlling most political and economic resources at the same time (Wheatley 2005: 110). In Ukraine under Kuchma, similarly, there were 'five or six economic clans that enjoyed a close relationship with the president' (Puglisi 2003: 114). The Kuchma regime rested partially on its control over the economy (D'Anieri 2007). The interwovenness of the economic and political spheres in Georgia and Ukraine entailed a large measure of state capture, the situation 'when powerful groups buy influence and shape the laws to their benefit', at the expense of responsible, good governance (Brinkerhoff and Goldsmith 2002: 29).

The international dimension
Democracy promotion and assistance, discussed later on in this chapter, is the most visible, though not necessarily the most potent international factor related to the prospect of democracy in individual states. Variables lying outside the domestic realm that can have an impact on the chances of democracy include cross-national diffusion (or 'contagion'); different types of linkage besides mere geographical proximity; and leverage, understood as the possibility to exert influence over foreign states or actors. The overarching concepts of linkage and leverage collectively subsume both democracy promotion and democracy assistance.[29]

The fact that democracies tend to exist in geographical clusters suggests that a diffusion effect between adjacent states is at play in democratization or the preservation of democracy (Gleditsch 2006). Examples of authoritarian states surrounded by democratic states, and vice versa, are rare. Macroquantitative studies indeed reveal a correlation between geographical proximity to democratic states and democratization (Coppedge and Brinks 2006; Wejnert 2005). Ukraine in this regard has been in an ambiguous position, located quite literally between the successful cases of democratization of Central and Eastern Europe, and two cases of clear failure of democratization, Russia and Belarus. Georgia's location, outside Europe or on its farthest southeastern border, and in the largely undemocratically governed Caucasus (both North and South), has been a disadvantage. Considering the even more doomed geography of a democratic state such as Mongolia (Fish 1998; Fritz 2008), however, this factor does not necessarily rule out democratization. Geographic proximity is a strong determinant of the degree of linkage to foreign states and IGOs. The extent of linkage, in the form of, among others things, information flows, transnational civil society, international travel and trade, and intergovernmental ties, correlates with the prospects of democratization. Levitsky and Way (forthcoming) find that competitive authoritarian states with extensive linkage to the West are much more likely to undergo democratization than states without such linkage.

With respect to the extent of linkage to the West, Georgia and Ukraine have been, in a cross-national comparison of the post-communist world, in an intermediate category: they benefit from less linkage than CEE states, largely due to a greater distance to the West and the absence of an EU membership perspective, but are certainly more linked to the West than Central Asia, and arguably also Armenia and Azerbaijan. Linkage to the West in the case of Ukraine, and less so in the case of Georgia, has been offset by a great extent of linkage to Russia, which may have partly unmade the possibly positive effects from linkage to the West. In the latter years of the Kuchma regime, increasingly warm ties with Russia compensated for the icy relations with the West. During the presidential elections in 2004 and on other occasions, Russia has sought to directly influence political outcomes in Ukraine (Petrov and Ryabov 2006). Also, according to various sources, Russia has taken punitive measures, foremost economic, vis-à-vis Georgia and Ukraine (e.g. Ambrosio 2007).

Undemocratic states can be vulnerable to a pressure to democratize, first, when they are linked with democratic states, and second, when these democratic states are able to exert leverage over the undemocratic states. One of the most visible instruments of leverage is a policy of conditionality. As the experience of EU accession of Central and Eastern European states has demonstrated, conditionality can be very effective in inducing actors to comply with given norms, rules, and policies (Schimmelfennig 2007; Vachudova 2002). Since Georgia and Ukraine have lacked any perspective on accession to the EU and NATO during most of the post-communist period, the potential of conditionality there has not been tested. The example of other former Soviet republics shows that membership in the Council of Europe and OSCE do not have the capacity to instill democratic values on member states. Western leverage over Georgia could be substantial, given the country's small size, its economic feebleness, and the interest that is associated, domestically, with good ties with the West, and especially with integration into European IGOs and NATO. Due to the country's larger size, population, and economy, the extent of leverage is somewhat smaller in relation to Ukraine, but still substantial. The West, however, has barely used available levers to impact on the political process in Georgia and Ukraine. There has been no push to integrate Georgia and Ukraine into IGOs with a credible policy of conditionality. Also, Western governments and IGOs have often been relatively uncritical of authoritarian tendencies in Georgia and Ukraine. As with linkage, a second source of leverage - Russia - arguably has counterbalanced the democratizing pressure that comes from Western leverage.

Agency

With the partial exception of institutional design and choices in nation-building and state-building, the explanations for the failure of democratization discussed so far in this section are by and large structure-oriented. Decisions made by elite actors, however, have helped to determine the course of political transformation in Georgia and Ukraine. The weight of agency has been particularly enhanced as a result of the high degree of concentration of power in the presidency in both states. Georgia's first president Gamsakhurdia, who ruled as president from his election in May 1991 until he was deposed in a coup in January 1992, has been widely depicted as a colossal political failure. Probably most damaging were Gamsakhurdia ill-conceived economic policy and the measures, inspired by a radical nationalist sentiment, taken with respect to minorities, triggering the two armed clashes in Abkhazia and South Ossetia. Georgia's second president, Shevardnadze, and Ukraine's first, Kravchuk, were both communist-era leaders, which has shaped their style of governing. Especially with regard to Ukraine, the relative lack of elite turnover since Soviet times has been seen as a constraint on democratization (D'Anieri 2007: 81). While Kravchuk was voted out of office in 1994, Shevardnadze stayed on until the Rose Revolution of 2003. The corruptive practices of patronage, clientelism and state capture which marked Shevardnadze's presidency were also present when Shevardnadze led the Georgian Soviet Republic in the 1970s and 1980s. With Shevardnadze and Ukraine's second president Kuchma unwilling to allow a change of power through fair elections, regime turnover in the end could seemingly only transpire in the form of extra-constitutional action.

Both Georgia and Ukraine have experienced an inauspicious start as independent states, which may have locked the two countries in a dynamic which made a turn to democratization unlikely in the short term. The two states suffered very substantial socioeconomic degradation. Georgia, in addition, fought a number of armed conflicts with separatist regions and a brief civil war in which first president Gamsakhurdia was overthrown, while Ukraine went through years of relative political deadlock during which the adoption of a new constitution was put off and reforms were stalled. The inauspicious developments of the initial years resulted to a large measure from poor decisions by the countries' leaders. Kuchma's and Shevardnadze's self-interested advocacy for strong executive power at the expense of the legislature, moreover, resulted in the type of executive-legislative relations which, as argued above, facilitated authoritarian persistence.

Conclusion

As the next chapter will demonstrate, the prolonged existence of semi-authoritarian rule in Georgia and Ukraine has had direct implications for the types of political parties that have occupied the political playing field over the years. This, in turn, has helped to suffocate the potential of successful norm diffusion through political party assistance. A palette of factors, both proximate and remote in time, both structural and hinging on agency, both domestic and international, help to explain why Ukraine, at least until 2005, and Georgia have not gone past the stage of less-than-democratic government. A few of the constraining factors appear to have been remedied in Ukraine as an outcome of the Orange Revolution: most significantly, executive power has been curbed, and major political elite actors from both the opposition and the ruling forces now adhere to democratic norms. Concomitantly, Ukraine's performance in Freedom House's and other ratings has improved. Most of the factors which constrained democratization in Georgia under Shevardnadze, on the other hand, are still in place.

3.3. REGIME CHANGE THROUGH ELECTORAL REVOLUTION

In 2003 in Georgia and in 2004 in Ukraine, incumbent regimes were involuntarily removed from power in the aftermath of fraudulent elections. The Rose and Orange Revolutions occurred according to a largely similar pattern: following accusations by the political opposition of electoral fraud in elections - parliamentary in Georgia, presidential in Ukraine - large and protracted street protests erupted, at which the opposition demanded a fair vote count and then government resignation. After weeks of mounting domestic and international pressure, the regimes were eventually forced to step down, after which new elections were held that were won by the opposition. Because of a striking similarity between the Revolutions in Georgia and Ukraine and other instances of regime change, most notably in Yugoslavia in 2000 and in Kyrgyzstan in 2005, and because of an alleged diffusion effect connecting the Revolutions, these events have often been collectively termed 'electoral revolutions'. The electoral revolutions were widely expected, particularly in the West, to have 'liberalizing outcomes' (Howard and Roessler 2006). Whereas liberalizing outcomes have indeed been observable in the cases of Ukraine and Yugoslavia (Serbia), liberalization of the political domain has been less forthcoming in Georgia and Kyrgyzstan. Relevant to the topic of this thesis, the events surrounding the electoral revolutions have raised political and scholarly questions about the impact of international factors, including democracy promotion and its subareas such as party assistance. Chapters five and six provide information on the activities around the Revolutions of the main actors involved in party assistance.

An already long line of scholarly work has sought to contribute to an explanation of the occurrence of the electoral revolutions. Most accounts can be distinguished along two dimensions: first, emphasis on the societal origin against the elite origin of the Revolutions; and second, emphasis on the weight of international factors at play in the Revolutions, versus explanation of the Revolutions from domestic factors (see table two).

	societal origin	elite origin
domestic factors	-civil society capacity (detecting electoral fraud, mobilizing voters and protesters) -civic participation and mobilization, most notably by youth movements	-divisions within the regime and coercive apparatus, aggravated by 'lame duck syndrome' -some degree of opposition unity
international factors	-Western support of domestic civil society -diffusion effect, both purposeful (imitation) and indirect (contagion)	-Western support to opposition parties and politicians -diplomatic pressure -mediation, conflict resolution by Western actors

Table 2. Accounts of the Rose and Orange Revolutions

On the domestic side, much has been made of the remarkable extent of grassroots civic activity (Demeš and Forbrig 2007; Diuk 2006). Civil society organizations proved effective in exposing electoral fraud, monitoring the media, mobilizing voters, etc. In addition, larger numbers of people than expected, especially in Ukraine, turned out onto the streets to demonstrate, creating the impression of opposition strength both to the regime and to outsiders. The activity of youth movements has particularly been ascribed a crucial role in firing up protests and motivating young people to challenge the regime (Bunce and Wolchik 2006b; Kuzio 2006). Explanations that emphasize the role of elite actors point to divisions within the regime and within the coercive state apparatus against some degree of unity among the opposition. In Ukraine, president Kuchma was to leave office at the time of the elections, to be replaced by his hand-picked successor. In Georgia, president Shevardnadze was nearing the end of his last term. Hale (2006) suggests that the nearing end of the presidents' last term lowered the loyalty to the regime of elite actors. Division within the coercive apparatus of the regime meant that police and armed forces were not ready to apply force to defend the regime (Binnendijk and Marovic 2006). The failure of the Kuchma and Shevardnadze regimes to unite elites, and division within their coercive apparatuses were clear symptoms of weak state capacity, which more generally is seen as a driver of regime breakdown (Levitsky and Way forthcoming; Way 2008). Against divisions within the regime, the Western-oriented democratic opposition in Ukraine was able to nominate a single candidate for the presidency, a feat that was probably key to the success of the Revolution, as it has been in other cases of regime change (Howard and Roessler 2006). Large parts of the Georgian opposition, by contrast, united only after street protests against the regime had already started.

The contribution of Western governments and international organizations has in part consisted of democracy assistance efforts in the years preceding the Revolutions. These efforts were sometimes specifically targeted at enforcing regime change, but more often they were not: in any event, they did strengthen the civil society organizations that were at the forefront in the Revolutions (Wilson 2006). A second international factor in the Revolutions concerns diffusion from one Revolution to the next. In addition to an ideational contagion effect, there are clear indications that the revolutionaries in Ukraine took cues from previous successful Revolutions. Revolutionaries sought to imitate or emulate the 'model' of these Revolutions (Beissinger 2007). Furthermore, revolutionaries have formed transnational activist networks with the aim of passing over knowledge and techniques to opposition movements in states that had not yet experienced regime change (Bunce and Wolchik 2006a). Finally, international factors have also impacted on actions and decisions by elite actors in Georgia and Ukraine. Against Russia's open endorsement of the Yanukovich candidacy, some Western actors supported Yushchenko in his bid, while most actors that were more bound politically, maintained a neutral position, at least officially. A number of high-ranking, mostly U.S. politicians visited Georgia and Ukraine and met with the country's leadership in the months ahead of the elections to advocate a fair election process.[30] Also, during the days of political crisis Western actors frequently had contact with the main players in the events to promulgate a non-violent solution of the conflict. Lastly, European actors took the lead in the mediation effort that led to a compromise solution to the conflict in Ukraine, and eventually made Yushchenko's election possible (Pifer 2007). A necessary condition of success in the Revolutions has been the pluralistic, semi-authoritarian, rather than repressive authoritarian nature of the regimes undergoing regime change. The Revolutions could occur because the regime did not block alternative political assembly and a degree of media pluralism, and did not systematically or widely repress opposition politicians. Realizing the potential of electoral revolution in these semi-authoritarian settings, governments in other post-Soviet states have taken measures to inoculate their regimes from ouster by further curbing political rights (Silitski 2004).

3.4. DEMOCRACY ASSISTANCE

Financial and technical assistance to Georgia and Ukraine aimed at promoting democracy has followed a largely similar pattern after 1991. During the 1990s Georgia and Ukraine emerged as significant recipients of European and U.S funds. Both countries received large amounts of U.S. assistance relative to other countries, worldwide and in the FSU. Some sources note that Georgia has been the third largest recipient of overall US aid per capita after Israel and Egypt (Lieven 2001; Matveeva 2003: 8), another that Ukraine has been the third largest recipient, again after Israel and Egypt, in absolute terms (Kubicek 1999: 21). A likely reason for the large volume of funds to Georgia is the favorable reputation that president Shevardnadze enjoyed in the West at least until the late 1990s (Lieven 2001; Metreveli and Hakobyan 2001). A strong Ukrainian lobby in the U.S is seen behind the large amounts of aid to Ukraine, particularly between 1996-1998 (Tarnoff 2003: 11). Partially driving the high levels of U.S. aid to Georgia and Ukraine also was a barely warranted degree of optimism about the countries' prospects of democratization. According to a 1996 USAID document, for instance, "President Eduard Shevardnadze enjoys great respect in America originating from the time he served as foreign minister of the Soviet Union and his outspoken support of democratic development since his return to Georgia. In 1992, he has presided over a halt to civil conflict and the beginning of notable democratic and economic reforms. Georgia's elections last November were relatively free and fair, and the new parliament is active and reformist." (USAID 1996: 7-8). Similarly, 'the Clinton administration stubbornly continued to insist that Ukraine was making "progress" which warranted generous American aid' (Prizel 2002: 382). In order to secure further aid, the efficacy of democracy aid programs were sometimes aggrandized: "USAID overstates the success of democratization in Georgia to maintain federal appropriations levels; USAID-funded organizations overstate their successes to USAID; and local NGOs overstate their successes to their international NGO partners" (King 2001: 103).

Until 2007, Georgia and Ukraine were recipients of EU Technical Assistance to the Commonwealth of Independent States (TACIS). TACIS and similar instruments in other parts of the European neighborhood were renamed European Neighborhood and Partnership Instrument in 2007. Georgia and Ukraine have also been eligible to funds from the EU administered European Initiative for Democracy and Human Rights (EIDHR). Around the turn of the century, optimism regarding democracy in Georgia and Ukraine faded among donors. From that moment, policy documents more often speak critically of the governments' reform record, a shift in outlook that has been reflected in democracy aid programs. [31] Particular damage to the reputation of Ukraine's government was done by the Gongadze murder, in which Kuchma and his entourage were implicated, and by arms sales to Iraq. The inability to stem corruption was seen as the biggest flaw of the Georgian government in these years. Both U.S. and EU actors have claimed a significant role in the occurrence of the Revolutions. EU foreign policy advisor Robert Cooper is reputed to have said that the EU has 'done regime change' in Ukraine through its diplomatic effort (Youngs 2006: 116). A USAID publication has it that 'the United States has been a major contributor to recent peaceful democratic transitions in Georgia and the Ukraine' (USAID 2006a). Another USAID publication details U.S. contributions to instances of democratic breakthrough in different parts of the world, including also Georgia and Ukraine (USAID 2005). Figures two and three display tendencies in USG expenditures on Democracy and Governance (figure two) and Electoral Assistance and Political Party Support programs (figure three) from 1992 until 2004.

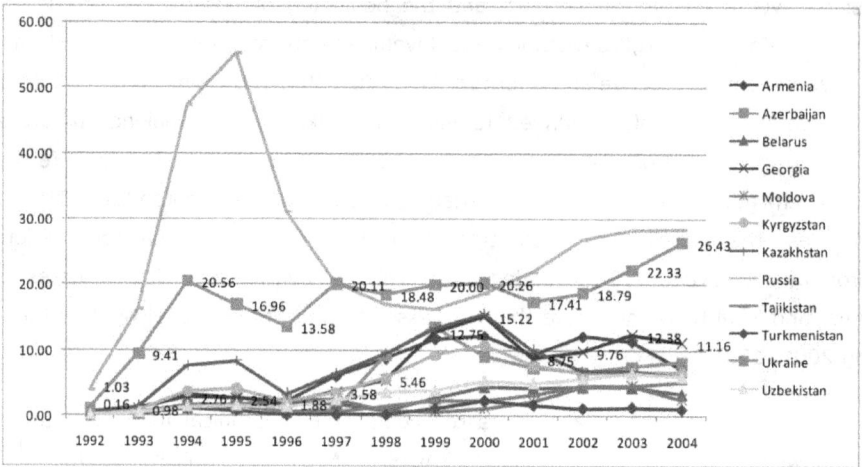

Figure 2. Total USAID investment for all Democracy and Governance (DG) programs in millions of constant 1995 US dollars in the NIS. Amounts of funding are from Finkel et al. (2006-2007).

Figure two displays the bulk of USG expenditures on democracy assistance in the newly independent states of the FSU. Similar data on the exact amounts of democracy assistance by the EU and their member states are not readily available. As this figure reveals, the size of DG aid to Ukraine has been comparable to that of Russia since 1997. Trailing behind Russia and Ukraine are the other FSU states. Despite being one of the smallest of these states, Georgia is still among the biggest recipients, during some years coming in third after Russia and Ukraine.

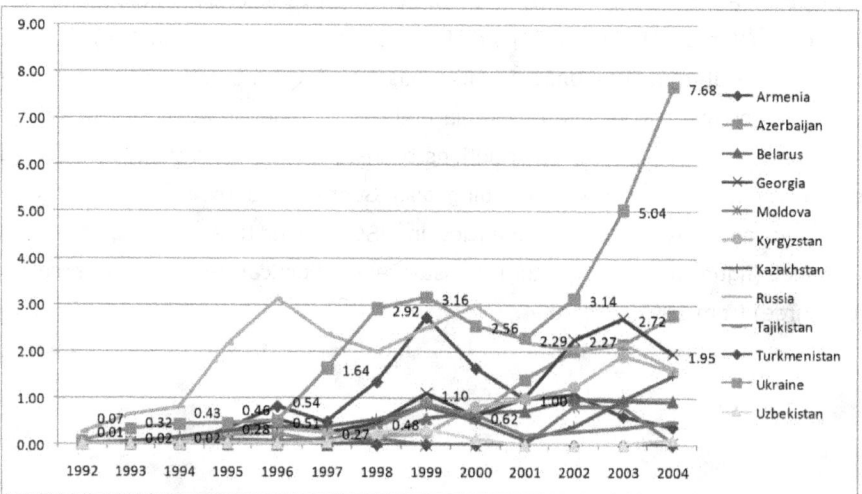

68

Figure 3. USAID investment in Electoral Assistance and Political Party Support programs in millions of constant 1995 US dollars in the NIS. Graph by the author. Amounts of funding are from Finkel et al. (2006-2007).

As for U.S electoral assistance and political party support, Ukraine and Russia received comparable amounts of assistance from 1997 until 2001 (see figure three). From that year, remarkably, assistance to Ukraine started to grow fast, leaving all other states, including Russia, behind. The increase is the more remarkable since overall USAID investment in Ukraine after 1999 fell sharply year by year. These figures, obviously, could give rise to suggestions that the U.S. worked towards changing the Kuchma regime. Electoral and political party assistance to Georgia similarly increased substantially in the two years leading up to the Rose Revolution. As with DG assistance overall, Georgia has often been the third biggest recipient among the NIS, during some years even surpassing Russia.

The Revolutions in 2003 and 2004 induced new optimism regarding the prospects of democratization in Georgia and Ukraine. USAID funding for Georgia in the immediate years after the Rose Revolution increased markedly, before falling to below pre-Revolution levels, consistent with the overall trend of decreasing USAID funds for the FSU (Tarnoff 2003; Tarnoff 2007). After the Revolution, Georgia was hailed by U.S. president Bush as a 'beacon of liberty', and a special Support to the New Government of Georgia program was installed, fed by the assumption 'that the Government of Georgia has made a concerted effort to bring in democratic principles' (USAID 2006b). In a less sanguine assessment, another 2006 USAID document notes that 'despite remarkable progress, a democratic deficit persists' (USAID 2006c: 4). USAID funding for Ukraine increased for only one year, and insignificantly, after the Revolution (Tarnoff 2003; Tarnoff 2007). Reflecting more intense relations with the EU within the framework of the European Neighborhood Policy, Tacis and ENPI funds to Georgia and Ukraine increased after the Revolutions,[32] an increase that, unlike the increase of U.S. funds, was sustained.

3.5. THE INTERNATIONAL DIMENSION OF PARTY DEVELOPMENT

Besides non-profit assistance provided by specialized organizations, political parties are exposed to a number of other external influences. These external influences, together with party assistance, constitute the 'international dimension' of political party development. The most obvious but least apparent forms of influence are demonstration and contagion: parties in Georgia and Ukraine are influenced by political ideologies that originate from party politics in Western democracies, and by models of party organization that are equally associated with parties in Western democracies. The fact that many parties bear names similar to the names of parties in Western democracies - liberal-democratic, socialist, republican, etc. - while in reality these parties are often ideologically diffuse, points to a demonstration effect. Also, the way parties are formally organized, including the existence of procedures of internal democracy, seems to implicate that Western models of party organization and operation are imitated. It is of course difficult to establish the precise diffusion mechanism at play in the imitation of Western models. Other, more tangible types of external influence on parties - association with transnational party organizations, fraternal contacts with parties in the post-communist world, and for-profit consultancy - are discussed separately in this section.

Transnational party organization

437 political parties worldwide are members of one of five party internationals, which unite parties of analogous ideological stripes, and offer a platform for dialogue and exchange (Hällhag 2008). Next to the party internationals with their global span, European transnational party organizations comprise parties from member states of the European Union, and reach out to parties in the EU's neighborhood by granting these parties observer status or a different form of affiliation (Desoldato 2002). Both the party internationals and the European parties have youth wings. Parties in Georgia and Ukraine generally have been eager to join or become affiliated with the transnational party organizations, and some have been successful in this regard. Of Ukrainian parties, Batkivshchyna, Our Ukraine, and NRU have observer status in the European People's Party; the CDU is a member of the Centrist Democrat International; and SPU and SDPU are 'consultative parties' in the Socialist International (SI). Remarkably, SPU changed its official ideological position from 'socialist' to 'social-democratic' in order to become eligible for inclusion in the SI.[33] Of Georgian parties, the Republican Party is a member of the European Liberal Democrats and has observer status in the Liberal International; the Christian-Democratic Union of Georgia, the National Democratic Party, and the People's Party are members of the Centrist Democrat International; the New Rights Party is an associate member in the International Democrat Union; and the United National Movement has observer status in the European People's Party. Furthermore, a relatively large number of youth wings of political parties and independent political youth movements have joined the youth wings of transnational party organizations. Some parties seem to have put their interest in joining the transnational party organizations before the decision to which of the party families they are closest ideologically or ideationally. The United National Movement of Georgia initially sought to join the Liberal International, but then

changed course to affiliate with the European People's Party. Batkivshchyna in Ukraine, similarly, first attempted to join the Socialist International, and later acquired close contacts with the European People's Party.

German and Dutch political foundations have played a role in lobbying on behalf of Georgian and Ukrainian parties for membership in the transnational party organizations, or have provided their partners with useful contacts within these organizations. For the *Stiftungen*, lobbying for fraternal parties is considered part of *Parteiförderung* (support for one specific party), distinct from *Parteienförderung* (assistance to several parties at once) (Saxer 2006a: 13). Until some time ago, the *Stiftungen* only assisted parties that had already gained membership in one of the party internationals. In recent decades, this criterion has been loosened, probably because the *Stiftungen* have started working in a large number of countries where membership in the party internationals was or still is rare. Representatives of the *Stiftungen* on the ground can now select parties for assistance independently, and are no longer bound to work intensively with parties that are in the party internationals.

The practical use of (partial) membership in transnational party organizations is not always evident. Among the reasons why association with the transnational party organizations is nonetheless sought are: first, association lends prestige, which is recognized both by other parties and by voters;[34] abroad, association adds respectability, opening doors which otherwise remain closed;[35] and lastly, during the foreign trips that result from association, party leaders and activists become acquainted with how parties are run elsewhere, and thus learn skills that can be implemented to the benefit of their own parties.[36] A specific reason was given by an informant from Batkivshchyna who remarked that contacts with European transnational party organizations will be helpful for Ukraine's integration into Europe once the party's leader, Tymoshenko, is president.[37]

Fraternal ties in the post-communist world
Besides the contacts that have been established with transnational party organizations, most relevant parties in Ukraine, and a few in Georgia, have developed fraternal relations with parties in the geographical neighborhood of Ukraine and Georgia. A look at the choice of partners sheds some light on the political outlook of parties. Notably, since the Rose and Orange Revolutions a particular increase in contacts between Georgian and Ukrainian parties has taken place. The People's Movement of Ukraine (NRU) has informal contacts with the Belarussian National Front, the New Rights Party of Georgia, and an unspecified party in Moldova.[38] Our Ukraine has informal contacts with like-minded parties in Moldova and Latvia, and with the

United National Movement of Georgia.[39] PORA is related with the Polish Law and Justice (PiS) party, with the Other Russia opposition movement, and with opposition parties in Azerbaijan and Kazakhstan.[40] The Communist Party of Ukraine, reportedly, has maintained relations with (ruling) parties in Cuba and China, and with communist successor parties in Russia and Serbia.[41] The Party of the Regions is involved in meetings with representatives from the ruling One Russia and Yeni Azerbaijan parties, while its youth wing has relations with One Russia's and Yeni Azerbaijan's youth wings, and with a youth movement that supports Belarusian president Lukashenka.[42] The youth wing of the New Rights Party of Georgia, finally, has established relations with political youth movements in Ukraine.[43] Apart from the symbolic value of these relations, and a mere exchange of experience and opinions, informants have not indicated reasons why their parties benefit from the ties with fraternal parties in neighboring states.

For-profit aid

Soliciting the services of foreign and domestic political strategists has become common practice for political parties in Ukraine in recent years. Since the political strategists shy away from publicity, and parties are often not keen to digress on the consultancy services that they solicit, little reliable information is available about these activities. A general trend has been that Russian agents have been partially replaced by Western, mostly American agents, especially after the Orange Revolution (Khmara 2007). American consultants have not only advised Ukrainian parties on the conduct of electoral campaigns and image improvement, but have as well sometimes promoted their political interests in the United States. The more palatable image and Western-style type of campaigning adopted by the Party of the Regions since the Revolution are ascribed to the work of the Davis, Manafort and Freedman consultancy firm (Page 2006). Because the Party of the Regions was already involved with the Davis, Manafort and Freedman firm, the party allegedly rejected to receive assistance from NDI for some time.[44] According to different sources, the firm previously consulted the governments of a number of (semi-)authoritarian Third World states (Nayem 2007: Voitsekhovskii 2006). Paul Manafort, leader of the firm's acitivities in Ukraine, has also been an adviser to former presidential candidate John McCain (Jacoby and Simpson 2008).

The BYuT electoral coalition has hired a number of American consultancy firms, including TD International, the Glover Park Group, and Dezenhall Resources (McKenna 2007). Instead of providing advice on political strategy, TD International has mainly lobbied for BYuT in the United States, and was heavily involved in a visit of BYuT leader Tymoshenko to the U.S. in 2007 (Lynch 2007; McKenna 2007). Also, Russian political strategist Aleksei Sitnikov, head of the Image Contact consultancy company, is said to have worked with BYuT (Khmara 2007). Working for the American consultancy firm Aristotle Inc., NDI chief of party from 2002 until 2005 Andreas Katsouris advised former ally of the Kuchma regime Viktor Medvedchuk for some time after he left NDI (Voitsekhovskii 2006). Aristotle Inc.'s links with Medvedchuk are remarkable because the firm has also taken credit for lending consultancy services to the 2004 opposition election campaign.[45] Katsouris' successor as NDI chief of party in Ukraine, David Dettman, worked for Aristotle Inc. prior to his engagement with NDI.

The only well-documented case of Western consultancy to a political party in Georgia is the involvement of American political strategist Michael Murphy with the New Rights Party in the campaign for the 2003 parliamentary elections. Among other things, Murphy, who has also worked for electoral campaigns of Jeb Bush, Arnold Schwarzenegger, and John McCain, advised the New Rights Party on how to position itself in the campaign, and, after the example of American election campaigns, proposed a bus tour throughout the country (Areshidze 2007: 84-9). Since Murphy's tactics did not resonate well with part of the party's leadership and with party activists, Murphy's advice was barely implemented, and the consultancy was suspended before the end of the campaign (Mitchell 2008: 55-6).

Chapter Four: Political Party Development in Georgia and Ukraine

Characterizations of political parties in Georgia mention 'a lack of clear ideology, values or vision; excessive role of leaders' personalities; heightened degree of political opportunism and populism; lack of internal democracy' (Tarkhan Mouravi 2006: 243). Instead of broad-based, institutionalized organizations with a serious degree of political clout, parties in Georgia have been 'more like political clubs with loose organizational structures, small memberships and no real influence' (Dolidze 2005: 2). During the 2003-2004 parliamentary elections, 'none of the political parties presented a meaningful or more-or-less comprehensive election program' (Usupashvili 2004: 98). Wheatley argues that parties were all 'highly centralized, top-down organizations', 'elite-led and leader-driven', with a 'complete subordination of ordinary party members to the leadership', lacking 'a clear policy profile', and failing to 'forge links with Georgian society'. In sum, 'Georgian political parties were fundamentally different sorts of organizations from their Western counterparts' (Wheatley 2005: 155-9).

Authors speak of the 'weakness of political parties' both at the outset of Ukraine's 'transition' in 1993 and fourteen years onwards (Wilson and Bilous 1993: 693; D'Anieri 2007: 43), and in 2008 still, 'Ukraine's party system is undeveloped and fluid' (Slomczynski et al. 2008: 93). Indeed, 'the parties' status and role have been persistently and deliberately undermined for more than a decade and a half' (Riabchuk 2008: 44). Parties in Ukraine are 'of marginal importance in Ukraine' and 'often vehicles for oligarchic interests' (Van Zon 2005: 17). Also, 'most parties' "ideologies" are very similar and ideology does not play a decisive role. Ukrainian parties are for the most part of the clientelistic leadership type that relies on other mechanisms for electoral success than on representing and aggregating voters' preferences and societal interests.' (Zimmer 2003: 11). Finally, '[p]arties, as it has turned out, are short of a broad social base, their ideology and program inadequately reflect current problems, they do not have a vision on the development of society, and they lack the capacity to function properly.'[46]

The above characterizations suggest that providers of assistance in Georgia and Ukraine have a formidable job at hand in helping parties transform into more democratic and representative organizations. Providers of assistance face an uphill struggle in which they can expect to achieve modest results at best. In any event, the state of party development in Georgia and Ukraine at different moments has important implications for what types of assistance programs are called for, as well as for the potential effectiveness of these programs. This chapter looks into the material with which providers of assistance have worked in Georgia and Ukraine - political parties during the second decade of multi-party politics, from the late 1990s until 2007-2008. The first section identifies the defining outcomes of party politics in Georgia and Ukraine over the course of this period - an extraordinary degree of volatility in party politics, and the impact on party politics of (semi-)authoritarianism - and sets these off against the outcomes of party politics in Western half of the post-communist world, Central and Eastern Europe,. The second section explores the extent of volatility in party politics in Georgia and Ukraine, and discusses the difficulties of studying party politics in conditions of 'fluid' party politics. The following three sections explicate three variables that have enabled the particular outcomes of party politics in Georgia and Ukraine - elite 'ownership' of parties, undemocratic practices in party creation and operation, and the limited leverage of parties. Starting from the observation that party creation and operation are almost exclusively led by elite actors, the sixth section sheds light on party politics in Georgia and Ukraine by looking into the incentive structures of political party 'entrepreneurs'. The following two sections, which move away from theory to a more empirically grounded discussion, review the dynamics of party politics in Georgia and Ukraine in the second decade of multi-party politics, and argue for a classification of parties in these countries on the basis of variables – foremost incentive structures and party origin – that have been most distinctive for these cases. The chapter concludes with a summary of the key implications for party assistance which flow from the analysis in previous sections.

4.1. DIVERGENT TRAJECTORIES

In most countries that were once part of the 'third wave of democratization', political parties are subject to a 'standard lament' (Carothers 2006a: 3-21). According to this lament, parties lack programmatic distinction, do not genuinely represent people's interests, spring into action only around election time, are leader-centric, and are ill-prepared to take up the responsible task of governing. These defects, unsurprisingly, are rife throughout both halves of the post-communist world. A diverse and sophisticated body of literature details the deep-seated shortcomings and growing pains of parties in Central and Eastern Europe (CEE). A frequent theme in this literature is the difference between party politics in CEE and in older democracies (Innes 2002; Toole 2003; Webb and White 2007). The gap between Western and

Eastern Europe, however, appears to have narrowed somewhat: a number of party systems in CEE have stabilized (Bakke and Sitter 2005; Lewis 2006), electoral volatility has gradually dwindled (Lane and Ersson 2007), and voters have turned out not be less versatile than may once have been expected (Kitschelt et al. 1999). Much less analysis has been directed to party politics in the former Soviet Union (FSU). A large share of the available literature centers on individual countries, mostly Russia, and has a limited focus, while few studies engage in cross-national comparison.[47]

When viewing party politics in the FSU in a wider perspective, the closest point of reference, naturally, remains the other, more democratic half of the post-communist world. In many former Soviet republics the party landscape changed radically from election to election since independence was gained, and on average more so than in CEE states.[48] Whereas in the majority of CEE countries one can reasonably speak of the gradual emergence of party systems, whatever was there in terms of parties at random moments in FSU states by and large constituted a loose collection of transient political forces which failed to develop patterns of interaction. As Sanchez (2008a) argues, these loose collections of parties should not be referred to as 'inchoate' or 'weakly institutionalized' party *systems*, but rather as party 'non-systems'. Changes in the supply of parties in these non-systems were less the outcome of changes in voters' preferences, as electoral volatility is often understood, than of the creation of new forces and abandonment of existing forces by political 'entrepreneurs', who tended to view parties as disposable 'projects' which had been designed to satisfy short-range objectives. Parties mostly remained utterly weak institutions, more so than in CEE countries, where in most cases a core of stable parties over time has become visible and has started to interact according to more or less understandable patterns - the hallmark of a party system (Mainwaring and Scully 1995: 4).

Party politics in the FSU over the post-communist period has been most obviously distinct from party politics in the democratic states of CEE primarily in two respects: first, the more volatile nature (a difference in degree) of party politics in the FSU, expressed by higher levels of electoral volatility (Bielasiak 2005: 341) and a higher replacement rate of parties (Birch 2001: 17), but also by other factors; and second, the impact of authoritarian practices (a difference in kind), a direct correlate of the political context of (semi-)authoritarianism in most of the FSU. As will be argued in the following sections, these two outcomes, in the cases of Georgia and Ukraine, have been foremost conditioned by three explanatory variables. Volatility is explained by the circumstance that parties have only very limited leverage over the political process in Georgia and Ukraine, which in turn is an outcome of institutional factors - mainly executive-legislative relations and electoral legislation - as well as by the fact that party operation is driven almost exclusively by elites. The elite-led nature of party politics is a proximate cause of volatility, in that the actions of the elite (party 'entrepreneurs') have a direct impact on party politics. The limited leverage of parties, on the other hand, has an indirect, albeit very powerful impact on party politics, and is therefore a remote cause of volatility. The uneven playing field in party politics is a direct consequence of the political context of (semi-)authoritarianism.

The enabling conditions of the outcomes of party politics in Georgia and Ukraine have constrained the development of a stable, democratic party system and, as will be argued later on in this chapter, have presented major dilemmas for the party assistance effort. The next four sections discuss the specific outcomes of party politics in Georgia and Ukraine over the post-communist period and the impact of the variables which explain these outcomes. After the extent and impact of fluid party politics in Georgia and Ukraine are laid out (4.2), it is argued why elite behavior rather than sociological factors shapes party operation in Georgia and Ukraine (4.3). Next, the impact of the political context of authoritarianism on party politics is demonstrated (4.4). Finally, arguments are put forward why specific elements of institutional arrangement in Georgia and Ukraine have bred party system volatility (4.5).

4.2. STUDYING FLUID PARTY POLITICS

In his classic treatise, Sartori (1976) reserves the term 'fluid polities' for 'polities whose political process is highly undifferentiated and diffuse' (idem: 244). Party politics in these states is formless, unstructured, not yet institutionalized, and therefore excluded by Sartori from his categorization of party systems (idem: chapter 8). It only takes a look at election results to get an idea of the low level of party system institutionalization in Georgia and Ukraine. The election results in appendices one and two display the turnover of political forces between elections and reveal the instability of electoral coalitions in Georgia and Ukraine over the course of the most recent four parliamentary elections.

It is widely acknowledged that some degree of party system institutionalization is imperative for the consolidation of democracy (e.g. Diamond and Linz 1989: 21; Mainwaring and Scully 1995).[49] Quantitative studies accordingly point to a correlation between levels of democracy and levels of party system institutionalization (Casal Bértoa 2008). Thames and Robbins (2007) find that 'the highest levels of democracy' do not go together with 'low levels of institutionalization'. Whether party system institutionalization is a necessary prerequisite for democratic consolidation or not, it has at least several important positive consequences for the performance of democratic rule (Powell 1982; Tóka 1997). Weak party system institutionalization is believed to undermine democratic consolidation in a number of ways. In the absence of strong and stable parties, it is impossible for voters to hold parties accountable for their actions in government or in the legislature, to develop a relationship with a party, and to engage in strategic voting based on available knowledge of party behavior, while for parties it is difficult to strategically position themselves vis-à-vis political opponents (Birch 2001; Mainwaring and Zoco 2007; Thames 2007). Also, more institutionalized parties are in a better position to aggregate and channel citizen's demands and to interact in a constructive manner in the legislature (Siaroff 2006: 198).

Since most parties in Georgia and Ukraine have shallow organizational structures and lack deep-reaching roots in society, they can be easily dissolved by their leaders when they do not bring in anticipated benefits. Party turnover has been accompanied by fractionalization. Relatively permissive laws on political parties in both Georgia and Ukraine[50] have allowed for the proliferation of parties: 183 parties were registered with the Ministry of Justice in Georgia in 2006 (Nodia and Pinto Scholtbach 2006: 152) against 138 in Ukraine in 2007 (Golubitskii 2007). Party system fractionalization in Georgia and Ukraine is fed by personal ambitions, as party leaders have been rarely willing to give up their organizations, no matter how insignificant, in favor of a merger with other parties (Boyko 2005).

Rapid changes in the supply of parties are the clearest indicator of the fluid nature of party politics in Georgia and Ukraine. Individual parties, however, have been unstable in more respects. Parties have been subject to far-reaching internal change resulting from defections or the arrival of new leadership. The degree of change could be such that the affected party should be regarded as a different entity. Furthermore, parties often did not compete as independent political forces, but as constituents of larger electoral alliances, that almost invariably proved to be short-lived. Sometimes, the line between parties and blocs became difficult to draw, contributing to the low profile of parties as autonomous political forces. Also, once parties got into parliament, they tended to disintegrate into several rivaling factions from which new parties were sometimes formed (e.g. Herron 2002). As with electoral coalitions, the distinction between parties and factions often became blurred.

As will be argued in subsequent sections, a compelling explanation for the weakness and instability of parties lies in the limited relevance of parties in Georgian and Ukrainian political life, providing potential political party 'entrepreneurs' with insufficient incentives to invest in the development of viable parties. Volatility has been a continuous feature of party politics in Georgia since independence. Both under Shevardnadze and under Saakashvili, a more or less dominant party of power was surrounded by a large number of weak and unpopular opposition parties, which in many cases enter and leave the fray fast and without trace. Whereas volatility was similarly marked in Ukraine until the 2002 parliamentary elections, since that moment a number of political forces, for the time being at least, have appeared to be sustainable. Some of these forces, however, are blocs which display a large degree of intra-bloc volatility and are not likely to prove sustainable in the longer run.

Political parties in Georgia and Ukraine, unlike long-standing parties in Western Europe but like parties in large parts of the world outside Western Europe, by and large have not grown out of social cleavages, do not represent large segments of society (though they may articulate their sentiments) and are often difficult to identify on the left-right, or conservative-progressive, spectrum of classical political ideologies. For these and other reasons, concepts from the study of parties in Western societies often travel poorly to non-Western contexts, as Erdmann (2004) has cogently demonstrated in relation to sub-Saharan Africa. As noted, a significant literature has appeared on party politics in Central and Eastern Europe, while little attention has been directed at political parties in the former Soviet Union, where the level of party system institutionalization is even lower than in Central and Eastern Europe, and party development mostly takes place under (semi-)authoritarian regimes or in a context of uncertain democratization at best. Understandably, it has been asked whether it is of much use to study parties in a political system as volatile and a party system as unstructured as that of Georgia and Ukraine during most of the post-communist period.[51]

No systematic analysis of party politics in Georgia exists in the academic literature, and, except from large-n quantitative studies, Georgian political parties are left out of cross-national comparative studies. The limited number of studies on parties in Ukraine have a narrow focus and mostly do not take on comparison with party politics in other (post-communist) countries. The difficulty of studying parties in circumstances of fluid party politics becomes evident when we attempt to apply common analytical concepts to party development in Georgia and Ukraine. Three basic characteristics of any party system are its size plus shape (or fragmentation), its degree of ideological polarization, and its degree of institutionalization (Mainwaring 1998; Siaroff 2005: 184-5). The first two of these form the basis of Sartori's influential classification of political parties, while the third characteristic features more often in more recent studies of party systems.[52]

The most widely applied indicator for party system institutionalization is Pedersen's (1983) index of electoral volatility, which primarily seeks to reveal aggregate changes in support levels for parties between subsequent elections. Any discussion of electoral volatility in Georgia and Ukraine, however, would have to start with the observation that the volatility score of the Georgian and Ukrainian party systems, considering that party creation and dissolution are almost exclusively elite-driven, is more a function of the 'whim of elites' than of changes in voters' preferences (Birch 2001: 3; Neff Powell and Tucker 2008: 3). The high turnover rate of parties as well as incessant fluctuations within parties and electoral alliances pose challenges to coding and therefore render calculating electoral volatility for Georgia and Ukraine since independence a very complicated and ultimately futile undertaking.[53] Moreover, official elections results may not reflect the actual relative strength of parties (as expressed by voters' preferences) given credible allegations of fraud in most elections in Georgia and Ukraine since 1991. This straightforward realization is too easily overlooked or ignored in many studies.[54] Those who do calculate scores of electoral volatility in Georgia for the purposes of large cross-national studies of post-communist countries find that it is either average (Tavits 2005: 85) or one of the highest in their sample (Bielasiak 2005: 341). Electoral volatility scores for Ukraine range from one of the lowest in post-communist Europe (Tavits 2005: 85) to one of the highest (Lane and Ersson 2007: 99; Bielaslak 2005: 341; Mainwaring and Zoco 2007: 60). Difficulties in calculating electoral volatility in inchoate party systems can, in theory, be overcome by looking separately at volatility of a stable core of parties on the one hand, and volatility from party entry and exit on the other (Neff Powell and Tucker 2008), or by calculating bloc volatility instead, whereby blocs are put together from ideologically akin parties (Bartolini and Mair 1990). In the absence of even a core of stable political parties, such strategies are bound to be problematic with regard to the Georgian and Ukrainian party universes. If one moreover wants to assess party system institutionalization in Georgia and Ukraine by applying other popular indicators instead, such as party age or stable roots in society,[55] then this would *ex ante* lead to the conclusion that the level of party system institutionalization in both countries is extremely limited due to the only brief existence of multi-party politics and the elite character of party creation.

While political polarization, primarily around a pro-regime/anti-regime fault line, tends to be high in Georgia, ideological polarization is not. Most relevant parties define themselves as centre-right, speak out in favor of pro-market reforms, and consider Euro-Atlantic integration a top priority of foreign policy. Only the Labor Party defines itself as left-of-centre, while the ruling United National Movement purports to be 'nonideological' and to 'represent the whole population' (IDEA 2006: 7). Evidently, differences between parties in Georgia do not hinge on different ideological positions, and, to the extent that differences in ideological positions are discernable, are they of secondary importance in shaping voters' choices.

Polarization over policy-related issues, such as pro-reform versus reform-averse, has been more readily discernable in Ukraine, particularly during the 1990s. Dividing Ukrainian political forces into three ideological blocs (left, centre, right), as Wilson and Birch (2007) have attempted, however, overstates the weight of programmatic positions in interparty competition. In the years leading up to the Revolution, the anti-regime contra pro-regime stance of parties was a more important signpost shaping voters' preferences. The two most popular electoral blocs since the 2006 parliamentary elections - Party of Regions (PR) and Yulia Timoshenko Bloc (BYuT) - have moved to the center in what may be called a catch-all electoral strategy and correspondingly lack a clearly identifiable ideological position. Both parties are said to contain within them political groups with diverging ideological outlooks. The foremost cleavage in Ukrainian politics, in terms of electoral effects, is regionally defined and related to questions of identity and value systems (Shulman 2004; Wilson 2002a). People in southern and eastern regions of the country view the Soviet past and the historical ties with Russia in a positive light, while voters in Western and eastern regions are more likely to adhere to the idea of Ukrainian (ethnic) nationalism. Although this cleavage is seldom openly alluded to in electoral campaigns, it does have a crucial impact on electoral behavior (Barrington 2002).

The degree of party system fragmentation is most commonly assessed by computing Laakso and Taagepera's (1979) Effective Number of Parties (ENP) score, in which the strength of parties is either determined by their vote share or by the percentage of seats they occupy in the legislature. As with electoral volatility, it is not obvious what the best strategy is to calculate the ENP for Georgian and Ukrainian parties due to, among other things, the high turnover of parties, the abundance of unstable electoral coalitions, the incongruence of parliamentary factions and political parties, and the high number of independent MPs. The effective number of parties in Ukraine has steadily been very high until 2006 among different samples of post-communist states (Dawisha and Deets 2006: 692; Wilson and Birch 2007: 57). Bielasiak (2005: 336) finds that that the Effective Number of Parliamentary Parties in Georgia between 1992 and 2004 on average was 4.5. This however conceals major fluctuations over the time period in question, from a high point of 21.16 in 1992 to a low point of only 2.60 in 1999 (Dawisha and Deets 2006: 691). More crucially, as Bogaards (2000: 165) has demonstrated, 'different party constellations can hide behind the same effective number of parties'. With regard to the Georgian party system, then, it seems more appropriate to identify the constellation of the party system, determined by the shape of the system and mode of competition within the party system, which over the last fifteen years almost continuously has been that of a dominant ruling party versus a fragmented opposition.

4.3. ELITE OWNERSHIP

The classic sociological account of party politics explains the origin of parties from societal cleavages (Lipset and Rokkan 1967). According to the cleavage hypothesis, social conflict is translated into party alternatives, i.e. different political parties essentially represent different groups in society (Mair 2006). The cleavage hypothesis presumes the existence of definable cleavages, e.g. along religious, class, ethnic, or linguistic lines, which split up separate electorates. Together with institutionalist explanations, sociological explanations, of which the cleavage hypothesis is the best-known representative, are dominant in theory on the origin of parties and party systems (Gel'man 2006: 548; Mainwaring 1998; Tavits 2008a; Ware 1996). A number of authors have argued that the cleavage hypothesis also holds up to a considerable extent in the case of CEE countries (McAllister and White 2007; Toole 2007; Whitefield 2002), while others exclusively stress the weight of institutional factors (Bielasiak 2002; Fesnic and Ghindar 2004). With respect to Georgia and Ukraine, there is less reason to take cues from the cleavage hypothesis. At the outset of party politics in the post-communist world, it was hypothesized that as a result of the 'leninist legacy', no immediately identifiable cleavage structures would be present that could serve as the foundation of strong interest-based parties (Geddes 1995; Lewis 2006: 565). Moreover, post-Soviet states like Georgia and Ukraine contained a weak, embryonic civil society (Howard 2003), a political culture unconducive to the development of programmatic parties (Kitschelt 2001), and lacked meaningful experience with pre-communist multi-party politics, which in some CEE countries has contributed to structure the relaunch of political competition (Toole 2007). For these reasons, the emergence of broad-based political parties with deep roots in society did not appear likely. The political party landscape in post-Soviet states would presumably resemble a tabula rasa on which a wide variety of different players would try their luck to catch the votes of a floating electorate. At the end of the first post-communist decade there were signs in CEE (Kitschelt et al. 1999) as well as in some FSU states (Korasteleva 2000; Miller et al. 2000; Miller and Klobucar 2003) that the electorate was no longer adrift. During these years, at least two types of programmatic parties with well-definable and more or less stable constituencies - namely communist successor parties and liberal-democratic parties - were still viable forces in Ukraine. Since then, however, these parties have lost much of their clout.

The disattachment of the Georgian and Ukrainian societies from political parties is reflected in membership figures of parties and in levels of popular identification with parties. Membership of political parties has been recorded at 1% of the adult population in Ukraine in 1999.[56] 63% of respondents did not perceive ideological attachment to any of the political parties, and slightly more than half at the time thought that political parties are necessary institutions for democracy (Kubicek 2001: 126). According to a different survey, less than twenty per cent of respondents deem a 'multi-party system as "absolutely necessary" for the functioning of democracy in Ukraine' (Walecki and Protsyk 2007: 26). At 10-15% of eligible voters in the early 1990s, Ukraine has recorded the lowest level of party identification in the whole of post-communist Europe. By 1998, this number had risen to barely 25% (Birch 2000b: 32). According to one survey, only one out of twenty respondents believed that parties serve the interests of the people, while more than half of respondents were convinced that parties instead serve economic interests, and close to half that parties exist the careers of their leaders (Yakimenko and Zhdanov 2003). Party membership rates in Georgia were higher, and according to one survey stood at 4.4% in 2001 (Nodia 2003: 30), against 2.6% in 2004 according to another survey (Nodia and Pinto Scholtbach 2006: 105). The exact number of party members in Georgia is difficult to measure because, first, most parties do not maintain a computerized database of their membership, and second, because parties tend to overstate their membership figures (idem: 152). Positive identification with parties is limited: in 2007, 58% of survey respondents had an unfavorable view of all political parties (IRI et al. 2007: 67) The leader-centric nature of parties in Georgia is to some degree vindicated by popular attitudes: more than half of voters admit to vote primarily for a party because of its leader, and only one quarter think a party's program is more important than its leaders (idem: 28).

The disattachment of society from parties in Georgia and Ukraine goes hand in hand with the absence of meaningful mechanisms of internal democracy within parties. In Georgia, 'Across the political spectrum, political parties lack internal democracy and meaningful distribution within the party' (Black et al. 2001: iii). With regard to Ukrainian parties it has been remarked that 'all serious decisions are often made by 'a "club" of about one or two dozen individuals' (Barca et al. 2006: 25). Consequently, as has been noted with respect to Georgian party politics, 'competition remains largely confined to elite circles' (ARD, Inc. 2002: 13). In terms of organizational strength, regime-initiated parties tend to be somewhat more full-fledged relative to opposition

84

parties, which, according to a USAID publication, 'in countries undergoing democratic transitions are often little more than a handful of leaders in search of a constituency' (USAID 2000: 45). It was found in 2001 in Georgia that the ruling CUG 'is the only party that has chapters throughout the country and is likely to field candidates in each district' (Black et al. 2001: 15). Despite its apparent organizational strength, CUG disappeared overnight following the Rose Revolution.

While cleavages may explain voters' preferences even in Georgia and Ukraine, they do not account for the rapid and frequent changes in the supply of political parties. Partly as a result of the pro-active interference by the executive branch in party politics, the creation of parties in Georgia and Ukraine was increasingly less driven by societal factors than it was by the interests of political and economic elites. Especially as the regimes sought to consolidate their rule, did they interfere in the electoral arena by creating and sustaining support parties and loyal satellite parties and by blocking off unwelcome contenders. For the regimes, this became one element in their strategy to predetermine the outcome of elections and, with that, to strengthen their hold on power.

It had been anticipated by Kitschelt (2001) that the legacy of the type of communist rule that was characteristic of the Soviet Union - what Kitschelt has called 'patrimonial communism' - would be less conducive to the emergence of programmatic parties than the types of communist rule that had existed in CEE. The reappearance, or continuation, of authoritarianism in the region would further constrain the prospects of programmatic, cleavage-based parties that truly represent the interests of societal groups, because the regimes had an interest and the means to check these parties' standing. The impact of the legacy of patrimonial communism on party development in FSU states, therefore, can barely be isolated from other elements in the political trajectory of these states. Irrespective of whether there are cleavages or issues in Georgia and Ukraine on the basis of which viable parties can be built, regimes and regime-proximate elites have acted to reduce the likelihood that these cleavages and issues would come to dominate party politics. The regimes, in other words, have intently reduced the weight of sociological factors in party politics. Furthermore, as the next section will outline, regimes in Georgia and Ukraine have taken the initiative to create different types of parties which have crucially altered party politics.

Once we realize that the operation of parties is led by elite actors, much insight can be gained from studying the motives of these elites. As Tavits (2008b: 549) notes, 'much more emphasis should be put on understanding the incentive structures of elites that encourage or discourage stability on their part.' Section six in this chapter will take up this challenge to help explain the dynamics of party creation and disintegration in Georgia and Ukraine.

4.4. PARTY POLITICS IN AN UNEVEN PLAYING FIELD

The (semi-)authoritarian political regime context has affected interparty competition and party development in Georgia and Ukraine (until 2005) in a profound manner. By focusing on the types of parties that have been at the forefront in Georgia and Ukraine, this section demonstrates how the political party landscape is to a large extent shaped by the impact of authoritarian practices. Party politics in a less-than-democratic setting should be expected to display a different dynamic from settings in which fair competition can be taken for granted. This straightforward but crucial assumption is insufficiently appreciated in studies of party politics in 'third wave' states. [57] In less-than-democratic settings, executive authorities often intentionally distort the electoral playing field in order to tighten their grip on power or to extract the rents that are accessible to regime actors by virtue of holding office. Distortion of the playing field is achieved both by checking the opposition and by becoming involved in party-building. Some regimes opt to establish a 'party of power' that towers over other parties in terms of financial and personnel resources and exposure. As will be demonstrated below, regimes may also deploy other types of parties, including satellite parties and spoiler parties, to keep a check on genuine pluralism.

Competition between parties in less-than-democratic conditions is often less about policies than about the rules of the political game. Elections may become 'nested games': 'At the same time as incumbents and opponents measure their forces in the electoral arena, they battle over the basic rules that shape the electoral arena' (Schedler 2002: 110). Moreover, the decisive fault line in electoral competition is that of support for the regime versus opposition to the regime, with little room for political accommodation. Opposition parties will often declare democratic convictions an important motive in their struggle against incumbents, and organize protests to voice their opposition to the regime. In the process, issue-based appeals, which are believed to better structure electoral competition in democracies (Croissant 2002: 346), are pushed to the background. Finally, the party system configuration under (semi-)authoritarianism often lasts only as long as the regime lasts, since regime change often brings about a radical shake-up of the party landscape. Party system change in less-than-democratic settings is therefore conditioned upon the regime's capability of survival.

86

Under each of the three Georgian presidents' regimes since 1990 have there been serious restrictions on the observance of full political rights. Leaders in Georgia have tended to tilt the political playing field in their favor by abusing their executive powers, though hardly ever to such an extent that pluralism and competitiveness were entirely thwarted. Although little consensus exists over the nature of the political regimes under Shevardnadze and Saakashvili, in part due to the dearth of scholarship on modern Georgia, it is clear, and corroborated by democracy indices such as Freedom House's, that they should be regarded as highly defective democracies in terms of the degree to which full political competition was inhibited. The Kuchma regime in Ukraine also, and increasingly, impeded fair political competition, as was particularly noticeable in the 2004 presidential election which triggered the Orange revolution. Ukraine under Kuchma is located in the less-than-democratic group of regimes, sometimes termed 'competitive authoritarian' regimes (Levitsky and Way 2002), with obvious authoritarian leanings but meaningful, contested elections at the same time. The Orange Revolution was widely perceived as a democratic breakthrough. Several years into the Orange Revolution, incessant political struggles notwithstanding, the democratic gains appear to have been sustained, with two parliamentary elections, in 2006 and 2007, held in a fair and competitive atmosphere.

Parties of power

Parties of power are created at the instigation of the executive branch of government, benefit extensively from state resources, are affiliated with the president - irrespective of whether the president does or does not have a formal role in the party - and, unlike other regime-initiated parties, are created with the purpose of becoming a dominant force in party politics. Parties of power for various reasons do not always succeed in becoming dominant forces, as the example of the National Democratic Party (NDP) in Ukraine shows. It is assumed here that the dominant position of a party in the party system is reflected in the control of more than half of seats in the legislature. Parties of power sometimes fail to get more than half of the vote but still succeed in becoming a dominant force because they attract 'independent' deputies or win most contests in single-member districts (SMDs). The key functions that parties of power are designed to fulfill are to amass popular support, primarily in the form of raw votes, and to bind elite actors to the regime. When they are successful in elections, parties of power send a signal of regime strength, which has the dual effect of seemingly conferring legitimacy on the regime and deterring possible contenders from attempting regime change (Geddes 2005). Binding elite representatives to the regime through a party of power has the effect of curbing the ambitions, which may be against the interests of the regime, of these elites, and of mitigating possible conflict between elites and the groups that these elites may represent (Geddes 2005: Gel'man 2008). In order to bind elites to a party of power, the party assumes the features of a patronage network; in this patronage network, jobs, economic gains, and other benefits are distributed in return for loyalty to the party and, by extension, the regime (Greene 2007; Resende and Kraetzschmar 2005). By uniting otherwise disparate elites, deterring potential contenders, and conferring legitimacy, parties of power can make a crucial contribution to regime survival (Brownlee 2007; Gandhi and Przeworski 2007).

Because they purposefully benefit from state resources in electoral campaigns, the operation of a party of power. as understood here, implies an uneven electoral playing field. In a description of the less-than-democratic aspects of the Georgian regime, Freedom House, for instance, notes 'a markedly uneven playing field in favor of the ruling United National Movement party' (Puddington 2009: 16). Concurrently, it has been found that UNM 'has not taken adequate steps to ensure a fair opportunity for the opposition' (Mitchell 2008: 91). State resources can range from 'administrative resources' (offices, supplies, mobilization of public servants, etc.) to direct monetary transfers from state coffers to the party budget, to the distribution of government jobs and other perks to loyalists (Greene 2007). Mostly, but not necessarily, parties of power do not propagate a distinct political ideology. The existence of a party of power is common in (semi-)presidential regimes with authoritarian leanings, and is especially common for former Soviet republics. In Georgia, parties of powers have dominated legislatures both under the Shevardnadze (Citizens' Union of Georgia) and Saakashvili (United National Movement) presidencies.

Over the course of the second half of Shevardnadze's presidency a second dominant party of power was present, pointing to the existence of an alternative centre of executive power outside Tbilisi, *in casu* in the autonomous region of Adjara, ruled by strongman Abashidze, and in many ways until 2004 a de facto independent entity which unlike Abkhazia and South Ossetia did not seek full secession. Regime change in authoritarian states is often brought about by splits within political elites (Geddes 2004). Around the turn of the century, the Citizens' Union of Georgia lost its ability to unite the political elite, when influential young politicians like Saakashvili, Zhvania and Burjanadze defected and started setting up their own opposition parties. The political forces of these politicians subsequently were at the forefront of the Rose Revolution. Attempts by Kuchma's administration to establish a 'party of power', uniting a large share of the country's political elites, have repeatedly fallen through, which can be partly explained by the same societal (geographical) divisions that have determined party system development in Ukraine as a whole. Arguably the most concerted effort at creating a nationwide ruling party, the People's Democratic Party (NDP) in the

1990s, garnered a paltry five per cent in the PR section of the ballot in the 1998 parliamentary elections. A partial explanation of the failure of parties of power in Ukraine, in addition to the geographical cleavage, indicates the existence of alternative forms of interest aggregation of Ukrainian elites. These 'substitutes' (Hale 2005) to parties, most notably financial-industrial groups and regional political machines, were better positioned to defend the interests of elite actors, who may otherwise have joined a party of power. The phenomenon of parties of power has not entirely gone past Ukraine, as in some regions parties, often connected to the economic interests of local elites, have been relatively successful in monopolizing power and aggregating popular support. The failure to unite political elites under one umbrella on a nationwide scale ensured that Ukraine's party system has always maintained a great deal of pluralism. Parliamentary elections, equally, have always been highly competitive and bitterly fought.

Other undemocratic party types

The mobilization of 'virtual parties' has been testimony to the authoritarian leanings of the Kuchma regime. Wilson (2002b) contends that from the ten most successful parties in the 2002 elections, no less than six were virtual projects. The 'virtual' in virtual parties refers to the shallowness of their organizational structure and support base. Virtual parties pursue specific short-range objectives which typically do not extend beyond the next elections. Two types of virtual parties in Ukraine can be distinguished (Wilson and Birch 2007: 72-3). First, 'spoiler' parties were created to drain away votes from political opponents. The 2002 parliamentary elections in Ukraine, for instance, witnessed the sudden appearance of the Rukh for Unity party, which copied the Rukh party, and a 'renewed' communist party, which, so it was hoped by its creators, would drain away support from the major communist successor party (Birch 2003: 526). Even when spoiler parties receive decimals of percents of votes, their mission of draining away votes and stirring confusion in a specific segment of the party landscape is successful.

Second, 'façade parties' concealed the actual, primarily economic interests of the party leadership under a programmatic shell. In Ukraine, façade parties, which were particularly widespread until at least 2004, acted as vehicles for individual 'oligarchs' or groups of businessmen, also called 'financial-industrial groups' (FIGs), that were often regionally based. Electorally, these parties benefited from the funds that their wealthy sponsors would contribute. Some parties that were not primarily oligarchic façade parties were equally associated with particular oligarchs whose sponsorship was sought. The involvement of oligarchs and business groupings in party politics corrupted legislative politics. It was widely believed that parliamentary seats could be bought and individual parliamentarians bribed. Parties, once elected in parliament, would often make way for factions whose primary purpose similarly was to promote the interests of a business grouping. Åslund (2006: 16) counted nine such 'oligarchic factions' in the parliament of late 2002. Sometimes, façade parties had once been more or less serious programmatic parties before at some point they were 'captured' by oligarchic groups (Protsyk 2002). The women's party ZPU, for instance, from a 'normal' party had turned into a vehicle for business interests by the 1998 elections (Kuzio 2003: 43); similar takeovers were carried out at the expense of the Social Democratic Party of Ukraine (united) and the Green Party. There is little evidence that virtual parties, of the types that were common in Ukraine, have been employed on a significant scale in Georgia, although many parties have been rumored either to pose as an opposition party while being loyal to the regime, or to serve as a front for American or Russian interests.

Parties of power and virtual parties are outgrowths of authoritarian politics. Since pluralism was far from entirely eliminated in Georgia and Ukraine, there has also been some room for other types of parties, including programmatic, policy-seeking parties, which correspond to an image of what parties should be like in a liberal democracy (Wolinetz 2002: 150), and that are deemed to be more readily compatible with democratization than other types of parties that are widespread in young party systems (Croissant 2002: 346). A significant presence on the party landscape in Georgia and in Ukraine until 2005, nonetheless, has been taken by parties that worked to distort the level playing field and that were not interested in reforming to become democratic forces.

4.5. THE LIMITED LEVERAGE OF PARTIES

Volatility in party supply and volatility within parties, which together determine the fluid nature of party politics in Georgia and Ukraine, hinge on the lack of incentives for political actors to invest in the formation and development of viable parties. The absence of strong enough incentives stems from the limited role of parties in policy-making, in elections, and even in legislation. As will be argued in this section, the limited role of parties, in turn, is largely predicated on the institutional make-up of the political systems of Georgia and Ukraine. The elements of institutional design that are most often considered to have an impact on party (system) development, and that will be consecutively discussed here, are executive-legislative relations and the electoral system (Croissant 2002; McFaul 2001; Meleshevich 2007). This section additionally discusses the impact of parliamentary rules on party cohesiveness.

Executive-legislative relations

Until the Rose Revolution, Georgia was a purely presidential republic, with the popularly elected president heading the executive while not being subject to the confidence of the legislative assembly. [58] Ukraine has had a semi-presidential arrangement throughout the post-communist period, while Georgia turned semi-presidential shortly after the Revolution as a result of the introduction of a second locus of executive power in the person of a prime minister.[59] Until 2006, the semi-presidential system in Ukraine heavily favored the president, putting Ukraine in the class of 'highly presidentialized semipresidential regime' (Elgie 2005: 102-5). Highly presidentialized semipresidential regimes 'often suffer the same problems as their purely presidential counterparts' (idem: 102), and may even be more 'presidentialized' than some purely presidential regimes, a state of affairs which, with regard to the FSU, is sometimes captured by the term 'superpresidentialism' (Fish 2005: 224-244; Herron 2004; Ishiyama and Kennedy 2001). The introduction of the post of prime minister in Georgia was accompanied by a simultaneous increase in presidential powers, so that, despite the fact that executive power was now formally shared, Georgia became even more 'presidentialized' (Fairbanks 2004) after the Revolution.

There is a reasonable consensus that presidential, or highly presidentialized, systems are less conducive to democratic consolidation than arrangements with strong legislatures in states moving away from authoritarianism (Bunce 2000; Frye 1997). Among other things, the 'perils of presidentialism' include the personalization of power, the often limited checks on executive authority, the blurring of prerogatives and spheres of accountability of the executive vis-à-vis parliament, and the lack of accountability of presidents due to their fixed terms of office (Fish 2006; Linz 1990). With regard to political parties specifically, it is argued that there is an 'inverse relationship' between presidentialism and party strength (Shugart 1998; Shugart and Carey 1992: 177). From the wealth of arguments linking presidentialism to problems with stable, democratic party development, four arguments with particular relevance to Georgia and Ukraine are highlighted here.

First, under presidentialism, the relevance of political parties is diminished as a direct consequence of the way powers are distributed. Most importantly, with the presidency being the main prize of competition, political actors will be inclined to place their bets on securing the presidency (Croissant and Merkel 2001: 7; van de Walle 2003: 310-1). In doing so, they often circumvent parties, especially in places where association with a political party is regarded a liability. Furthermore, while a parliamentary majority, typically consisting of one or more parties, is central in forming the government in parliamentary regimes, it is mostly the president, with or without *ad hoc* approval by a parliamentary majority, who is in charge of forming government cabinets under presidentialism. Particularly in countries where parties are unpopular, presidents prefer nonpartisan, technical cabinets. None of the ten cabinets formed in Ukraine between 1991 and the Orange Revolution, for instance, had a genuine party affiliation (Protsyk 2003: 1079). This circumstance exacerbates the situation by prompting ambitious, careerist politicians who are interested in assuming government posts not to join parties. Last, given that parliament is the main platform for parties to manifest themselves, especially when parties are not involved in cabinet formation, the weakness of the legislature reinforces the image of parties as inconsequential organizations.

Second, because of the centrality of the presidency, presidential regimes are more characterized by the 'politics of personality' than are parliamentary regimes, in which parties rather than persons - partisan or not - take center stage (Ishiyama and Kennedy 2001; Samuels 2002). The personalization of politics, where it affects parties, works at the expense of the development of viable party organizations. Most party organizations in FSU countries are dominated by 'big men' (rarely women) who personify their parties.[60] Concomitantly, only few parties have experienced leadership succession. Outside of parties, most of the highest-ranking politicians, including presidents and presidential candidates, often eschewed to affiliate with a party. Kuchma, for instance, in 1994 after his first election victory, declared: '[T]his is good that not a single political party supported me during the election, as I am going to serve people and not the party' (cited in Meleshevich 2007: 151). Following in part from the personalization of politics, parties in presidentialized regimes are less often of the programmatic type and tend to have a stronger electoral focus than in parliamentary regimes. Taking on Kitschelt's (1995: 449) distinction between the broad categories of programmatic, charismatic, and clientelist parties, under presidentialism the two latter types are more widespread (Croissant 2002: 355). Although neither charismatic nor clientelist parties necessarily obstruct the consolidation of democracy,[61] the effective interest aggregation and larger degree of institutionalization of programmatic parties go together with democratization more readily.

Third, related to the diminished leverage of parties under presidentialism, parties tend to be less cohesive (Carey 2002; Croissant 2002: 354; Kitschelt and Smyth 2002), lending support to the suggestion that parties in presidential systems are differently organized than in parliamentary systems (Samuels 2002). In non-programmatic parties, leaders and activists are quicker to abandon their party when the expected benefits of party affiliation are not met. Their excessive focus on elections and lack of cohesiveness obstruct the institutionalization of parties under presidentialism (Croissant and Merkel 2001). Finally, executive authorities in presidential regimes may have an interest in checking the development of strong (opposition) parties which potentially pose a challenge to the regime. Especially in a less-than-democratic setting, the regime may be tempted to block parties from becoming too influential, for instance by amending legislation, detaining party leaders, or rigging elections.

Electoral Legislation

The impact of electoral laws on political parties and party systems is extensively studied. Following Duverger (1959), a distinction is commonly made between mechanical and psychological effects of electoral laws. While the mechanical working of electoral formulae translates votes into seats in a specific way, the psychological element prompts voters and parties to rethink the possible consequences of their actions and to adapt their voting and electoral strategy to fit anticipated outcomes. As in the relation between strong legislatures and democracy, there is much evidence, from both case-oriented and large-n studies, that proportional representation (PR) is more conducive to democratization than single member districts (SMDs) in states moving away from authoritarianism (Hoffman 2005; Moser 1999; Norris 2008).

All parliamentary elections in Georgia and two in Ukraine (1998 and 2002) have been conducted according to a mixed electoral system, combining PR and SMDs in different proportions - equally divided in Ukraine and two-thirds to one-third in favor of SMDs in Georgia until 2008. The 1994 elections in Ukraine were all-majoritarian, while party list voting in a single nation-wide district was applied in the 2006 and 2007 parliamentary votes. The main reason why SMDs have a depressing effect on viable party development is straightforward: individuals are elected rather than parties. In the 1994 Ukrainian parliamentary elections, in which all seats were filled from single-member districts, only one fourth of candidates were members of a party, and only half of those were backed by their parties (Birch and Wilson 1999: 277). Especially when parties are unpopular forces, as is the case in Georgia and Ukraine, candidates in majoritarian races have weak incentives to join a party, contributing to the limited visibility and significance of parties. Party development in Ukraine received a considerable boost with the introduction of PR for half of the seats in parliament. A second reason why SMDs, either in combination with PR or not in combination with PR, has the ability to stem the development of a pluralist and competitive party landscape lies in its propensity to sustain and strengthen regionalized political bases. In the less-

93

than-democratic conditions of Georgia and of Ukraine until 2005, however, regimes are reluctant to allow alternative power bases which potentially challenge central authorities. A more serious threat is the emergence of one-party dominance (Birch 2005). In mixed electoral systems, the party list result for a party of power is often inflated by the outcome of SMD elections. Particularly state-sponsored parties of power, or otherwise parties with more resources than their competitors, are disproportionally successful in SMD elections. While the ruling United National Movement in Georgia, for instance, won close to sixty per cent of the party list vote in the 2008 parliamentary elections, the party received eighty per cent of seats in parliament because it won almost all SMDs races.

Two arguments why the mixed electoral system, which 'involves the combination of different electoral formulas (plurality or PR; majority or PR) for an election to a single body' (Massicotte and Blais 1999: 345) has been detrimental to the development of viable parties in Georgia and Ukraine, are singled out here. The first argument is similar to the one already mentioned in relation to SMDs. Candidates in the majoritarian section of the vote often refrain from joining parties. As a result, a large ratio of MPs is likely to be nonpartisan, a situation which decreases the leverage of parties and can augment the creation of unstable factions in parliament, which sometimes draw (former) members from party factions. Secondly, the SMD section provides an alternative route for parties and individuals into parliament (D'Anieri 2007: 159), holding back parties from merging into bigger, more viable forces, and individuals from seeking party affiliation. Individuals with no interest in joining one of the existing parties, as well as parties that see no chance in gaining representation in parliament independently or for whatever reason refrain from joining electoral blocs, have the opportunity to try their luck in the SMD section of the ballot (Ferrara and Herron 2005). Since small parties out of strategic calculation often concentrate much of their effort on winning seats through SMDs, do they not spend as much time and effort on national campaigning, developing a platform and a party organization as they may otherwise. These arguments make clear that mixed electoral systems in Georgia and Ukraine have not turned out to deliver the 'best of both worlds' (Shugart and Wattenberg 2001) of the proportional and majoritarian principles, that has been anticipated by proponents of the mixed system. In the 'best of both worlds' scenario, 'the PR system would channel activity into the parties, and the majoritarian section would create strong incentives to party consolidation' (D'Anieri 2007: 159). Instead, the mixed system has in most cases revealed itself to be, in Sartori's (1997: 74-5) formulation, 'a bastard-producing hybrid that combines their defects'.

Besides SMDs, a second alternative route for small parties and for individuals to gain representation has in Georgia and Ukraine been provided by the opportunity to form electoral coalitions (alternatively, blocs or alliances). The fact that parties often team up with other parties in electoral coalitions has been a major driver of party fragmentation. Parties with no chance of getting into parliament on their own still have the chance to jump on the bandwagon of more prospective parties and by doing so win a small number of seats, despite their lack of an autonomous support base. For these weak parties, winning a few seats is enough of an incentive not to disband their organizations. Electoral coalitions furthermore work against viable party development by allowing movements (instead of parties) and non-partisan individuals on their lists. A final manner in which electoral laws could have a negative impact on party development was when they were frequently amended or replaced. In both Georgia and Ukraine, electoral legislation has been subject to several major amendments.[62] Consistent with the hypothesis that electoral laws are amended to benefit those who control the legislative process (Andrews and Jackman 2005; Colomer 2005; Ishiyama 1997), amendments to electoral legislation in the FSU has been often driven by the intention of regimes to skew party competition in their favor. The awareness among parties that electoral laws are not fixed and may be subject to amendment in the near future heightens insecurity about the electoral prospects of parties, which could induce them to focus on more immediate goals and put off organizational development. Furthermore, changes in electoral legislation should also be expected to cause shifts in voting behavior, contributing to even greater party system volatility (Remmer 2008).

In addition to executive-legislative relations and electoral laws, parliamentary rules have had distinct effects on party (system) development. Rules pertaining to the creation and operation of parliamentary factions and to the status of individual mandates have often undercut party discipline and consequently party consolidation. The relative ease with which deputies have been able to establish factions separate from parties has decreased the salience of parties in parliament. In an extreme example, only four out of a total of fourteen parliamentary factions in the Ukrainian parliament in 2001 coincided with parties that had been elected to parliament three years earlier (Wilson 2001: 62). The widespread 'floor-crossing' (switching between factions), which is seen as an inhibition to party system institutionalization (Shabad and Slomczynski 2004) has triggered the adoption of an imperative mandate, which assigns seats in parliament to parties instead of individual MPs, in Ukraine. MP mobility has also provided an additional opportunity for political corruption: it is widely believed that MPs in Ukraine were offered large sums of money for joining a certain faction.

The overarching effect of the institutional framework in Georgia and Ukraine on party politics has been to diminish the 'positions of leverage' of political parties. Parties have often been irrelevant, or at best not crucial, in the presidential contest and in government formation; presidentialism and electoral laws encourage a focus on persons rather than on issues in both presidential and parliamentary elections; electoral laws provide alternative routes for non-party actors and weak parties to gain parliamentary representation; and a number of party functions are substituted by electoral coalitions and factions in parliament. In the next section it will be argued how the diminished leverage of parties has played out on party development by looking at the incentive structures of party actors.

Constitutional amendments enforcing a more balanced power equilibrium between president and parliament, as well as the introduction of party list voting for all seats in parliament in 2006 have brought Ukraine closer to the kinds of institutional arrangements that are believed to be more conducive to party development. Crucially, as a result of the reforms the role of parties in Ukraine has been significantly enhanced. Georgia has so far retained its 'superpresidential' system and a mixed electoral system.

4.6. INCENTIVE STRUCTURES AND MODELS OF PARTY BEHAVIOR

It has been noted that parties in Georgia and Ukraine states seldom have a societal origin. Among the explanations for this are the absence of clear-cut cleavages in post-Soviet societies (Lewis 2006), the weakness of civil society (Howard 2003), as well as the fact that party system development to varying degrees is steered by the post-communist (semi-) authoritarian regimes. As is to some extent true for the entire post-communist world, the creation and subsequent development of parties are typically instigated by elite actors without an immediate grassroots constituency (van Biezen 2005: 155; Birch 2001: 2; Tavits 2008b; Toole 2003). Since these elite actors 'owned' their parties entirely, studying their incentives should provide insight into the dynamics of party creation and operation.

Especially in the initial stage of multiparty politics, party-building in Georgia and Ukraine involved much 'small-scale political vanity, fanaticism, and whimsy, which have generated a penumbra of tiny "divan" or "taxi" parties' (Wilson and Birch 2007: 54). These mostly irrelevant small parties, which are typically headed by a self-interested leadership and of which there are still dozens in Georgia and Ukraine, may defy classification. Considering the meager electoral prospects and the very limited

96

leverage over politics of these parties, their prolonged existence is not easily explained from an inquiry into their incentives. It is assumed here, nonetheless, following a key premise in rational choice approaches, that the more relevant political party actors by and large behave purposefully (Hershey 2006: 75). The principal rationale underlying the activity of these actors is the benefits that they anticipate receiving from electoral success; borrowing from political economy terminology, they may be thought of as political party 'entrepreneurs' (Strom 1990). These entrepreneurs can be divided into those who operate separately from the regime and do not have access to state resources, and those who belong to the inner circle of the regime and therefore do have access to state resources that can be employed in party-building.

Because of the limited leverage, conditioned by elements of institutional design, of political parties in FSU states, nonregime actors have had few compelling incentives to invest in party-building. Parties have remained weak institutions, with the exception of a number of parties of power whose ultimate purpose was to entrench a consolidated authoritarian regime. Weak parties were prone to be abandoned by their leaders at some point. Many of them had been launched as not much more than 'projects' that had to satisfy short-range objectives. As soon as they failed to deliver, these parties were discarded by the leadership. A considerable number of weak parties have been sustained despite their failure to deliver: often, however, did these forces continue to exist merely in name, without a leadership willing to invest in them, and without any serious degree of leverage. Incentives to create and sustain viable parties, to the extent that they did exist, moreover, have been offset by a number of other factors that have discouraged political actors to invest in parties. At different times potential party entrepreneurs have anticipated repression from the authorities when they would engage in opposition activity. In effective authoritarian systems, party entrepreneurs may furthermore refrain from party-building because they do not expect to gain electoral success in an uneven playing field. Also, alternative types of organization, such as financial-industrial groups or clan structures based on kinship, may substitute parties with respect to aggregating and defending the interests of elites. Political parties traditionally carry out a number of functions which, at the risk of oversimplification, can be divided in procedural functions (nominating candidates for office, legislative tasks, forming government) and representative functions (aggregating interests, issue formulation, mobilization) (Bartolini and Mair 2001: 332; Erdmann 2004; Gunther and Diamond 2001). Parties are indispensable for the fulfillment of at least a minimum of procedural functions, but can be substituted regarding their representative functions. Hale (2005), in a highly insightful account of party politics in Russia before the emergence of the One Russia ruling party, argues that on the 'marketplace' where political interests are 'traded', parties were outflanked by 'substitutes' for parties, most notably financial-industrial groups and regional political machines, that were more effective in aggregating and defending the interests of elite groups. To the extent that these groups engage in electoral competition, do they merely employ parties as 'vehicles' to secure parliamentary representation. After this narrow goal has been achieved, the party is readily abandoned. In other FSU states besides Russia where regimes have not been able to direct party system development, and where elites were disunited, the party universe was fragmented and individual parties were weak, alternative forms of organizations have also operated as networks that aggregated interests of elite actors, who otherwise would likely have been drawn to parties or would have created parties. Wheatley (2005: 218) has identified four such interest-based networks of elite actors in Shevardnadze-era Georgia. Similar to Russia, financial-industrial groups in Ukraine, mostly with a regional origin, wielded much influence and were involved in politics (Puglisi 2003).

Taken together, a wide range of factors hold back individual actors - likely party entrepreneurs under different conditions - from joining parties or from engaging in party-building: the limited leverage of parties in the overall political process; the poor career prospects in political systems in which executive posts flow to non-partisan actors only; the poor electoral prospects for partisan candidates in single-member constituencies where parties are unpopular; the availability of 'substitute' organizations with more effective mechanisms of interest aggregation; the likelihood of repression; and the limited chance of electoral success in an uneven playing field. Despite the generally weak incentives to invest in parties for actors not intimately connected to the regime, parties have fulfilled if not the representative, then at least the procedural functions which make parties indispensable in elections with more than one party.[63] Some parties were steered by the executive powers in the FSU states or by oligarchic forces and were driven by stronger and more specific incentives, and incentives of a different type, than those of actors from outside the regime. Parties of power mainly served the purposes of checking the opposition and providing a patronage network for elite actors. Satellite parties equally served to pull in elite actors and keeping the opposition small by winning as large a share of the vote as they could, while spoiler parties, a subtype of the satellite party, singularly served to drain away votes from the opposition. A more remote intended effect of these regime-initiated parties was to contribute to regime survival. Next to the regime-initiated parties, self-interested businessmen in some countries created 'oligarchic parties' to win office in order to then reap the benefits related to holding office.

A way to picture the incentives that drive party creation and operation in Ukraine and Georgia is by extending Strom's 'three models of party behavior' (Strom 1990) - policy-seeking, vote-seeking, and office-seeking - to the less-than-democratic context of Ukraine (before 2005) and Georgia. According to Wolinetz (2002: 149-50), 'a policy-seeking party is one which gives primary emphasis to pursuit of policy goals, a vote-seeking party is one whose principal aim is to maximize votes and win elections, while an office-seeking party is primarily interested in securing the benefits of office - getting its leaders into government, enjoying access to patronage, etc.'.

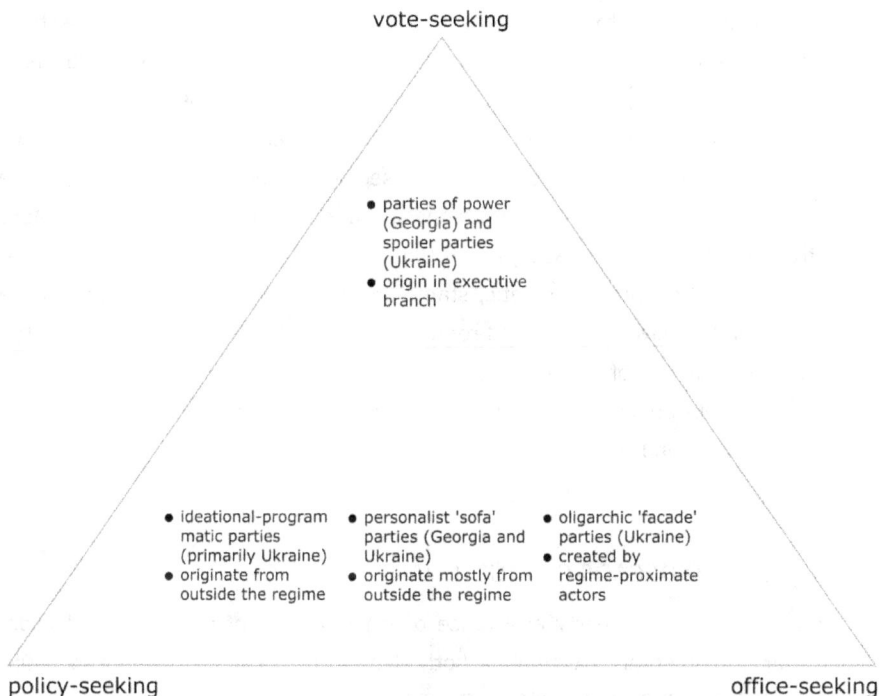

vote-seeking

- parties of power (Georgia) and spoiler parties (Ukraine)
- origin in executive branch

- ideational-program matic parties (primarily Ukraine)
- originate from outside the regime

- personalist 'sofa' parties (Georgia and Ukraine)
- originate mostly from outside the regime

- oligarchic 'facade' parties (Ukraine)
- created by regime-proximate actors

policy-seeking   office-seeking

Figure 4. Incentives, party types and party origins. Adapted from Wolinetz (2002: 161)

Figure four depicts how the incentives for party-building in Georgia and Ukraine are related to the types of parties that have been prevalent in these states. Naturally, the three types of incentives are ideal-types: real-life political parties are functional hybrids whose leaders can be driven by intricate combinations of incentives. Rather than laying a claim on precise classification, the above figure for that reason primarily serves a heuristic purpose.

The dominant parties of power of Georgia and the frequent spoiler parties of Kuchma-era Ukraine have been first and foremost interested in securing as many votes as possible, in the case of the parties of power mostly to signal regime strength and derive legitimacy from elections, and in the case of spoiler parties to spoil the chances of anti-regime forces. Virtual 'façade' parties, common in Ukraine under Kuchma, sought office more than anything else in anticipation of receiving the (economic) benefits that were associated with office. With the disappearance of virtual parties after the Revolution, fewer parties in Ukraine are ostensibly office-seeking. A large number of mostly not so relevant, small, personalist political parties in Georgia and Ukraine are neither clearly policy-seeking, nor clearly office-seeking. Often, these parties are sustained for many years, without enjoying any prospect of electoral success or gaining access to office, except when they become part of an electoral coalition. Finally, a number of parties in Ukraine, and arguably a few in Georgia, have primarily pursued policy goals. These parties, however, have almost invariably been kept outside of executive power, and have lost much of their clout over the years. Of all these party types, only some of the policy-seeking parties can boast a credible degree of organization, societal rootedness, and internal democracy. More importantly, only few parties in Georgia and Ukraine have been seriously interested in developing their parties into democratic, stable and representative forces, and future constituents of a democratic, stable and representative party system in a consolidated democracy. The majority of parties, therefore, would be dubious recipients of party assistance, a conclusion with important implications regarding the efficacy of party assistance in Georgia and Ukraine.

4.7. THE SECOND DECADE OF MULTI-PARTY POLITICS

This thesis studies political party assistance over the course of roughly one decade, spanning four parliamentary elections in both Georgia (1999, 2003, 2004 and 2008) and Ukraine (1998, 2002, 2006, 2007). Considering that multipartism commenced in the two former Soviet republics near the end of the 1980s within the framework of the political reforms of perestroika, the time period under investigation here comprises, roughly, the second decade of multipartism. During this second decade of multipartism, party politics in Georgia and Ukraine has remained highly volatile. In Georgia, both before and after the Rose Revolution, and even more so than in Ukraine, voters have been confronted with a radically different set of parties and electoral blocs from one election to the next (see appendices one and two). In the 2002 parliamentary elections in Ukraine, similarly, only 4 out of 33 forces that competed had been at the ballot in 1998 in the same form (Birch 2003: 530). Results from elections since 2002 suggest some degree of continuity. Intra-bloc volatility, in the form of frequent changes in the composition of electoral blocs, however, has been substantial. Moreover, previously successful parties (in electoral terms) have lost much of their clout, and by 2008 one of the major parties of previous years, People's Union Our Ukraine, was seemingly in a process of dissolution.

As noted in section 4.5, the strengthening of the role of parliament and the cabinet of ministers after the Orange Revolution, and new electoral legislation according to which all MPs are now elected from party lists, have created more fruitful conditions for stable party development in Ukraine. In Georgia, on the other hand, factors which are considered to have a negative impact on stable party development have remained in place. The shape of Georgia's party 'system', characterized by a dominant ruling force surrounded by a flurry of small and weak opposition parties, has equally remained unchanged. The only notable change after the Revolution in this area has been the disappearance of a second party of power, previously signifying the existence of a second locus of executive power in the autonomous republic of Adjara. As much as before the Revolution, the main fault line in electoral competition has revolved around whether parties do or do not support the ruling forces: besides the charisma of party leaders, the stance of parties' vis-à-vis the regime has defined their identities. Electoral competition has not been strongly marked by geographical cleavages. The most significant geographical factor in elections has been the generally greater support for the regime outside the capital Tbilisi, as suggested by official election results, than in the capital.

Compared to Georgia, electoral competition in Ukraine has been more multidimensional, with a slightly bigger role for substantial issues, a still notable but less overpowering pro-regime/anti-regime divide (mainly before the Revolution), and a much greater weight for geographical differences in voting patterns. In the absence of successful ruling parties, party politics in Ukraine on a national level has been more pluralist than in Georgia, reflected in, among others, a larger number of parties in the legislature. It has also been somewhat easier to tell Ukrainian parties apart on the basis of programmatic issues, although the election campaign for the 2002 parliamentary elections, for instance, was said to be 'virtually policy-free' (Birch 2003: 527). Arguably the most defining aspect of electoral competition in Ukraine has been the geographical voting patterns. Although the actual picture is a bit more complex, a distinction if commonly made between, on the one hand, the southern and eastern regions of the country, and the Western regions on the other, with central Ukraine occupying, literally, a middle ground between the two. In the Western half of the country, the Lviv region embodies Western Ukrainian voting behavior. There, president Yushchenko's party Our Ukraine came in first at the parliamentary elections of 2006.[64] The Party of the Regions, which won the national race with one third of the vote, garnered only three per cent of the vote in the Lviv region. The east is most vividly represented by the Donetsk region, considered to be the home base of the Party of the Regions (PRU), led by former prime minister and losing candidate in the 2004 presidential elections Yanukovich. PRU received 74% of the vote in the Donetsk region in 2006, while the parties that occupied second and third place in the national vote received a scant 1–3% per cent of votes in the Donetsk region, according to official data. In parliamentary elections before the Orange Revolution, the electoral schism between regions was equally clear-cut. In 2002, the Our Ukraine bloc won 75% in the Western Ivano-Frankivsk region, against less than 3% in the Donetsk region. The Communist Party of Ukraine won 40% in the Luhansk region, and less than two per cent in some Western regions. Geographical concentration of party support has in some cases been limited to one city, typically the home city of a certain party leader. In the 1998 parliamentary elections, the Hromada party scored 35% in Dnipropetrovsk, with a second best result of 6% in the city Kirovograd, and 5% of the overall national vote. These figures invite the observation that 'there is no real national party system in Ukraine, only a series of (partially) interlocking regional subsystems' (Wilson and Birch 2007: 74).

4.8. COMMONALITY AND VARIATION IN PARTY DEVELOPMENT

The bulk of political parties in Georgia and Ukraine have shared a number of characteristics which more generally are rather common for political parties outside Western democracies and which make up much of the 'standard lament' about parties. First, parties in Georgia and Ukraine were poorly institutionalized, as has been most apparent in the high turnover rate of parties. Further manifestations of weak party institutionalization have been the lack of dense organizational structures, the failure to forge links with society and to attract active members, and shallow organizational capacity outside the capital. Partial exceptions to this have been the Communist Party and Rukh in Ukraine, and arguably also the Republican Party and the Labor Party in Georgia. During the 1990s, the Communist Party and Rukh were often held to be the only true parties on the Ukrainian party landscape (Wilson and Birch 2007: 53). The Communist Party of Ukraine, however, has been kept out of executive power with rare exceptions in southern and eastern regions, and lost most of its support base after 2000, while Rukh, one of the biggest forces in the first years of multi-party politics in Ukraine, suffered a split in the late 1990s after which its two successors were unable to become as influential and popular as Rukh before. In Georgia, the Republican Party and Labor Party have never taken part in government and moreover have never been very successful in electoral terms. Besides these parties, other parties that have proven durable generally did not have credible organizations: most of them are small 'sofa' parties that, facilitated by low maintenance costs, have continued to exist rather out of inertia than out of purpose. Second, parties have been dominated by one leader or, more rarely, a small clique of leaders. The most obvious indication of personalism in parties is that hardly any of them has experienced leadership succession. One exception among currently existing parties is the Republican Party of Georgia, whose former leaders, however, still wield much power within the party. The strong position of a party leader sits uneasily with internal democracy. Parties typically do have the trappings of internal democracy, but lack the content: as noted with respect to Georgian parties, 'their structures are democratic, yet this merely hides the real distribution of power inside the parties (Dolidze 2005: 8). Third, most parties in Georgia and Ukraine are indistinguishable in terms of political program. Especially the more influential parties often do not bother to define a program. Party names in many cases do suggest an ideological orientation, but the actual weight of ideology is small. In Georgia, the remarkable situation exists that a large majority of opposition parties define themselves as 'centre-right' (IDEA and CSS 2006: 7). The reason people vote for a party rarely reflects a programmatic linkage between them and the parties: more often, personal reputation, and sometimes clientelistic practices, shape voters' choices (Kitschelt 2000). To be sure, some relevant parties, particularly in Ukraine, do have a distinct ideological profile: for Ukraine these are mainly the Communist Party, the Socialist Party, People's Union Our Ukraine, and the successors of Rukh. In Georgia, the Labor Party and the Republican Party, not by chance also parties with relatively strong organizations, enjoy some recognizability as ideological forces.

Meaningful variation between parties as organizations is to a large degree captured by two factors: the primary incentive driving parties' operation and continued existence, and secondly, their origin. As noted in section six of this chapter, authoritarian practices in party politics in Georgia and Ukraine translate into vote-seeking and office-seeking incentives in party operation against program-seeking incentives, which are more commonly associated with party development in democratic societies. [65] Strom's tripartite division of program-seeking, office-seeking, and vote-seeking models of party behavior provides a useful framework to understand the different incentives that drive party operation in Georgia and Ukraine. Second, three types of origins of parties can be distinguished: parties may be initiated at the direct instigation of the executive branch; actors from within the regime or with close ties to the regime, such as 'oligarchs', may engage in party-building; and parties may originate entirely from outside the regime. Party origin, conceived in this way, is indicative of whether parties turn out to be pluralistic (as against proto-hegemonic) and of the incentives which drive their operation. Purely program-seeking parties in Georgia and Ukraine, for instance, are invariably created from outside the regime, while parties that are created at the instigation of the executive branch work to distort the electoral playing field and by doing so thwart pluralism.

A more circumstantial feature of parties is their political relevance. Relevant are those parties which possess, in Sartori's well-known formulation, 'blackmail potential' and 'coalition potential' (Sartori 1976: 122-3). Broadly interpreted, parties are relevant when they have some stake in how the country is governed, either by being in government or being seen as a possible future coalition partner, or by presenting an influential force in the legislature. Of the 100-200 parties that are registered with the Ministry of Justice in Georgia and Ukraine, only 10-20 at any moment are said to be truly functional, and have some prospect of winning representation in parliament.[66] A much smaller number of parties still, sometimes only one, has actual leverage over how the country is ruled. Finally, parties vary according to their ideological self-positioning, or, if no explicit ideology is proclaimed, the type of policy that is consistently advocated. The ideological self-positioning of parties, obviously, does not necessarily reflect the true objectives of those parties. As noted, policy and ideology are often largely absent in electoral races. Parties with clear ideological profiles, as much as parties which do not reveal an ideological position, may not give precedence to emphasizing programmatic issues.

Tables three and four list the most prominent parties in Georgia and Ukraine during the period under investigation, and score these parties on the variables of variation between parties identified above. Because of their relative prominence, the parties listed in these tables have been the primary material with which providers of assistance have worked. Some of the parties no longer exist; others have surfaced only in recent years.

	relevance (low-medium-high)	dominant incentive (program-seeking, office-seeking, vote-seeking)	origin (regime, regime-near, outside regime)	ideological self-positioning
CUG	high	vote	regime	indefinite
UNM	high	vote	opposition turned regime	indefinite
Revival	high	vote	regime	indefinite
CUG bloc partners	low	office	regime-near	indefinite
United Democrats	medium	program/office	outside regime	indefinite
LP	low	program/office	outside regime	center-left
RPG	low	program/office	outside regime	liberal
NRP, CP, IWSG, Georgia's Way, Freedom Movement, For a United Georgia	low	program/office	outside regime	center-right, conservative

Table 3. Variation between the most significant political parties in Georgia

	relevance (low-medium-high)	dominant incentive (program-seeking, office-seeking, vote-seeking)	origin (regime, regime-near, outside regime)	ideological self-positioning
PRU	high	office	regime-near	indefinite
Batkivshchyna	high	office	outside regime	indefinite
NSNU	high	program/office	outside regime	nationalist, liberal
KPU	medium	program	outside regime	socialist
SPU	medium	program/office	outside regime	social-democratic
NDP	low	office	regime-near	indefinite
SDPU(o)	low	office	regime-near	social-democratic
NU bloc partners	low	program/office	outside regime	nationalist, liberal
BYuT bloc partners	low	office	outside regime	various
ZYEU bloc partners	low	office	regime/regime-near	indefinite
spoiler parties[67]	low	vote	regime	various

Table 4. Variation between the most significant political parties in Ukraine

These tables demonstrate that, in both Georgia and Ukraine, political parties with a more pronounced ideological position tend to be less relevant. Formulated reversely, the most relevant parties in both countries are not primarily driven by the incentive to implement a specific set of policies, and in addition, and relatedly, fail to associate with a definable political ideology. The only parties with a serious degree of leverage in Georgia, before and after the Rose Revolution, have been the parties of power. As auxiliary organizations of the regime, these parties of power are ideologically diffuse and are driven primarily by a vote-seeking incentive. The wide range of small opposition parties which have been somewhat more explicit ideologically, have invariably remained inconsequential forces. Unlike in Georgia, there have been no dominant parties of power in Ukraine. Most of the parties that have been highly relevant in Ukraine, however, have, with the partial exception of People's Union Our Ukraine, equally been short on ideology and a program-seeking incentive. The parties that have been most consistent in advocating a coherent program, particularly the Communist Party and Rukh, have become less relevant over time. The greater degree of pluralism and competitiveness of the Ukrainian party system, relative to the Georgian party system, is demonstrated by the fact that more parties that have their origins outside the regime have gained some degree of relevance.

4.9. IMPLICATIONS FOR POLITICAL PARTY ASSISTANCE

The implications for party assistance that follow from the discussion on the domestic constraints on party development in Georgia and Ukraine in this section, are simple. Most evidently, the effectiveness of party assistance has been impaired by the large degree of volatility in party politics in Georgia and Ukraine. Parties that were assisted were likely either not to survive or to become subject to far-reaching internal change. Indeed, most parties that have been assisted over the years subsequently withered. The Georgian party landscape in 2009 is still highly in flux. New parties, led by former regime actors, have recently presented themselves, and the survival of the ruling United National Movement seems to hinge solely on the survival of the regime. In Ukraine, a modicum of continuity has become discernable in recent years. Within-bloc volatility, however, is considerable. Moreover, the party that has by far has received most attention from providers of assistance, People's Union Our Ukraine, in 2009 is near extinction.

Even more crucially, a substantial share of the more relevant Georgian and Ukrainian parties that have received assistance were really unsuitable to receive assistance because the operation of these parties was driven by incentives that were incompatible with the norms and values that party assistance sought to infuse in party politics. This applies foremost to the regime-initiated vote-seeking parties (parties of power and spoiler parties) and to office-seeking 'oligarchic' parties. These parties were not interested in becoming constituents in a future stable and democratic party system, an observation that was echoed, for instance, in a USAID-commissioned assessment of political parties in Georgia in 2001 which found that 'limited interest exists within the major political parties to transform themselves into well-structured democratic organizations presenting the public with credible, differentiated policy platforms' (Black et al. 2001: iii).

106

Finally, even if parties would be receptive to assistance, as a form of democracy promotion party assistance would still have been unlikely to be particularly effective given the limited leverage of parties in political life and as vehicles of representation. To really make a difference, providers of assistance not only would have needed to work with parties, they also would have had to address the structural constraints on the development of stable and democratic parties. Addressing these structural domestic constraints, including institutional arrangements and the unevenness of the electoral playing field, however, goes beyond the capabilities and the mandate of party assistance.

CHAPTER FIVE: POLITICAL PARTY ASSISTANCE IN GEORGIA AND UKRAINE

This chapter presents the bulk of data on party assistance in Georgia and Ukraine that have in part been collected from interviews, and in part are documented in reports by the institutions on the supply-side of party assistance. The next chapter, in turn, drawing on the data from the current chapter, explains why the assistance effort has failed to help parties become more stable, democratic, and representative. Data are presented in the current chapter primarily when they are vital to the discussion in chapter six. The first two sections provide a basic, descriptive overview of party assistance in Georgia and Ukraine, respectively. These sections outline the types of activities that have been undertaken by the principal actors involved in party assistance, as well as the approaches that have shaped these activities. The latter two sections address central questions in party assistance, in relation to Georgia and Ukraine, with distinct ramifications for the effectiveness of the effort. First, which parties have been selected to receive assistance, and on the basis of which criteria have they been selected? Second, to what extent has the assistance favored certain forces over other forces? These two issues coincide with the two key standards of good practice in party assistance that have been identified in section two of chapter two. The discussion in sections three and four makes clear that providers of assistance have frequently fallen short of adhering to these two standards, and besides reveals much about the form that party assistance in Georgia and Ukraine has taken. More crucially, the two questions are related to the discussion of the failure of party assistance in chapter six. As will be demonstrated there, a combination of unfortunate and misguided decisions made by providers of assistance with regard to party selection have contributed to their inability to overcome domestic constrains on party development.

5.1. POLITICAL PARTY ASSISTANCE IN GEORGIA

NDI

NDI was involved in political party assistance in Georgia from 1996 until 2004. During these years, NDI in Georgia also implemented a civic program, primarily through support to the local election watchdog ISFED, and a parliamentary program, aimed at improving the functioning of the legislature. Before the 1999 parliamentary election, NDI conducted political party seminars primarily with three parties: the ruling Citizens' Union of Georgia (CUG) of president Shevardnadze, the National Democratic Party (NDP), and the People's Party (PP), which emerged from a split in NDP in 1996. Political party assistance was concentrated on these 'three main democratic parties' in order to intensify training (NDI 1998: 2). Seminars with CUG focused, among other things, on how to address voters' concerns, media strategies and press relations, and included training-of-trainers. Activists and leaders of NDP were trained in 'party communication and cohesion', campaign skills, and message development. Training to PP was mostly on election-related issues (NDI 2000a: 18-20). During these years, NDI to a lesser extent also worked with the Socialist Party, the Traditionalist Party, and the Green Party. Between the 1999 and 2003 parliamentary elections, most of NDI party assistance in Georgia was with six parties: CUG, NDP, Labor Party, the New Rights Party (NRP), the United Democrats (UD), and the (United) National Movement (UNM). Especially in 2002-2003, much more assistance went to the latter three than to other parties. After several splits occurred within CUG, the party lost much of its interest in participating in party assistance programs. NDP and Labor equally were not as eager to receive NDI's assistance as NRP, UD, and UNM were.[68]

Party assistance by NDI included the standard components of educational seminars, consultations with party leaders, and study visits.[69] Four objectives of assistance programs during these years can be discerned: strengthening organizational capacity, enhancing the campaign skills of parties, training-of-trainers, and coalition-building.[70] Much of training related to organizational development targeted the expansion of the regional and local representation of parties. Other training aimed at strengthening party organizations focused on issues such as recruitment of members, media relations, and internal coordination within parties. Training was typically organized for individual parties. In 2001 and 2002, a number of seminars were organized, and consultations held with party leaders, on the topic of coalition-building. These events had the explicit purpose to encourage a variety of small parties to look for partners. The most visible and controversial party assistance effort by NDI in the years leading up to the Rose Revolution was the unsuccessful attempt to help forge a coalition of three new opposition parties - UNM, NRP, and UD. The Traditionalist Party was initially included in this effort, but soon dropped out.

Different sources indicate that coordination between NDI in Georgia and the head office in Washington during these years was scarce. Allegedly, NDI in Georgia took decisions that it did not coordinate with main offices.[71] From 1999, there was no clear division of labor with IRI: the party institutes took the freedom to work with any party they selected themselves, and as a result there was some overlap of political parties that were assisted by both NDI and IRI.[72] After the Rose Revolution, the party institutes agreed to establish a strict division of labor: while IRI continued to work with parties outside parliament, NDI from that moment shifted its focus almost entirely towards legislative strengthening, for which it received a multi-year grant.[73] The fact that one of the party institutes now dedicated most of its work to improve the functioning of parliament is seen as a reflection of the heightened interest that the U.S. government took in supporting institutions of government after the Revolution, at least in part at the expense of support for civil society. Because of its new mandate, NDI in Georgia from 2004 has not to any significant degree been involved in party assistance as it is understood here (see section one of chapter two).

IRI

IRI has been continuously involved in political party assistance in Georgia since it opened its country office there in 1998. Throughout the years, party assistance has taken up about half of IRI's overall activity in Georgia. The main other areas of activity of IRI in Georgia include support to youth and women's organizations and opinion polling. IRI's chief partner among youth organizations is New Generation New Initiative, an NGO that, among other things, runs information campaigns in relation to Georgia's possible accession to NATO, and that is generally believed to be close to the Saakashvili administration.[74] IRI in Georgia has also organized several get-out-the-vote campaigns targeted at youth, which, it claims, have led to a 30 per cent increase in the percentage of voter turnout among young people (IRI 2004: 14). Although not an intrinsic part of its political party program, IRI's polling, which is also done in many other countries where IRI works, at least partly serves to promote party development. IRI surveys typically consist of a part on general topics, the findings of which are made public, and a part which contains questions on individual parties and party leaders, and that is disseminated to these parties only. The findings of these surveys are thought to enable parties to develop a message which reflects voters' concerns and thereby make parties more responsive.[75]

In 1998, NDI and IRI agreed to divide available parties between the two party institutes in order to avoid overlap. The agreement, however, was abandoned one year later because both institutes wanted to work with the ruling party, CUG.[76] IRI consequently provided assistance to roughly the same set of parties, including CUG, UNM (from 2002), People's Party, the Labor Party, and the Socialist Party, that NDI

111

also provided assistance to before the Rose Revolution. Since the Rose Revolution, IRI, now the one U.S. party institute that works with parties outside parliament, has provided assistance to a wide range of parties, which are selected by IRI on the criterion of alleged political relevance.[77] Training by IRI in Georgia is mainly demand-driven.[78] To parties eligible for party assistance, IRI disseminates an overview of around fifty-five topics on which it can provide training. Reflecting an overall emphasis on election-related programming, most of these topics, including for instance 'psychological types of voters', 'how to defend results', and 'agitation', are related to campaigning. Concurrently, a frequent topic in party assistance training by IRI in Georgia is 'message development', which has the aim to better connect with voters. A second, altogether less frequent type of party seminars by IRI, in addition to those on campaign management, are on party building. Seminars on party building by IRI are primarily concerned with reforming the organizational structures of parties.[79]

Most seminars are for individual parties, particularly those with an election-related topic, because it is believed that training is more productive when party activists are in the company of their fellow party members.[80] Participants in party assistance events by IRI in Georgia are more often from the upper levels within the parties than they are rank-and-file party activists. At least as frequent as training to larger groups of people are 'consultations' with selected persons from parties. Dozens of these consultations are held each quarter.[81] Moreover, some events are specifically targeted at party leaders, such as the 'party building schools' for 'parties' top managers' that were organized in 2005. In addition to training and consultations with party leaders, since the Rose Revolution several study visits for political party leaders to Lithuania were organized, over the course of which party leaders from the two former Soviet republics exchanged ideas and know-how. Lithuania was selected for this purpose due to personal ties of IRI's former chief of party with that country.

ODIHR-NIMD

In response to the 'democratic opening and momentum offered by the so-called Rose Revolution' (OSCE ODIHR 2006: 31), the Office for Democratic Institutions and Human Rights (ODIHR) of OSCE, in cooperation with NIMD, in 2005 initiated a multi-faceted political party assistance program that eventually would run until the May 2008 parliamentary elections. Implementation of the project was in the hands of NIMD in tandem with local experts from the Caucasus Institute for Peace Democracy and Development (CIPDD), while ODIHR provided funding and fulfilled a coordinating role.

The initial stage of the project consisted exclusively of an 'interactive assessment' of the political situation and party development in Georgia. During this stage, expert teams met to identify issues in party development, and workshops were organized in which participating parties were requested to engage in self-analysis in order to identify shortcomings in party development in Georgia. The six biggest parties in Georgia, as suggested by the results of the 2004 parliamentary election, were selected to participate in the project. These were the United National Movement, Labor Party, Conservative Party, Industry Will Save Georgia, Republican Party, and New Rights Party. The initial stage of the project culminated in the publication of the book Political Landscape of Georgia - Political Parties: Achievements, Challenges and Prospects (Nodia and Pinto Scholtbach 2006), which provides a comprehensive assessment of political party development, and of the environment in which parties operate in Georgia. In the ensuing stage of the project, which stretched from 2006 until 2008, and which built on the 'interactive assessment' of the first stage, the project comprised three separate 'tracks': educational seminars; preparation and implementation of VoteMatch; and a 'special track' aimed at promoting interparty dialogue. Two types of educational seminars were organized: first, training-of-trainers (ToT), mostly by Dutch experts, and targeted at mid-level activists. Participants in these trainings went on to conduct trainings within their respective parties. Second, multi-party seminars or workshops in which mainly the higher tier of party organizations participated, and which featured topics such as party funding, strategic planning, and regional party politics.

The VoteMatch track of the project was modeled after the online voting advice application StemWijzer, developed in the Netherlands by the Institute for Political Participation. The primary aim of VoteMatch in the context of the ODIHR-NIMD program was to compel parties to formulate policy positions and to identify a target electorate in the run-up to the 2008 parliamentary election. It was envisaged that a more lasting effect of the program would be that the significance of programs in electoral competition would be enhanced. As part of VoteMatch, parties received a long-list of ninety-three questions to which they were requested to provide answers. From the answers, a number of issues would be distilled on which parties apparently disagreed, and that would form the basis of the VoteMatch application which voters could then use to determine which parties is closest to them in terms of program or ideology. Because of the limited reach of internet in Georgia, VoteMatch was to be distributed on cd-rom, in a paper format outside metro stations, and at various events, in addition to an online version. The execution of VoteMatch was cancelled shortly before the elections because the United National Movement deliberately omitted to provide answers to all ninety-three questions on the long-list.[82]

The 'special track' of the project sought to promote interparty dialogue by bringing together party leaders. To this end, among others, dinners were organized at the residency of the Dutch Ambassador to Georgia in Tbilisi, and several party leaders were sent to the Netherlands to participate in an election observation mission.

Among the broad objectives of the project were to strengthen party organizations, to stimulate cooperation between parties, and to help parties develop recognizable party programs so as to make them more responsive and representative. [83] Strengthening party organizations should lead, among other things, to a more pluralist playing field, in which the ruling party would face serious competition. It was argued by a representative from NIMD that UNM itself was interested in seeing stronger opposition since this would be conducive to the country's democratic development.[84] More specific objectives that have been mentioned by the project's coordinators were to invigorate political competition by strengthening the opposition, to contribute to coalition-building among participating parties, and to enhance the significance of women and youth within parties.[85] An ultimate objective of the project was to establish a 'multiparty centre' in Tbilisi. The project was not extended beyond the 2008 parliamentary elections primarily because funding by ODIHR was discontinued. The decision to halt funding for the project was part of a wider stop to funding of politically sensitive democratization projects of ODIHR, and reportedly was influenced by criticism of prominent OSCE member Russia concerning this type of projects. [86] Considering the highly contentious political situation in Georgia prior to and after the parliamentary elections, it is unlikely that the project had been extended if funding would not have been discontinued.

Stiftungen

FNS has provided training to its partner the Republican Party of Georgia (RPG) since not long after the Rose Revolution. RPG was selected to become FNS' partner in Georgia due to that party's observer status in the Liberal International. Training to RPG has revolved around three themes: party organization in the regions, the role of youth in the party, and campaigning.[87] The ruling United National Movement was initially viewed as a potential partner by FNS, but the party's decision to move closer to a rival party family cut short its ties to FNS in Georgia. Besides providing assistance to RPG, FNS in Georgia have worked in two other areas: advocacy of liberal free-market values, and promoting dialogue between Georgians and the peoples from the two conflict regions on Georgia's legal borders. The reluctance of

FES throughout and KAS until 2007 to engage in party assistance was informed by their assessment of party development in Georgia. A 'natural' partner in Georgia for FES would be the Labor Party, given that party's stated ideological position as a center-left or social-democratic party. The Labor Party, however, was not considered an appropriate partner by FES as the FES questioned the social-democratic credentials of the party.[88] KAS did not work with parties in Georgia until 2007 because it was unable to identify a viable Christian-democratic partner party.[89] With the establishment of a permanent office in Tbilisi in 2007, however, KAS set out to start a party assistance program in Georgia. Until the 2008 parliamentary elections, only a few informal meetings with party representatives were organized. The objectives of KAS' party assistance in Georgia have been, first, to promote interparty dialogue, and second, to increase the weight of programs in political competition. Regarding future party assistance programs, KAS intended to work with an inclusive range of parties, but direct a disproportionately large share of its assistance to the United National Movement and the New Rights Party, which are both affiliated with the European People's Party.[90]

Dutch party institutes

Following fact-finding missions in 2004 after the Rose Revolution, the three biggest Dutch party institutes - Eduardo Frei Stichting (EFS), Alfred Mozer Stichting (AMS), and the International Bureau of VVD - have, on a modest scale, become involved in party assistance in Georgia. Since 2005, the three party institutes have collectively organized annual 'leadership academies' for youth from the most relevant parties. During these 'academies', participants are familiarized with political ideologies in Western democracies, are taught media skills, and reflect on the shortcomings of their respective parties. Besides this collective effort, the three party institutes also have individual partners among parties and youth organizations. EFF has organized several seminars for Saqda, the youth branch of the marginal Christian-Democratic Union of Georgia. AMS has conducted seminars for the youth branch of the Labor Party. VVD, finally, has cooperated with the Republican Party. Like FNS, VVD initially worked with the United National Movement, but terminated this relation when UNM started seeking affiliation with the European People's Party. In addition to party assistance, EFF and VVD provide support to civil society organizations in Georgia.

5.2. POLITICAL PARTY ASSISTANCE IN UKRAINE

NDI

NDI has assisted political parties in Ukraine since 1992 when it opened an office in Kyiv soon after Ukraine became an independent state. For most of the period since 1992, NDI's programming in Ukraine has consisted of three elements: political party assistance, legislative strengthening, and promoting civic organizations. NDI's work in parliament has been strictly distinct, in organizational terms, from party assistance. The chief beneficiary of NDI's support to civic organizations over the years has been the Committee of Voters of Ukraine (CVU), an election monitoring organization. In many other countries where NDI is active, including Georgia, a large part of its civic program has been devoted to cooperation with a local election monitoring organization. After the Orange Revolution, NDI received funding from USAID for a fourth program, aimed at providing support to reform of the presidential apparatus.[91] Allocation of funding by USAID for this program reflected the heightened expectations on the part of the U.S. government regarding Ukraine's post-Revolution leadership.

Party assistance by NDI in Ukraine has been viewed as consisting of three separate elements: seminars, efforts aimed at coalition-building among parties, and individual consultations with political leaders.[92] Unsurprisingly, seminars have made up the bulk of party assistance. While most seminars by IRI in Ukraine were conducted with several parties at once ('multi-party seminars'), NDI has opted to train parties individually. Different than in Georgia, where NDI and IRI at one point have simply divided up available parties, and NDI later ceased doing party assistance while IRI continued working with parties to avoid overlap in programming, the division of labor in Ukraine has been along geographical lines: NDI has worked in about ten of Ukraine's twenty-five regions, and IRI in slightly more, while both have simultaneously worked with parties in the capital.

Three stages of party assistance by NDI in Ukraine can be distinguished, with the first and second divided by the wave of mass demonstrations against the Kuchma regime in 2000, and the second and third by the Orange Revolution. In all three stages, much attention in party assistance in Ukraine, a heterogeneous country where political life is nonetheless very much concentrated in Kyiv, has gone towards strengthening the local and regional representation of political parties. A second element of continuity is that NDI throughout has encouraged like-minded parties to forge alliances and coalitions, which were supposed to halt fragmentation and lead to a more comprehensible and better organized party system.

Before 2000, NDI assisted a limited number of 'reform-oriented, democratic' political parties, including foremost Rukh, the Reform and Order Party (PRP), and the People's Democratic Party (NDP), which was the most prominent attempt to establish a party of power in the 1990s. Since 1992, NDI has maintained a particularly close relationship with Rukh and its two successors, informally known as Rukh-Kostenko and Rukh-Udovenko after their respective leaders, following a schism in Rukh in 1999. Assistance to parties that were deemed not 'reform-oriented', such as the Communist Party of Ukraine (KPU) and a range of social-democratic and socialist parties, was purposely declined. In addition to common objectives of party assistance such as party strengthening and improving campaign skills, an explicit objective of party assistance in the 1997-1999 period was to strengthen the 'reform-oriented, democratic' parties at the expense of the purportedly undemocratic and reform-averse KPU (NDI 1999: 3).

Informants who worked for NDI in Ukraine during the years concerned have stated that most party assistance from 2000 until the Orange Revolution was aimed at helping democratic parties against the regime.[93] Changing the balance on the electoral playing field in favor of democratic parties was attempted foremost by pressing for coalition-building among a number of opposition forces. Two episodes of the coalition-building effort between 2000 and 2004 stand out. First, in 2001, around ten opposition parties gathered in a hotel in Poland at the initiative of NDI to discuss opportunities for cooperation. At the occasion, NDI representatives convinced party leaders of the necessity of an alliance in order to be able to challenge the regime and come out as the biggest force in the 2002 parliamentary election.[94] Although a formal electoral coalition of a number of the political forces present in the hotel in Poland materialized only later, the event is regarded as the genesis of the Our Ukraine electoral bloc, which won the parliamentary election in 2002 and subsequently named Viktor Yushchenko as their candidate for the 2004 presidential election. Second, it is alleged that NDI, in the run-up to the 2002 election, convinced the Our Ukraine bloc with two other opposition forces, the Yulia Tymoshenko Bloc (BYuT) and the Socialist Party of Ukraine (SPU), to nominate only one candidate from these forces collectively per SMD in the 2002 election to maximize the combined opposition share of MPs in the new convocation of the parliament.[95] Also, through its seminars for political parties, NDI now sought to contribute to a mass grassroots movement of primarily young people, that was hoped to become successful, in contrast to the Ukraine without Kuchma movement of 2000, in truly challenging the regime, as eventually happened during the Orange Revolution.[96] Political party seminars were organized in these years for 'a wide range of parties that support political reforms to help democracy take root' and emphasized 'basic skills training, internal management, public communications and regional growth' (NDI 2000b: 2). At the instigation of the NDI's chief of party of that moment, NDI now also provided assistance to SPU and the Social Democratic Party of Ukraine, which were previously regarded as insufficiently 'reform-oriented'.[97] Since the Orange Revolution, the range of parties for which NDI has organized seminars includes both opposition forces and pro-government forces. Most assistance since the Revolution has gone to individual constituent parties of the Our Ukraine bloc and to BYuT, all of which were in the 'Orange camp' at the time of the Revolution; less often, seminars have been conducted for the Party of Regions, SPU, and other parties. On order of the U.S. embassy in Kyiv, NDI and IRI party assistance programs were put on hold for a few months in 2007 after PRU and KPU accused the U.S. government, but not specifically NDI and IRI, of having provoked the dissolution of parliament and consequently the fall of the PRU-KPU-SPU government. [98] The PRU-KPU-SPU government succeeded the 'Orange' government coalitions of 2005-2006. Two of its coalition parties, PRU and KPU, had previously been skeptical of the purported role of the U.S. in the Orange Revolution.

IRI

Two years after NDI, IRI became engaged in political party assistance in Ukraine in 1994. For most of the time since, party assistance has taken up the bulk, roughly eighty per cent, of IRI's activity in Ukraine.[99] Besides party assistance, IRI runs programs in Ukraine for political active women and youth, supports civic organizations, and, as in Georgia and in many other countries, conducts opinion surveys. In addition, similar to NDI, IRI implements a governance assistance program, reflecting the trust that was placed in the authorities after the Revolution.[100] This program helps 'government officials in their efforts to improve communication with voters, develop policies that address issues of concern to Ukrainians, and manage public expectations' (IRI 2006: 17). The role of women and youth in politics is a subject that IRI has pressed for outside party assistance, but, other than for NDI, is also a frequent topic in party assistance seminars.

Three sorts of activities are common in party assistance by IRI in Ukraine: seminars, study visits of political party representatives to the United States, and consultations with party leaders. The goal of one typical study visit was 'to demonstrate the methods that U.S. political parties use between elections' (IRI 2001: 4). Consultations with party leaders are held to receive feedback on current programs, and to inquire on parties' needs. IRI political party training in Ukraine is distinct from that of NDI in two significant, and related ways. First, whereas NDI seminars are in principal with individual parties, a large majority of IRI seminars are 'multi-party'. The main reason for IRI to organize seminars in a multi-party format is that, by gathering groups of people from several parties at once, more people are reached with fewer funds. Moreover, it is hoped that a multi-party setting will induce increased dialogue between parties.[101] Considering that a multitude of parties attend most seminars, the second difference from NDI assistance is that the range of parties which receives IRI party assistance is more inclusive. While in 1998 IRI maintained that it only provided assistance to 'reform political parties' (IRI 1998: 3), in later years parties from very different stripes took part in seminars or were at least were invited to seminars. With the exception of a few parties that were staunchly anti-American, ahead of the 2006 parliamentary election, for instance, all forty-four parties which participated in the election were offered assistance. Despite the fact that a larger number of parties takes part in IRI seminars, an estimated four out of five are seminars for the two, three biggest parties, for the simple reason that these parties have bigger organizations and therefore more people to send to seminars.[102] Sometimes, representatives from parties that are known to be not so Western-oriented, such as PRU and KPU, participate in seminars without discussing beforehand their participation with the party leadership. It has been said that while in earlier years the topics of the between fifty and one hundred seminars that IRI organizes on average per year, addressed basic skills, they have become more sophisticated and specialized to continue to be of interest and relevance to participants.[103] One topic that is sometimes included in IRI party seminars is coalition-building, though it has been less of a priority than it has been for NDI.

KAS

The Konrad Adenauer Stiftung has focused on three themes since it opened its office in Kyiv in 1994: fostering democracy and the rule of law, European and Euro-Atlantic integration, and social market economy. Support to political parties is provided under the heading of 'fostering democracy and the rule of law', and, in 2007, amounted to about one fourth of KAS' activity in Ukraine in terms of the number of events around political parties as a share of all events organized that year.[104] The central objective of political party assistance by KAS in Ukraine - strengthening the centre-right part of the party spectrum - has essentially remained unchanged since 1994. KAS seeks to strengthen centre-rights parties both by educating them on issues of party organization and management, and by encouraging them to cooperate, engage in electoral coalitions, or even to merge. During the 1990s, KAS' centre-rights partners included Rukh, the Reform and Order Party (PRP), and the People's Party. Since 2001, the Our Ukraine bloc, and later the People's Union Our Ukraine (NSNU) party have become KAS' principal partner, with the smaller People's Movement of Ukraine (NRU) and the marginal Christian

119

Democratic Union (CDU) counting as secondary partners. NSNU and NRU, by virtue of the fact that they enjoy observer status in the European People's Party, are regarded KAS' 'natural partners' (Wachsmuth 2006: 66). Because NSNU is a much more relevant force in Ukraine than NRU, however, most of the fraternal assistance has gone to NSNU. KAS explicitly takes credit for the initial emergence of the Our Ukraine bloc in 2001, for which, it contends, the foundation was laid at a KAS-organized gathering of centre-right parties.[105] After the election victory of the Our Ukraine bloc in the 2002 election, KAS directed many of its efforts at convincing the participating members of the bloc to create one united party on the basis of the electoral bloc. There is little, however, that indicates that KAS has played a role in the eventual merger of six parties which established the People's Union Our Ukraine in 2005.

For its partners, KAS organizes trainings and seminars on a wide variety of topics, touching on the general themes of party organization and electoral campaign management, that are not unlike those of seminars of other providers of assistance. Reflecting the fraternal nature of its partnership with NSNU, KAS even advises the party and the electoral bloc of which it is the leading party on the contents of their election programs. In addition to the party-to-party seminars, multi-party seminars are organized for only the most relevant political parties and their youth branches, which have included, after the Orange Revolution, particularly NSNU, the Party of Regions, and Batkivshchyna. The practical organization of seminars is often outsourced to the Kyiv-based NGO Institute for Political Education, whose director is a former international secretary of the Christian-Democratic Union, and which has ties to both NSNU and Rukh. Besides seminars, party assistance by KAS also holds consultations with a range of political leaders and organizes study visits to Germany, primarily for NSNU representatives.

FES

The Friedrich Ebert Stiftung, present in Ukraine since 1993, works in three project areas: labor relations and social dialogue, democratization and civil society, and international co-operation and European integration. One element of the democratization and civil society project area is 'development of the political parties and parliamentarism in the context of democratic and social values'.[106] At an estimated one tenth of overall activity, party assistance takes up a smaller part of FES' work in than it does of KAS' work in Ukraine.[107] Party assistance activities by FES in Ukraine comprise both multi-party seminars and single-party seminars, and consultations with party leaders. Ever since 1993, FES in Ukraine has involved a

120

wide range of parties in its party assistance programs simultaneously, and left-wing parties merely somewhat more than others. Training is most often organized for several parties at once. Despite the fact that SPU counts as a 'sister party' because it has observer status in the Socialist International, FES has been reluctant to accept SPU as an exclusive and close partner. During the 1990s, several parties vied for recognition as the prime social-democratic party of Ukraine. One contender, SDPU, after 1998 was pushed to the margins after its leader Buzduhan was not re-elected to parliament. Another, SDPU(o), had dubious credentials, mainly because of its strong economic interests and its complicity in the Kuchma regime. Following the Orange Revolutions, relations with SPU were intensified, as it was hoped that the party would now consolidate and become one of the main parties in a more democratic Ukraine. SPU lost sympathy with many, however, when it joined a government coalition with PRU and KPU in 2006.

Other providers of assistance

FNS has started working in Ukraine only after the Orange Revolution, the achievements of which it sought to help consolidate. Whereas KAS divides its work almost evenly between four types of activities, and FES chooses to have a small party assistance program relative to its other activities, for FNS party assistance is a primary activity. Next to its work with parties, FNS organizes debates in Ukraine aimed at promoting liberal thought. FNS sees Our Ukraine as its 'natural partner' in terms of ideological and programmatic kinship, but cannot work with that party because KAS already is. When it started working in Ukraine, FNS therefore had to look for alternative partners. In the few years since it has provided party assistance, FNS has worked with the youth branch of Our Ukraine (but not with the 'mature' party) and the youth branch of BYuT, as well as with the Reform and Order Party (PRP) and the PORA party, which came out of the yellow PORA youth movement, one of the most vocal organizations in the Orange Revolution. Assistance to PORA was suspended after a schism occurred in the party.

Providers of party assistance in Ukraine without an office include EFS and AMS. EFS has conducted seminars on campaign management, some of which were organized through the Institute for Political Education, with which KAS has also cooperated, for activists from the Our Ukraine electoral bloc. In addition, EFS organized a study visit for youth of the Our Ukraine bloc to the Netherlands. AMS organizes seminars for the youth wing of SPU. In previous years, assistance was provided to the nominally social-democratic party SDPU.

5.3. PARTY SELECTION

The principal donors and providers of party assistance that have worked in Georgia and Ukraine bind themselves to only work with parties that are both democratic and viable (see section two of chapter two). A considerable share of the parties that have received assistance over the years, however, are either undemocratic or unviable, or both.

The standard of viability

Appendices one and two demonstrate that a large number of parties that won seats in parliament through the 1998 legislative election in Ukraine and the 1999 legislative election in Georgia, as well as many parties that came up at the next election, have not succeeded in maintaining popular support or upholding their organization. Among the parties that have disappeared or become marginal since 1998/1999 were many that received assistance from the actors whose programs have been outlined in the previous two sections. Two of the three core recipients of NDI party assistance in Georgia before 1999 - CUG and the People's Party - have disappeared, while the third, NDP, has at best turned into a marginal force. The three other parties with which NDI worked in Georgia until 1999 - the Socialist Party, the Traditionalist Party, and the Green Party - have equally withered. Of the six parties that received the bulk of NDI and IRI assistance between 1999 and 2003, two have withered (CUG and NDP); the Labor Party and the New Rights Party, which rose to prominence around the turn of the century, are still active; and the National Movement and the United Democrats have merged to become the ruling United National Movement after 2003.

One party, Industry Will Save Georgia, that has participated in the ODIHR-NIMD project, has been largely absent from public view since 2004. Another party, the Labor Party, through its self-positioning as a centre-left party, occupies a niche on the Georgian political party landscape, and has been a relatively consistent opposition force, albeit one that is particularly known for being ruled at the almost exclusive discretion of its leader Natelashvili, since the beginning of the decade. The New Rights Party, the Republican Party, and the Conservative Party, which also participate in the project, are three of a large number of small opposition forces, most of which designate themselves as 'centre-right', and which in highly volatile coalitions and occasional alliances lead a struggle against the regime. These parties were selected for the ODIHR-NIMD project because they had some representatives in parliament after 2004. A few years into the project, however, it was no longer evident that these parties were more relevant or viable than some of the many other opposition parties, such as Georgia's Way, the Freedom Party, of For a United Georgia. Moreover, it can be questioned whether these parties were relevant forces at all, given the degree of fragmentation among the opposition and the highly uneven playing field in which the ruling United National Movement, the sixth participating party in the ODIHR-NIMD project, towered over all other parties in terms of representation in parliament and available resources. Though UNM is clearly relevant, it is not necessarily also viable, because its continued existence depends on the sustainability of the regime and that of its president. Should the regime be overturned or a new president elected, UNM may be abandoned, as the previously ruling CUG was abandoned directly after the Rose Revolution.

The turnover of political parties and forces in Ukraine since 1998 has been less pronounced than in Georgia, but still very substantial, as appendix two shows. The three parties that received most of NDI's assistance during the 1990s - NDP, Rukh, and PRP - have lost much of their relevance, if they ever had much relevance. While NDP has subsided, both PRP and the successors of Rukh are reduced to the role of 'junior partner' in electoral coalitions, and in that role have little autonomous potential. The same can be said of almost all 'junior partners' in electoral coalitions, including the large number of small parties from the Our Ukraine bloc, many of which have eagerly participated in assistance programs. The political force that has received far more assistance than any other force in Ukraine since 2000, the 'presidential' People's Union Our Ukraine, which formally exists as a party only since 2005, obviously has been a highly relevant force. In 2008, however, splits occurred within the party, and it is unclear whether the party will be sustained after president Yushchenko leaves office. In early 2009 it was even reported that the party de facto had ceased to function (Topolianskyi 2009). The sustainability of Batkivshchyna is believed to be entirely dependent upon the future of its leader, Yulia Tymoshenko. SPU, long-time partner of FES and AMS, is at risk of becoming marginal after failing to cross the electoral threshold in the 2007 parliamentary elections. Two other nominally social-democratic parties, SDPU and SDPU(o), which have previously received assistance from several actors, have already become marginal.

Ironically, KPU, the one party that has been continuously represented in parliament since the early 1990s and by that token has proven to be the most durable political party in Ukraine, has barely received assistance. The party was often not invited to assistance programs; when it was, the party turned down the invitation. [108] Moreover, the most relevant party of recent years in terms of electoral support and political leverage, the Party of Regions, has received relatively little assistance, and admits not to have made any changes in the party following the little assistance it has received.[109] A large portion of the assistance that has been provided to political parties in Georgia and Ukraine since the late 1990s, in sum, has gone to parties which did not turn out to be relevant for the longer term, or even disappeared entirely. Providers of assistance, to the extent that their efforts were targeted first and foremost at assisting parties to become stable and democratic forces, as a consequence, have seen much of their effort go to waste. It could be argued that providers of assistance have too easily assumed that the parties with which they worked would either remain or become stable and relevant. The ODIHR-NIMD project is a telling example: its initiators were hopeful that the six parties that were invited to the project would present the nucleus of an impending stable party system. A few years into the project, however, they were confronted with a different reality. Since the project did not allow for quick adjustments, some of the original purpose of the project could no longer be fulfilled.

The standard of democracy

To be eligible for party assistance, parties need to adhere to democratic standards both regarding their internal organization and in relation to other parties and the political process. The requirement of democratic internal organization boils down to the existence of functioning procedures of internal democracy in the party, or at least an aspiration to install these procedures. As has been argued in section three of chapter four, a defining feature of party politics in Georgia and Ukraine is that parties there have been overwhelmingly elite-led and that, relatedly, few have implemented meaningful procedures of internal democracy. Parties are often described as the personal fiefdoms of their leaders, and formally existing procedures of internal democracy as merely cosmetic. While some parties, such as, arguably, the Republican Party of Georgia and the People's Movement of Ukraine, have implemented a reasonable degree of internal democracy, most others have not and did not intend to do so in the foreseeable future. If the criterion of internal democracy would have been strictly observed, few parties would have been left for providers of assistance to work with.

An extreme example of a leader-dominant party is the Georgian Labor Party: 'In a country where parties were often dominated by their leaders, Labor was extreme even by Georgian standards' (Mitchell 2008: 49). Still, the Labor Party has received assistance from both NDI and IRI, participated in the NIMD-ODIHR project, and counts as a 'sister party' for AMS. An example of a party of which the overly dominant position of its leader has been detrimental to the goals of party assistance, is SPU. According to a former international secretary of SPU, years of

124

receiving party assistance have not led to any changes within the party because its leader, Oleksandr Moroz, ruled the party as a dictator and did not allow change.[110] SPU is a participant in assistance programs by all major providers of assistance, and is the 'sister party' of FES and AMS.

On top of exercising internal democracy, parties need to have democratic credentials both in terms of attitude and in terms of actual behavior, and both in relation to other parties and to the political process. As has been argued in chapter four, many parties in Georgia and Ukraine, especially among the more relevant parties, essentially were products of undemocratic practices, or otherwise were led by incentives which are seen as inimical to democracy, such as the overriding aim to win office for economic gain. Together, these 'undemocratic' parties contribute to distort the electoral playing field. Undemocratic practices in party politics have been most evidently embodied in the parties of power which benefited extensively from state resources and patronage. Although CUG of president Shevardnadze contained most features of a party of power, the party counted as one of NDI's main recipients of assistance until not long before the Rose Revolution. NDI's lack of inhibition to work with CUG squares with the generally favorable opinion of Western governments towards the Shevardnadze regime until at least 1999. Since the Rose Revolution, all providers of assistance have been eager to work with UNM. Even after the 2008 parliamentary elections, which have been generally seen as suffering from serious flaws (e.g. Cooley and Mitchell 2009: 33-4; Lanskoy and Areshidze 2008: 165), NIMD staff maintained that UNM is a 'democratic' party and an appropriate partner for party assistance. [111] Providers of assistance have had reservations to work with other undemocratic forces in Georgia considering their refusal to offer assistance to the Revival party, which was a vehicle of the autocratic and repressive regime of Aslan Abashidze in Adjara, rather than the ruling party of a feeble, semi-authoritarian regime that CUG was. The Socialist Party and the Traditionalist party, which entered in an electoral coalition with Revival for the 1999 parliamentary election, however, were still eligible to receive assistance after 1999. Besides the parties of power, numerous other parties in Georgia with dubious incentives were offered assistance. Among them has been, for instance, Industry Will Save Georgia, which rather than seeking to promote the common good, sought to promote first and foremost the business interests of its leader Topadze (Mitchell 2008: 36).

As in Georgia, a party of power, albeit in this case the unsuccessful NDP, was one of the main recipients of assistance of NDI in Ukraine during the 1990s. Other parties that have received assistance in Ukraine, such as SDPU(o) and the Labor Party, have been equally associated with the exploitation of state resources for electoral gain. Providers of assistance generally have held back from offering assistance to parties that ostentatiously were virtual projects. Since IRI in Ukraine, however, as part of a very inclusive approach, has only declined assistance to a few extremist parties among the parties that took part in parliamentary elections, some 'virtual' and 'oligarchic' parties have inevitably been offered assistance. Several arguments could be put forward why the Party of Regions would not pass the test of being a democratic force and therefore should not be eligible to receive assistance. Among other things, its leaders sought to steal the presidential election in 2004, the party contains features of a dominant party of power on a regional level in southern and eastern *oblasti*, and is propped up by donations from the country's wealthiest businessman, Rinat Akhmetov. Still, all major providers of party assistance do not refrain from offering assistance to the party. The democratic credentials of SPU, one of the political parties which actively supported the Orange Revolutions, were shattered in the eyes of many when the party entered a government coalition with PRU and KPU in 2006. The example of SPU illustrates that providers of assistance often harbor unrealistic expectations concerning the parties they work with. Another example is CUG. A work plan of NDI in Georgia for the years 2001-2002 stated that NDI 'would try to help CUG remain true to its original democratic ideals' (NDI 2001c: 8). Given that CUG was a party of power which served the interests of a less-than-democratic regime, as became clear, for example, in the complicity of CUG in the large-scale fraud during the 1999 parliamentary election, it is far from evident that there was much sincerity to the 'original democratic ideals' of CUG.

A significant share of parties that have received assistance in Georgia and Ukraine, in sum, have not met the criteria of viability and democracy that the providers of assistance impose on themselves with regard to the selection of parties. This was to some degree unavoidable: if only those parties had been selected that were both credibly viable and democratic, then very few would have been eligible for assistance. Decisions to include certain parties in assistance programs have besides been driven by misguided perceptions of those parties. The problems with the selection of unviable and undemocratic parties for the effectiveness of party assistance are obvious: the possible effect of assistance on unviable parties is lost when these parties disappear, while undemocratic parties are a priori unreceptive to assistance.

5.4. PARTISANSHIP

A second standard of good practice prescribes that assistance should be provided to a set of parties that collectively are representative of the democratic section of the political party spectrum, so as not to influence the outcome of an election or to interfere directly in the domestic affairs of recipient states (see the second section of chapter two). If one provider of assistance through its individual efforts cannot attain non-partisanship, then the efforts of assistance providers from the same country should fill the gap to ensure a net effect of non-partisanship. Thus, NDI and IRI through their combined effort, in theory, are non-partisan, and so are the *Stiftungen.* As a consequence of the selection of parties or the type of activity that is carried out, however, party assistance in Georgia and Ukraine more often than not effectively favors certain forces over others. Some of the persons who have been interviewed for this research have acknowledged that party assistance by their organization indeed was at least partially aimed at increasing the electoral chances of certain forces over other forces.[112] A range of excuses are put forward by donors and providers to vindicate partisan outcomes of party assistance.

First, in a less-than-democratic or a non-pluralist setting providers of assistance can direct most of their assistance to disadvantaged forces in order to 'level the playing field' (USAID 1999b: 28). Doherty (2002: 5) notes that Ukraine is an example of a country where NDI was right to work mainly with 'reform-oriented' parties, because these were 'severely disadvantaged by a restricted political environment'. A 2007 USAID report contends that 'party assistance directed at providing democratic alternatives to UNM is critical for creating a level political playing field' (USAID 2007: 25). Since the Rose Revolution, however, there have been frequent allegations that IRI instead favored the ruling party. Leveling the playing field can also be pursued in a single segment of the political party spectrum. A representative of IRI in Georgia has remarked that it lends support to the small Kartula Dasi party with the aim of creating more competition in the left-wing part of the political spectrum, which is seen as being virtually monopolized by the Labor Party.[113] Second, supporting reform-oriented parties can be proposed not so much to give them better chances in a less-than-democratic or non-pluralist setting, but rather to help them in their competition against reform-averse parties. In a number of post-communist countries including Ukraine until, roughly, the turn of the century, reform-averse parties have been equated with communist successor parties.[114] A USAID report on NDI's Ukraine program during the 1997-1999 period openly states: 'NDI's focus on consolidation stems from concerns that the lack of cooperation among democratic forces would further undermine public support for democratic reform and result in another parliament dominated by the Communist Party' (NDI 1999: 3). NDI's efforts to check communist successor forces arguably compromised its objective to also contribute to a level playing field, since one of the three 'reform-oriented' parties with which NDI worked closely was the state-sponsored NDP. The 'restricted political environment' that NDI apparently wanted to oppose by working with reform-oriented parties was in no small measure a consequence of the interference in party politics by the regime through parties like NDP. Third, a partisan outcome in party assistance is excused by pointing out that parties which are not trained are invited to participate, but do not respond to the invitation. The fact that a party like KPU has barely received assistance, indeed, may be at least as much because the party is not responsive to invitations for party assistance, as it may be because of a possible partisan bias on the part of the providers of assistance. Fourth, parties can be excluded for being insufficiently viable. Decisions to exclude parties for being unviable, however, ultimately rest on a qualitative assessment, and may easily turn into decisions led by partisan motives. Fifth, a provider of assistance may opt to work with a small number of parties in order to intensify training programs. If they do so, selecting a representative sample of democratic parties is even more difficult than when a more inclusive range of parties is selected. NDI in Georgia before the 1999 parliamentary elections concentrated its training program on three parties: CUG, the People's Party, and NDP. These parties were earmarked by NDI as, respectively, centre-left, centrist, and centre-right, suggesting a balanced division of the three parties along the left-right spectrum (NDI 2000a: 17). It can be questioned, however, whether these labels really reflected the respective ideological positions of the parties concerned. Finally, when providers of assistance choose to conduct seminars with individual parties, as NDI in Ukraine has done, the number of parties they can work with is typically smaller than when they conduct seminars which are attended by representatives from several parties at once. As noted above, when a narrow selection of parties is made, the selection more often tends be non-representative.

Providers of assistance in Georgia and Ukraine have often been subject to criticism for alleged partisanship. The coalition-building efforts of NDI in Georgia were widely perceived as favoring the political forces of especially Saakashvili and Zhvania over other forces, both from the opposition and the regime. Criticism targeting NDI was voiced by the government,[115] by Shalva Natelashvili, leader of the opposition Labor Party (Mitchell 2008: 88), as well as by well-known Georgian political scientists.[116] IRI in Georgia since the Revolution has been criticized for allegedly favoring UNM or more generally for acting in cahoots with the ruling forces.[117] According to one IRI representative in Georgia, UNM receives a disproportionate share of party assistance by IRI because it is more advanced and better coordinated than all other parties.[118] IRI was also criticized for its partnership with NGNI, which 'was, in essence, hand selected by the governing UNM' (McGlinchey 2007: 20). Allegations by the opposition to the effect that IRI was pursuing a partisan line appeared to be substantiated when Dimitri Shashkin, long-standing program officer for IRI in Georgia who was promoted to become IRI's chief of party in 2008, accepted an offer to join the government as Minister for Penitentiary and Probation in February 2009. Reportedly, Shashkin stayed on as IRI chief of party for some time after he took up his cabinet position.[119] The ODIHR-NIMD project came under fire from a few participating parties because the director of the local partner organization CIPDD, Ghia Nodia, was rumored to be close to government circles, before he left CIPDD to join the government as Minister of Education.[120] In Ukraine, the Party of the Regions has accused NDI of support to the opposition ahead of the Orange Revolution.[121] A blatant expression of partisanship has been the active participation in party politics by two local representatives of the providers of assistance. One representative of KAS in Georgia was on the list of the Rightist Alliance-Topadze Industrialists in the 2008 parliamentary elections, while a representative of NDI in Ukraine has been one the list of the PORA-PRP coalition in 2006. Both were on unelectable positions.

Since coalition-building in Georgia and Ukraine has typically been promoted among parties from a particular part of the political spectrum, it has inevitably taken on a partisan nature. NDI has arguably been the most assertive actor in coalition-building in Georgia and Ukraine. In a 2003 publication by USAID entitled Political Party Assistance Policy, it is argued that coalition-building among 'a fragmented opposition' is permissible 'in a strict authoritarian system' (USAID 2003b: 10). It is a stretch, however, to typify Georgia under Shevardnadze and Ukraine under Kuchma as 'strict authoritarian', if only because a degree of political pluralism in these countries was preserved. KAS in Ukraine has actively promoted coalition-building among centre-right forces both before and following the Orange Revolution, with the explicit aim of a formal merger of these forces into one larger force. Especially before the Revolution, the balance of German party assistance in Ukraine was clearly partisan due to the fact that FES had only a small party assistance program that moreover comprised seminars for political parties from different parts of the political spectrum, and other Stiftungen were not, or only marginally active in party assistance. A secondary objective of the ODIHR-NIMD project was to contribute to coalition-building among the participating opposition parties, and more generally to strengthen the opposition so as to create a more level playing field.

According to an NIMD representative, this approach was justified because the ruling UNM had itself indicated that it wanted to be faced by a stronger opposition because this would enhance the country's democratic legitimacy[122] It is remarkable in this light that the authorities undertook measures, such as amendments to electoral legislation which reduced the number of parliamentary seats chosen from party lists, to ensure a particularly big win in the 2008 parliamentary election (Mitchell 2008: 94).

Partisan motives are obvious in the selection of partner parties by the *Stiftungen* and the Dutch party institutes. It has been argued before that claims by providers of assistance to the effect that the cumulative efforts of providers of assistance from one country guarantee non-partisanship, are untenable, in part because some of the *Stiftungen* and the Dutch party institutes work exclusively with partner parties, while others opt for a multi-party approach, whether on top of party-to-party assistance or not (see section two of chapter two). Despite claims that the U.S. party institutes do not engage in fraternal relations, in practice their party selection sometimes has seemed to strongly favor one particular party. This applies especially to NDI's relationship with Rukh in Ukraine during the 1990s. IRI's relationship with UNM after the Rose Revolution equally borders on a fraternal relationship.

The selection of a partner party by the *Stiftungen* and the Dutch party institutes has often involved decisions that were informed by incorrect assessments of parties. Too often, the decision for a partner party appears to have been driven by that party's membership or observer status in a transnational party or a similarity in party name or stated ideological position. It has been naïve of EFF, the party institute of the Dutch Christian-Democratic Appeal, to believe that the Christian-Democratic Union of Georgia, a fringe party, had the capacity to grow into a more viable force (EFF 2004). Both FNS and VVD were initially eager to accept UNM as their partner because that party had voiced its intention to become a member of the Liberal International. After some time, however, UNM changed course to seeking observer status in the European People's Party, which it received in 2008. FNS in Ukraine was not amused when it found out PRP, known up to that moment for them as a liberal party, had suddenly joined the BYuT electoral coalition, which, to many, has a populist centre-left outlook. Batkivshchyna, the leading party in BYuT, surprised providers of assistance by seeking affiliation with the European People' Party while it had previously stated an interest to join the Socialist International.[123] FES and AMS, for which SPU counts as a partner, were surprised when that party apparently betrayed the ideals of the Orange Revolution by joining a government coalition with PRU and KPU. SPU was shunned for years by NDI in Ukraine, before it became one of the vanguard parties in the anti-Kuchma opposition, and a regular recipient of NDI assistance. An evaluation of the Matra Political Parties Program, from which the party assistance programs of the Dutch party institutes are funded, has noted that the ideological indeterminacy of many parties in recipient countries renders partner selection virtually impossible (Verheije et al.: 2006: 59). Sometimes, providers of assistance have apparently shared this view: because they were unable to identify appropriate partners, KAS (until 2007) and FES, for instance, have refrained from engaging in party assistance in Georgia.

In sum, the outcome of the assistance that is provided to parties is nearly always to some degree partisan. The many possible excuses that are put forward for a partisan outcome are not all credible. More often than not, providers of assistance do not 'make a good faith effort to assist all democratic parties with equitable levels of assistance' (USAID 2003b: 1), as is generally required from them. The frequent instances of partisanship raise questions about the legitimacy of party assistance and have sometimes compromised the effort in the eyes of domestic stakeholders. Individual examples of partisanship show that providers of assistance in Georgia and Ukraine have often strayed from self-imposed norms in order to achieve desired effects. Even if they did so, however, party assistance has remained largely without a positive, lasting impact on parties. As the next chapter will argue in more detail, party assistance, despite the many irregular approaches that it has incorporated, has not been able to put up a challenge to the domestic constraints on party development in Georgia and Ukraine.

CHAPTER SIX: THE FAILURE OF PARTY ASSISTANCE IN GEORGIA AND UKRAINE

Political party assistance in Georgia and Ukraine has been unsuccessful in achieving its primary objective - contributing to making parties more representative, viable, and democratic forces. This chapter makes insightful why this is so. The first section discusses the effects that party assistance, despite the overall failure of the effort, *has* generated, both on parties and outside parties. Starting from the premise that party assistance will be ineffectual when it does not deliver an adequate response to the domestic constraints on party development that have been identified in chapter four, the second section explores the relation between party assistance and these domestic constraints. The core argument about the failure of party assistance, concerning its inability to overcome the domestic constraints on the development of stable and democratic parties, is contained in this section. Sections three and four provide complementary insight on the failure of party assistance in Georgia and Ukraine, first, by looking at the reasons why parties have failed to comply with the party assistance norm, and second, by taking a quick tour of the shortcomings in the input of the assistance. Through a synthesis of the insights into the domestic constraints on party development (chapter four) and the diffusion of the party assistance norm (section four in chapter two), section three sums up the main reasons why recipients of assistance have failed to comply with the party assistance norm. Section four, finally, subjects the supply-side of assistance to a critical assessment. It takes note of a number of flaws in the input of assistance in Georgia and Ukraine that point to more general problems with the implementation of party assistance.

6.1. THE QUESTION OF EFFECTS

Statements and reports by the providers of assistance sometimes mention examples of concrete impact of their work. A quarterly report of NDI in Georgia from 2001, for instance, notes that, as a consequence of NDI's work, several parties 'are currently evaluating the effectiveness of their organizations and campaigns' and have 'undertaken activities in coordination with NDI to improve voter outreach through canvassing and to refine their messages to their constituents' (NDI 2002b: 8). IRI in Ukraine claimed in 2005 that as a result of its work, parties 'are more focused on critical economic, social and governmental issues' (IRI 2005b: 9). NDI in Ukraine reported in 2000 that, following cooperation with NDI, a few parties had 'instituted regular office hours at regional offices where the public may meet with party officials and receive information about the party's activities and positions' (NDI 2002b: 7), while one party had 'solidified its infrastructure across the regions' and another had 'opened a new regional branch' (idem: 5). Most of what has been written by providers of assistance in Georgia and Ukraine, however, merely outlines past and future activities, while failing to explicate the effects from their work. The *Stiftungen*, in their very few writings on party assistance in Georgia and Ukraine, largely omit to report evidence of the effectiveness of their programs.

Apart from the effects of party assistance that are claimed by its providers, over half of representatives of political parties who have been consulted for this research were generally positive about the assistance that their parties have received. At the same time, most were unable to point to concrete positive effects of assistance on their parties, a finding echoed, among others, in an evaluation of the Matra Political Parties Program (Verheije et al.: 47). Likewise, a USAID assessment of party assistance in Kyrgyzstan has found that '[w]hile political party representatives told the assessment team that they found this assistance to be useful, the team felt that its impact on the development of a multi-party political system in the country was very limited' (Roberts 2001: 20). Some informants from political parties have admitted that assistance has not led to any changes within their respective parties.[124] Former employees of providers of assistance have equally indicated that the assistance programs in which they worked, were overwhelmingly ineffectual.[125] Despite generally positive assessments of assistance by party activists that were interviewed for this research, there have been complaints, for instance with regard to the multi-party ODIHR-NIMD project in Georgia, that parties did not participate to the degree that was required by the organizers of the project.[126] One former representative of KAS in Ukraine has bluntly noted that parties in Ukraine were 'beratungsresistent' (immune to counsel) during his tenure at KAS.[127]

Effects of party assistance that are reported by providers and recipients of assistance are sometimes not as impressive as they may seem to be for two principal reasons. First, most obviously, effects on party organizations are lost as soon as those parties are dissolved. An evaluation of NDI's work in Georgia between 1997 and 2000, for instance, details a score of instances of concrete effects on political parties, but none of the parties that these effects concerned is still active (NDI 2000a). The many small effects from assistance that NDI in Ukraine reported to USAID in 2000 likewise concern parties, such as the two successor parties of Rukh and the Reforms and order Party, which in subsequent years were no longer found among the more relevant parties (NDI 2000b). It could be that activists from dissolved parties who go on to establish new parties implement what they have learnt while participating in educational seminars as activists of those previously existing parties, but this is not evident, especially since the shortcomings of parties in Georgia and Ukraine that are widely noted today are not unlike those of ten, fifteen years ago. Second, changes that are made in parties following participation in party assistance programs may be short-lived or not much more than merely cosmetic. The single most tangible effect from party assistance in Georgia that has been mentioned in interviews by informants from across parties and outside parties, is that the Conservative Party, upon training and counsel by IRI, introduced primaries to select candidates for elections,[128] a novelty that attracted the attention of other parties, but was not imitated. When the primaries fuelled disagreements within the Conservative Party, however, the use of primaries was quietly abandoned.[129] A representative of IRI in Georgia has acknowledged that the type and extent of impact that was reached with respect to the Conservative Party, was not reached with respect to any other party in Georgia.[130] Rather than aiming for tangible and lasting effects, some representatives of the providers of assistance are resigned to the idea of contributing only indirectly to the development of more stable and more democratic parties. A NIMD representative has commented that instant and measurable results should not be expected from the ODIHR-NIMD project, since the emergence of viable parties in Georgia requires a process of 'cultural change'.[131] In a critical assessment of party assistance in general, a representative of CIPDD, NIMD's partner organization in Georgia, has contended that external assistance to parties is not capable of inducing structural change, and that most effect from assistance in reality consists of 'elite socialization'.[132] A FES representative in Ukraine, roughly in the same vein, has opined that party assistance should not even aim for effects, since the adverse political culture which blocks the development of stable and democratic parties can only be overturned over the course of several decades.[133] This view has been supported by a representative of the PRU party bureau, who deems cooperation with NDI and IRI merely 'symbolic', since it would take a sustained process of many years to really bring about change in his party.[134]

The immediate, primary goal of party assistance is to contribute to the development of stable, democratic and responsive parties with the overarching intention to promote democracy. Through party assistance, however, its providers have an indirect impact on political processes beyond party politics. Occasionally, providers of assistance seek to directly influence a political outcome. There has been considerable speculation about the role of especially the U.S. party institutes in the Rose and Orange Revolutions. The most significant form of impact on the occurrence of the Revolutions from the work of the providers of assistance consisted in their efforts to assist with the creation of coalitions ahead of the parliamentary election in Georgia in 2003 and the presidential election in Ukraine in 2004 around which the Revolutions took place. It is widely accepted that the creation of the Our Ukraine bloc, for which both NDI and KAS take credit (see section two of chapter five), has increased unity among the opposition, without which it would have been unlikely that a single candidate could be nominated to run for president on behalf of the opposition (Howard and Roessler 2006; McFaul 2005: 9-10). A representative of IRI moreover has claimed that when one of its opinion surveys showed that, of all opposition politicians, Yushchenko had the biggest chance to win the presidential elections, other opposition politicians withdrew their bid in favor of Yushchenko.[135] Besides coalition-building, the role of the providers of assistance in the Orange Revolution is seen rather in the cumulative effect of many years of assistance. IRI states in its annual report for 2004: 'The events that took place throughout Ukraine's 2004 presidential election showcased the Ukrainian people's willingness to fight for democracy and were a testament to the effectiveness of political party training conducted by IRI' (IRI 2005a: 4). Regional Program Director for Eurasia of IRI Steven Nix has similarly remarked: 'The International Republican Institute contributed to the triumph of democracy in Ukraine by educating its people and political parties on the values and practices of democracy since 1992.' (Nix 2005: 1). According to a representative of IRI in Ukraine, his organization did not undertake activities that were any different from activities that had been undertaken around previous elections, and that if IRI had an impact on the occurrence of the Orange Revolution, it was through the cumulative effect of a decade of training party activists.[136] NDI in Ukraine maintains that, by organizing hundreds of trainings to party activists over the years, it has contributed to the emergence of a class of politically active, and often young citizens many of whom helped form the vanguard of the protests against the regime in November 2004.[137] KAS in Ukraine actively supported the Orange Revolution while it was unfolding, but, like FES, has not claimed to have played a considerable role in the Revolution.

Even though parties were more central in the Rose Revolution, which happened following parliamentary elections, than in the Orange Revolution, providers of assistance have not claimed to have significantly contributed to the Rose Revolution. Efforts by NDI in Georgia to help create a coalition of three prominent opposition parties demonstrated that NDI in Georgia was not shy of being partisan. The

136

coalition-building effort, however, fell through. A representative of IRI in Georgia, like his colleague in Ukraine, has commented that IRI did not undertake any extraordinary activities which particularly increased the likelihood of regime change.[138] Other actors in party assistance have taken up work in Georgia only after the Rose Revolution.

On occasion, providers of assistance have sought to directly influence a political outcome, but not through political party assistance. NDI in Ukraine, for instance, convinced candidates of a number of opposition parties in 2002 not to run against each other in single-member districts.[139] After the Rose Revolution, a representative of IRI in Georgia, in informal conversations with government officials, has advocated changes in electoral legislation.[140] In addition to effects on the macro-level of political outcomes, party assistance has affected scores of individuals who, by participating in party assistance programs, have been exposed to elements of the party assistance norm. It could be assumed that exposure to the party assistance norm has had a positive impact on those individuals, even when it did not have an impact on their parties, and that this positive impact is more profound and lasting than the more immediate effects on existing parties that party assistance typically seeks to engender. Several party activists, most of them young, who have been interviewed have indicated that repeated participation in party assistance seminars has had a formative effect on them.[141] By training thousands of party activists over the years, the bigger players in party assistance have a broad reach. IRI in Ukraine, for instance, has calculated that 85 out of the 450 MPs in the Verkhovna Rada have at one point participated in a party seminar that was organized by IRI.[142]

In sum, the picture of effects from party assistance in Georgia and Ukraine is a mixed bag. Lasting effects on the operation of individual parties - the primary target of assistance - have been few; effects that were insignificant, isolated, short-lived, or merely cosmetic were many. Besides the limited receptivity of parties to assistance, effects have mostly not been durable because the parties that were affected have often subsequently broken up. Outside parties, assistance has been able to leave a footprint on different levels. On a micro-level, thousands of individuals, through participation in assistance programs, have been exposed to the party assistance norm. Moreover, there is ground - though little concrete evidence - to believe that party assistance has had an impact on political outcomes in Ukraine mainly through its contribution to the creation of electoral coalitions and of NSNU.

6.2. THE RESPONSE TO DOMESTIC CONSTRAINTS

Among the biggest constraints on the development of stable and democratic parties in Georgia and Ukraine are weak party institutionalization expressed primarily in a high turnover rate of parties, the impact of authoritarian practices on party building and operation, and the circumstance that the fate of parties is almost exclusively tied to their leaders (see chapter four). Providers of assistance are not mandated, and otherwise would not have the means, to counter two crucial enabling conditions of these constraints - the limited leverage of parties to the extent that this results from institutional arrangements, and the prevalence of an (semi-)authoritarian regime context in Ukraine (until 2005) and Georgia, leaving little optimism about the potential effectiveness of party assistance. Starting from the premise that party assistance must nonetheless provide an adequate response to the domestic constraints on party development if it is to be effective, this section reviews how party assistance has related to the three core constraints on party development identified in chapter four.

Fluid party politics

Providers of party assistance have employed two types of activities with the potential to work against volatility and instability of parties. First, educational seminars in the area of 'operational and structural development' were aimed at strengthening party organizations, which in turn should have prevented them from far-reaching internal overhaul or from disintegration. Typically, these seminars focused on topics such as membership recruitment, the development of regional branches, and cadre training. Next to seminars on election-related topics, seminars aimed at strengthening party organizations are the most common type of party assistance seminars. With seminars being a fixed component of party assistance, providers of assistance face the decision to direct their focus on either of these types, or to balance between the two types of seminars. It has been a frequent objection to party assistance in Georgia that a too large proportion of seminars has been about teaching campaign skills at the expense of seminars aimed at party strengthening.[143] This observation applies in particular to party assistance by IRI in Georgia. IRI party assistance in both Georgia and Ukraine generally has been more often around election-related topics than assistance by other providers. There is a widespread perception that party representatives are more receptive to training in campaign skills than to training on structural and operational development. Former chief of party of NDI in Georgia Lincoln Mitchell, indeed, sees the effect from party assistance in acquired campaign skills rather than anything else (Mitchell 2008:

121). Seminars organized within the framework of the ODIHR-NIMD project, on the other hand, have left out campaign-related issues, instead focusing entirely on internal organization and interparty dialogue. While it can be argued that gaining campaign skills by party activists is beneficial to overall party development, the objective of consolidating individual parties is probably better served by seminars which specifically address questions of party organization. It may even be argued that enhancing campaign skills within parties has contributed to an even stronger emphasis on elections, which is one element in the 'standard lament' about parties (Carothers 2006a: 3-21).

Second, efforts at coalition-building, understood here not as stimulating temporary electoral coalitions but rather as the pursuit of more far-reaching forms of cooperation between parties that ultimately may lead to formal mergers of several parties into one party, has the potential to reduce fractionalization of the party system. In Georgia, efforts at coalition-building have fallen through. As Mitchell (2008: 122) acknowledges, NDI was not able to halt fractionalization, despite a sustained effort. The large array of electoral coalitions that have been formed in Georgia, whether or not after NDI encouraged the concerned parties to join forces, have steadily disintegrated after elections. NDI and KAS take credit for the emergence of the Our Ukraine electoral bloc from a multitude of centre-right parties and, by extension, for the merger of six parties into People's Union Our Ukraine (NSNU) on the basis of the Our Ukraine bloc. The eventual emergence of NSNU appears to be an unequivocal success of coalition-building, but as the end of the Yushchenko presidency seemed to come to a close in 2008 and 2009, the party entered a process of disintegration, with little prospect that the party could be preserved as a viable political force. Representatives of the providers of assistance who have been involved in coalition-building in Ukraine for many years rather than successes stress the difficulty of reaching results in coalition-building. An often-heard complaint in interviews has been that coalition-building has often been quite ineffectual in Ukraine, but equally in Georgia, due to the unwillingness of party elites to give up their party organizations and due to personal differences between party leaders.[144] Party assistance could hardly manipulate the whims of these elites. The ODIHR-NIMD project, finally, has sought to stimulate coalition-building through interparty dialogue. Against assertions by the supply-side of the project (OSCE ODIHR 2006: 34), representatives of the participating parties in the project have indicated that not much constructive dialogue between the parties has taken place,[145] and coalition-building, accordingly, has not been forthcoming. By contrast, it may be argued that the position of the parties as autonomous forces has been affirmed through their participation in the project.

The impact of (semi-)authoritarianism

In the political context of post-communist Georgia and Ukraine (before the Orange Revolution), a number of highly relevant parties have been products of (semi-)authoritarian practices. This applies foremost to parties of power and spoiler parties that have been created at the behest of the regimes with the purpose of distorting the electoral playing field. In part flowing from regulations and in part by informal self-imposition, providers of assistance are barred from working with undemocratic parties. Nonetheless, especially parties of power have received ample assistance, and in the case of Georgian parties of power have received even more assistance than other parties. Shevardnadze's party of power CUG was one of NDI's three core partners until 1999, and remained a recipient after the fraudulent parliamentary elections of 1999. UNM has received a disproportionately large share of IRI party assistance, has been included in the ODIHR-NIMD project, and was perceived by FNS and VVD as a potential partner until the party started pursuing affiliation with the European People's Party. NDP in Ukraine, a party which benefited extensively from state resources, was one of the core recipients of NDI assistance in the late 1990s. A former chief of party of NDI in Ukraine has remarked that NDI's association with NDP was prompted by the objective to undercut KPU.[146] To battle one evil, then, NDI engaged with what was seen as a lesser evil.

While providers of assistance may sometimes work with a party of power in the understanding that the concerned party does not fully meet democratic standards, in some cases they seem to be unable to detect the undemocratic elements in parties. It has been naïve of FNS and VVD, for instance, to believe that UNM was serious in its initial self-positioning as a liberal party 'of the European type'. Similarly, even after the 2008 parliamentary elections, one representative of the NIMD-ODIHR project maintained that UNM was still a democratic force while by that time evidence pointed in the other direction.[147] Considering that they were driven by incentives that were incompatible with the elements of the party assistance norm that providers of assistance sought to infuse, parties of power have been unlikely to prove compliant with the party assistance norm. In Georgia, the VoteMatch element in the ODIHR-NIMD program resulted in failure because the ruling UNM did not follow the stipulations of VoteMatch. The project, in the end, suffered directly from the participation of the party of power. Providers of assistance in Georgia have been right to refrain from working with the Revival party, which over the course of a number of years existed as a second party of power alongside CUG and which was an instrument of the highly repressive Abashidze regime in the autonomous region in Adjara. With good reason, however, could the arguments not to work with Revival have been extended to CUG. Two parties which received NDI assistance, the Traditionalist Party and the Socialist Party, entered into an electoral coalition with Revival in the 1999 parliamentary elections. Despite their association with an obviously undemocratic party, these two parties have continued to receive NDI assistance after the 1999 elections.

Providers of assistance who have chosen an inclusive approach in party selection, have inadvertently worked with less-than-democratic parties. IRI in Ukraine, most notably, 'does not have stringent selection criteria for program participants' (IRI 2002: 1), and therefore has sent out invitations to all parties that participated in a given parliamentary election, bar the most extremist or virulently anti-American parties. Given that, for example, out of the ten top contenders in the 2002 parliamentary elections in Ukraine, six were identified as 'virtual projects pure and simple', (Wilson 2002b: 96) among the invitees were different types of parties that were products of semi-authoritarianism.

Elite ownership

A widely recognized brake on the development of stable and representative parties in many countries is the excessive power of party leaders who often regard their parties as personal vehicles which can be controlled and disposed of at will. If party assistance seeks to help overcome this constraint, it will have to work towards breaking the dominance of party leaders. Since internal democracy, or at least the intention to install procedures of internal democracy in the not too distant future, is an eligibility criterion for inclusion in party assistance programs, assistance, in theory, is only provided to parties in which the power of leaders is constrained. As has been demonstrated in the previous chapter, however, providers of assistance barely enforce the criterion of internal democracy.

Party assistance is for a large part about strengthening and broadening the organizational structure of parties, which, if successful, multiplies the number of persons within parties who can exert influence over their party's operations, and which consequently decreases the power of leaders. A still significant proportion of assistance, however, in effect affirms the role of leaders. This applies most directly to study and exchange visits that are organized for party leaders, and to consultations with party leaders. In the case of assistance to Georgian and Ukrainian parties, study and exchange visits came in two varieties: they were either for (young) party activists or for party leaders. Consultations, a fixed component of party assistance, were always with party leaders or with confidants of party leaders. Providers of assistance would typically be reluctant to acknowledge that their activities involve party leaders, and rather stress how rank-and-file activists gain influence in their parties as a result of their work. An exception to some degree is the ODIHR-NIMD project, which contained a separate 'leaders' track' aimed at stimulating dialogue and constructive relations between party leaders through informal dinners, collective study trips, and more.

One problem of the elite ownership of parties for party assistance is that potential effects from assistance are offset by leaders who sometimes have interests that run against the reforms proposed by party assistance, the simplest interest being the retention absolute power within the party. It has been frequently noted in interviews that while party activists were in favor of implementing a certain reform, nothing came of it because the party leadership resisted.[148] In an independent assessment for USAID of civil society (including political parties) in Georgia in 2001, the authors, along the same lines, note that 'party leaderships have to date taken few concrete actions that can be viewed as meaningful first steps towards building effective, internally democratic organizations, capable of presenting the voting public with credible, differentiated platforms' (Black et al. 2001: iii), Mostly for this reason the report recommends that 'USAID should consider a reorientation of party assistance to concentrate where possible on grassroots party structures' (idem: 2). There is little, however, that indicates that providers of assistance, whether in Georgia or Ukraine, have given up engaging with party leaderships.

It has been said in interviews that at the many trainings for party activists that are organized, most participants are relatively low in the party hierarchy and in any case are not in the position to enforce change in their respective parties. The problem, so it seems, is that participants in assistance programs who may be receptive to the contents of assistance have too little leverage, while those with the leverage are not interested in reform. Even if party assistance would reorient to only work with grassroots party structures, the issue of all-powerful leaders is left untouched. Assistance programs often include an effort to enhance the role of two groups in parties who are thought of as being unduly kept out of influential positions: women and youth. Against the backdrop of more imminent problems in parties, such as the dominance of leaders, these efforts rarely have much effect. A 2007 assessment of USAID party assistance in Eastern Europe and the former Soviet Union therefore suggests that supporting women and youth should not be a priority for assistance (USAID 2007: vi-vii).

This section has shown that providers of assistance are largely powerless against domestic factors which impede the development of a mass of stable and democratic parties, and it has revealed some of the dilemmas that providers of assistance face in their work in countries like Georgia and Ukraine. Much party assistance is, directly or indirectly, concerned with increasing the sustainability of parties, but rarely has assistance been able to halt parties from disintegrating or to convince parties to coalesce into bigger, more viable forces. It is moreover doubtful whether assistance could have had much more impact when a larger share of assistance would have been specifically targeted at making parties more viable. Providers of assistance could have been more cautious regarding assistance to undemocratic parties. Being stricter in this respect, however, would have involved very difficult choices in the selection of parties, and have rendered the effort even more politically contentious. Finally, it is virtually impossible to circumvent excessively powerful party leaders in party assistance when the assistance is interested in yielding real effects. Providers of assistance can choose to direct the assistance to grassroots elements within parties, but these are typically blocked from wielding any real influence.

6.3. WHY NOT COMPLY?

The previous section has made clear that domestic constraints on the development of stable and democratic parties in Georgia and Ukraine have invalidated party assistance in the form in which it has been implemented. Providers of assistance have been unable to effectively counteract or mitigate the domestic constraints. The current section adds a perspective to the failure of party assistance in Georgia and Ukraine by shifting focus to the recipients of assistance. Specifically, this section asks why parties have not been more receptive to the core of assistance programs - the party assistance norm. Three arguments are presented. The first and most hefty argument draws, as the previous section, on the insights from chapter four, while the latter two arguments draw on the discussion on the promotion of the party assistance norm in section four of chapter two.

First, most of the more relevant parties do not comply with the party assistance norm because they are disinterested in reforming into the type of party that assistance programs promote. Most likely without admitting to it, these parties oppose greater internal democracy, the development of a coherent program to which they can be held accountable, or an expansive organizational structure. They are often led by incentives, such as vote maximization or reaping the benefits associated with holding office, that make them disinterested in reforming in accordance with the tenets of the party assistance norm. They are, in sum, are a priori unsuitable recipients of party assistance. This applies most of all to consecutive parties of power in Georgia and to spoiler parties and office-seeking 'oligarchic' parties in Ukraine, but it also applies to the many parties that are essentially a vehicle for their leadership. While some party activists may be receptive to the message of assistance and would like to see change within their parties, it is especially party leaders who are disinterested in the type of reform that providers of assistance seek to help engender in parties, or who even may have explicit reasons to want to block reform. Installing procedures of intraparty democracy, for instance, could entail that the position of party leaders becomes subject to contestation. Carothers (2006b: 82) notes that 'the leaders of parties in [recipient] countries tend to resist the reforms that outside aid providers advocate'. A 2001 assessment of civil society (including parties) in Georgia has it that 'limited political will seems to exist within the parties to overcome their many institutional weaknesses, particularly among the national leadership who hold most of the authority within the party' (Black et al. 2001: 2). The circumstance that many relevant parties are plainly disinterested in reform is a sufficient explanation for why these parties have failed to comply with the party assistance norm. For the sake of the argument it is assumed in the remainder of this section that parties generally are not disinterested in reform. When this is the case, however, the odds of compliance with the party assistance norm are still small, because other factors, related to the diffusion of the party assistance norm, contribute to make compliance unlikely.

The first of two major reasons for the failure to comply that draws on the discussion of the promotion of the party assistance norm in chapter two, finds that incentives which could compel parties to comply with the party assistance norm, are few and weak. The strongest incentive that may induce compliance is the anticipation of electoral gains, but despite claims by providers of assistance to the contrary (see page 48), there is no evidence that compliance indeed delivers electoral gains, and neither do parties expect that it does. Moreover, parties in Ukraine (at least until 2005) and Georgia, rather than planning long-term organizational development, were mainly involved in a struggle against the regime, and consequently rarely looked beyond next elections. Even if parties would in principle be interested in reform, their limited time horizon, which was dictated by more short-term concerns, put off reform. Compliance is also not strongly associated with higher social status, which under different conditions may present a real incentive to comply. Parties tend to be eager to participate in assistance programs in part because participation

144

is seen as a feat of prestige, but compliance does not have a similar working. Providers of assistance do not systematically reward parties for 'good behavior', nor are they systematically reprimanded when they, for instance, display undemocratic behavior. Providers of assistance do not employ 'social influence' (see section four of chapter two) on parties to the extent that may produce noticeable positive effects.

When compliance is difficult to achieve from a lack of intrinsic incentives, a policy of providing external incentives, whether or not in the form of conditionality, by the providers of assistance may still have the potential to bring about compliance. Providers of assistance, however, do not have the means at hand to credibly effectuate a policy of external incentives. A possible external incentive is the inclusion, as observer, associate, or full member, of parties from Georgia and Ukraine into party internationals. Providers of assistance can play a role in this process by facilitating contacts or lobby on behalf of their 'partner' parties. The relation between compliance with the party assistance norm and inclusion in party internationals, however, is minimal, as, for instance, is illustrated by the inclusion of Batkivshchyna and the United National Movement in the European People's Party as observer members in recent years. As damaging as the inability to provide credible positive external incentives is that the providers of assistance neither take negative measures to retaliate a failure to comply. Since parties do not incur costs from non-compliance, many of them participate in assistance programs for years on end while remaining as unresponsive, unrepresentative, and leader-dominated as they were before participation.

A logic of consequentiality, in sum, has not applied to the diffusion of the party assistance norm in Georgia and Ukraine. A logic of appropriateness equally has not been at work in party assistance. The second major reason for the failure to comply that draws on the discussion of the promotion of the party assistance norm, accordingly, is that receiving assistance has not gotten Georgian and Ukrainian parties to see compliance with the party assistance norm as 'the right thing to do'. This should in part be attributed to inherent characteristics of the norm (see section four of chapter two), including a missing ethical dimension to the norm, as well as to the limited intensity and consistency of the party assistance effort. Between the providers of assistance and its recipients, there is mostly only a loose relationship, which, as discussed above, does not involve binding agreements or the provision of meaningful external incentives. Moreover, there is often not much of an incremental learning process in assistance programs (Carothers 2006a: 126-7): different components of assistance programs are implemented without a coherent underlying plan and are sometimes recycled after some time. Personnel turnover in the organizations of the providers of assistance and a turnover of party representatives who maintain contacts with foreign organizations (often called 'international secretary') contribute to undermine continuity in party assistance. Getting parties to see compliance with the party assistance norm as 'the right thing to do' is further complicated by limited degrees of normative fit and cultural match (see section four of chapter two) between the party assistance norm and existing local norms, and between the providers and recipients of assistance. Certain elements of the party assistance norm, such as internal democracy or increasing participation of women, are too divorced from the prevalent domestic political culture to make compliance attainable through party assistance alone. In the relationship between the providers and recipients of assistance, the providers have moreover been unable to persuade recipients to accept both the instrumental and the normative value of reform, in part due to a shortcoming in mutual understanding and the ability to empathize. Recipients were sometimes unsure of what was expected from them, while providers have often insufficiently grasped local settings of party development, including the incentives which drive the operation of parties.

6.4. SCRUTINIZING PROVIDERS OF ASSISTANCE

This section takes stock of the most glaring shortcomings in the input of assistance in Georgia and Ukraine in order to shed more light on the failure of party assistance in these two cases. While not a comprehensive assessment of the performance of donors and providers of assistance, this section takes them to task for a number of strategies and practices that should be considered as misguided in light of the challenges with which the party assistance effort was confronted in Georgia and Ukraine. A quick tour of the shortcomings of the input of assistance helps to understand why the assistance effort has been unsuccessful. The shortcomings have been grouped under four headings: obfuscation, fragmentation and contingency, feedback and accountability, and limited understanding and false judgment.

Obfuscation

The donors and providers of assistance have engaged in obfuscation regarding the effectiveness of their work, the degree to which they kept themselves to self-imposed standards of good practice, and in their assessments of parties and regimes in Georgia and Ukraine. First, party assistance has sometimes been depicted as a (modest) success, particularly in annual reports of donors and providers of assistance, when there were few facts to substantiate the claim of success with. A booklet outlining the USAID contribution to the wave of electoral revolutions that occurred between 2003-2005 notes that as a result of assistance provided by U.S.-supported groups, 'Georgian political parties learned how to organize and register their voters, train election observers, prepare party platforms and communicate their agendas to the public.' (USAID 2005: 2) The 2006 annual report of ODIHR speaks, in relation to the NIMD-ODIHR program, of a 'momentum based on an authentic commitment for further co-operation and multilateral dialogue between the parties involved in the program' (OSCE ODIHR 2007: 34), while representatives from the political parties have indicated in interviews that relations between the participating parties in fact have been strained throughout. Referring to the period before the Orange Revolution, a 2008 KAS publication notes: 'It can be concluded in hindsight that, both with regard to the rudimentary programmatic contours of the partner parties, and with regard to the approximation to European partners and concepts, some successes were achieved at this stage'.[149] It remains unclear, however, what these successes consist in. Official publications, unsurprisingly, keep silent about failures, which are more widely acknowledged in private conversations with providers of assistance and by former employees of these organizations. Overall, donors and providers present a picture of assistance in Georgia and Ukraine that does not reflect its inability to bring about real changes to party development. As Easterly (2008: 5) has described with respect to development aid, donors and providers prefer not to think much about past failures and instead express optimism about the opportunity to do it well this time around, even when current programs are not that different from previous ones.

Second, the latter two sections of chapter five have demonstrated how the core standards of good practice in party assistance, with regard to party selection and to maintaining a non-partisan position, have been commonly violated in Georgia and Ukraine. Providers of assistance have generally omitted to put forward the reasons behind these violations. The fact that they have not been scrutinized for these violations to any serious degree points to a gap in accountability.

Third, donors and providers have also often painted a brighter picture of political regimes and of parties than was warranted. In one example, USAID described Georgia around the turn of the century as a state that was still in a process of 'democratic transition' (USAID 1999b: *passim*). According to former chief of party of NDI in Georgia Lincoln Mitchell, however, 'It was clear by the turn of the twenty-first century that Georgia under Shevardnadze and what remained of CUG was not moving toward democracy, but was a nondemocratic country with a fair amount of political and civic freedom and "essentially illiberal traits."' (Mitchell 2008: 41). Linguistic obfuscation through the use of euphemisms has been common. Instead of acknowledging that the political party landscape was upset by a high degree of volatility and party turnover, IRI in Ukraine noted in its work plan for 2000 that 'Ukrainian political parties are in a state of transition' (IRI 1999: 1). Instead of pointing out the clear shortcomings in the political transformation of Georgia, NDI in 2001 had it that 'Georgia's government continues to face serious challenges in building a unified, democratic state' (NDI 2000a: 2).

Fragmentation and contingency

The implementation of political party assistance in Georgia and Ukraine has lacked concentration and intensity. The limited resources that are available to donors are spread over a large number of different programs. Most donors have opted to work in all post-communist states of Central and Eastern Europe and of the former Soviet Union, unless they had specific reasons not to work in a particular country. Moreover, the standards of good practice prescribe that providers of assistance work with a representative, inclusive set of parties, so that the amount of assistance per party is further decreased. Because the amount of assistance individual parties receive is small, the relation between recipients and providers of assistance a relatively loose one. In addition to fragmentation, the assistance effort has suffered from a large degree of contingency in Georgia and Ukraine. One representative of NDI in Ukraine, for instance, indicated that most of what NDI does in Ukraine depends on who heads the country office: under consecutive chiefs of party, programming had undergone substantial changes.[150] The future of the ODIHR-NIMD project, similarly, has been said to depend largely on personnel changes at ODIHR.[151] Interpersonal relations between representatives from different providers of assistance are often decisive for the degree and form of coordination between them. Generally, the different providers of assistance that are present in Georgia and Ukraine scarcely coordinate their activities; sometimes they are unaware of the activities of other providers in the same country.[152] Taken together, the impression is created that party assistance is insufficiently sustained and is short on informed understanding of how to proceed.

Feedback and accountability

Next, party assistance in Georgia and Ukraine has been characterized by a lack of feedback and accountability. Measures are rarely taken when assistance programs do not bring in desired effects, as evidenced by the fact that most ineffectual assistance programs have gone on for years on end. A gap in accountability, as noted above, is also noticeable in the fact that parties do not explain why they divert from prevalent standards of good practice in party assistance. The providers

148

of assistance as a result are virtually immune to scrutiny. Most evaluation of party assistance is done internally: independent evaluations are conducted infrequently and on an irregular basis. The few independent assessments of party assistance programs in Georgia and Ukraine have either been largely ignored, or rebutted by the providers of assistance. In 2007-2008, there was no indication, for instance, that a large assessment in 2007 of assistance programs in four countries, including Georgia, of 2007 had been taken note of.[153] A 2001 civil society assessment with respect to Georgia by USAID advised that 'party development efforts not be given priority among the areas of D/G program emphasis' and even more directly that 'the political party program could be scaled down' (Black et al. 2001: 17). An assessment of USAID's DG program in Georgia, commissioned by USAID, one year later similarly advised that 'USAID should reorient its party work away from attempting to build national party organizations to building or sustaining support for specific reforms or to blocking roll-backs of enacted reforms' (ARD Inc. 2002: 48). Assessments of party assistance in Kyrgyzstan and Armenia, where the environment for party assistance has been comparable to that of Georgia and Ukraine, have in similar terms suggested that existing party assistance programs could be decreased (Nelson and Katulis 2005: vii; Roberts 2001: 30). In its work plan for 2001-2002, IRI in Georgia rebuts the suggestion that downsizing party assistance is due, arguing that scaling down party assistance 'would hurt Georgia's fledgling democracy', and pointing out that 'the Institute's work with a range of democratic parties has begun to show results' (NDI 2001c: 7).

In addition to the fact that providers of assistance are not often held accountable or let themselves be held accountable for their work, they receive little valuable feedback that could help improve their activities. The most natural source of feedback, recipient parties, tend to report positively on the assistance that they have received, even if they do not expect that the assistance will have much effect on their organizations. As in much of development aid, party assistance lacks a 'market feedback' that provides a potential check when assistance goes awry (cf. Easterly 2006). An obvious reason why such a market feedback is missing lies in the asymmetrical relation between providers and recipients of assistance and in the fact that the effect of assistance is not subject to measurement with clear indicators. Instead, as noted under the heading of 'obfuscation', effects from assistance can be spinned to make the effort seem more successful.

Finally, it has been found in this research that the donors and providers of assistance are in part unable to present records of their past activities, making it more difficult for the public to scrutinize those activities. With a reference to the

Freedom of Information Act, a request was filed within the framework of this research project to USAID to receive all work plans from NDI and IRI in Georgia and Ukraine from the late 1990s until 2007-2008. USAID could only partially meet this request. The *Stiftungen*, for their part, keep very few systematized records of their activities that can be examined by the public.

Limited understanding and false judgment

The widely held contention that democracy promotion is compromised by a limited knowledge of local conditions (e.g. Carothers 1999: 261) applies in equal measure to political party assistance in Georgia and Ukraine. An evaluation of party assistance by the Dutch party institutes plainly notes that the party institutes have insufficient knowledge about the relations between different actors in party development in Georgia and about the complex political situation (Verheije et al. 2006: 60). Limited understanding of local conditions entails copying of programs from one recipient country to the next. Methods and strategies in party assistance in Georgia and Ukraine have in many instances not been unlike those used in a host of other countries, foremost other post-communist states, and conform to what can tentatively be called a 'standard method' (Carothers 2006a: 112-41). An implication of this unreflective 'one size fits all' approach is that some topics in party assistance in Georgia and Ukraine were not directly relevant to the local context, while topics that were omitted would have been more required. Representatives from political parties and local organizations have sometimes voiced their frustration over the insensitivity of international actors in party assistance, for instance with regard to the frequent use of foreign trainers.[154] Despite claims by providers that their assistance to parties is entirely demand-driven, there have been complaints by parties that assistance programs in which they participated were drawn up without their involvement and did not respond to their needs and wishes.[155] Limited knowledge and insight of the local setting have been reflected in incorrect assessments of party development and of individual parties in Georgia and Ukraine. Among the issues that providers of assistance have sometimes insufficiently understood regarding party development in Georgia and Ukraine are the real incentives which drive the creation and operation of parties. Also, providers of assistance have often too easily assumed that adjustments that were made by parties in their organization were more than mere cosmetic. Concerning the setting in which assistance programs were implemented, providers of assistance, moreover, sometimes failed to grasp the undemocratic leanings of consecutive political regimes, and how this less-than-democratic regime context contributed to invalidate the party assistance intervention.

CONCLUSIONS AND IMPLICATIONS

Among the small number of those who have written about the subject, there is a realization that party assistance rarely produces lasting and tangible effects. This is confirmed in the cases of Georgia and Ukraine: the state of party development in these two former Soviet republics suggests that party assistance over the course of roughly fifteen years of uninterrupted work has outright failed to achieve its primary objective of contributing to the development of a set of more stable and more democratic parties. The degree of effectiveness of party assistance is a function of the adequacy of the input of assistance plus the permissiveness of conditions on the recipient-side of assistance, ie. a combination of the international and the domestic sides to the assistance. The failure to generate desired effects in party assistance, accordingly, is explained from a combination of shortcomings in the input of assistance and domestic constraints on the reception of assistance. This thesis has not only pointed to the reasons why party assistance has been ineffective in Georgia and Ukraine; the account that is offered also carries distinct implications for other cases. The thesis has proposed a new way of viewing party assistance - as a type of norm promotion - and demonstrated that insights on party assistance can be gained by drawing from literature on norm diffusion. The thesis has besides emphasized the weight of domestic factors for the effectiveness of party assistance, and has explicated how these factors invalidate assistance. By doing so, the thesis presents the most comprehensive and theoretically informed account of the problems with political party assistance in particular cases to date. It has added substantial new insights, summarized below, for our understanding of why party assistance so often fails to deliver.

Regarding the supply-side of party assistance, it has been found beneficial to view the assistance as a type of norm promotion. From a range of standard-setting documents issued by the funding and implementing institutions of party assistance, three elements can be deduced that constitute the core of the 'party assistance norm': parties should have stable and broad-based organizational structures; parties should advocate coherent and recognizable programs; and power within parties should be dispersed so that parties themselves are democratically governed organizations. The party assistance norm informs the design of most party assistance programs by the major providers of assistance. One reason to lower expectations about the effectiveness of party assistance is that conditions that are generally seen as conducive to the diffusion of norms are largely absent in relation to party assistance. First, the party assistance norm lacks robustness because there are few explicit references to the norm, because its promotion falls short of intensity and consistency, and because it does not contain an obvious ethical dimension. Second, the relationship between providers and recipients of assistance is relatively loose and distant, while the misfit between the international party assistance norm and local norms tends to be excessively large. Third, recipients have insufficient incentives to comply with the norm against, in many cases, concrete incentives *not* to comply. Besides, the degree of success of party assistance is negatively affected by the requirement for providers of assistance to adhere to 'standards of good practice' which oblige them, whether individually or in conjunction with other providers from the same country, to work with an inclusive, representative set of democratic and at the same time viable parties. While providers of assistance have sometimes opted to work with only a very limited number of parties, more often the requirement of inclusiveness in party selection has led them to work with a relatively large number of parties. As a consequence, the amount of assistance for individual parties was decreased, and, for want of a range of more suitable parties, insignificant, unsustainable, or undemocratic parties were invited to participate in programs.

Since party assistance across the world is to a considerable degree characterized by a 'standard method', the arguments about the shortcomings of the input of party assistance - especially those regarding the party assistance norm - can be expected to apply to many cases. In other words, the arguments may provide hints as to the *general* ineffectiveness of party assistance that has been observed in scholarly literature. With respect to the *particular* ineffectiveness of party assistance in the cases of Georgia and Ukraine, however, the presence of domestic constraints on the development of stable and democratic parties constitutes a sufficient explanation of why assistance failed. Largely irrespective of the form or quality of the input of assistance, party assistance in these two states has been a priori invalidated due to existing domestic constraints on party development. The simplest reason for this is that most of the relevant parties that have been assisted during the decade that has been investigated here, have either disappeared or lost relevance. The remarkable degree of turnover of relevant political parties has in part been fed by the excessively powerful position of party leaders who tended to dispose of their parties at will and without giving much notice to other possible stakeholders within their parties. Often, these leaders proved most reluctant to reform. A second explanation for the weak institutionalization of parties - and relatedly, their often rapid and casual disintegration - hinges on the limited leverage that parties had over political

152

decision-making. The limited leverage resulted in large measure from institutional arrangements, particularly regarding executive-legislative relations and electoral legislation. Since parties were relatively inconsequential organizations, political party 'entrepreneurs' had insufficient incentives to invest in the creation and subsequent development of parties.

The second reason why party assistance has been invalidated by domestic constraints is that a large share of the more relevant parties that received assistance were not interested in reforming in accordance with the proposals of the providers of assistance. The operation of these parties was driven by incentives that were incompatible with the values that party assistance sought to infuse into party politics in Georgia and Ukraine. Put differently, these parties were not inclined to transform into the type of stable and democratic forces that were envisaged to constitute the core of a future stable party system in a democratic political system. This conclusion most obviously concerns parties that were created at the instigation of the Kuchma regime and consecutive semi-authoritarian regimes in Georgia. Besides secondary purposes such as deterring contenders and binding elites, the ultimate purpose of these parties was to contribute to ensure regime survival. In addition to the regime-initiated parties, a number of parties, especially in Ukraine, were primarily interested in gaining office or proximity to office and then reaping the (economic) benefits associated with holding office. Even if parties were not purely vote-seeking or office-seeking vehicles, did they often resist meaningful reform. Especially if party reform would imply the dispersion of power within the party, dominant party leaders had a clear interest in blocking reform. Taken together, in both countries the number of relevant parties which were credibly ready to reform into stable and democratic forces was very limited.

Defining outcomes of party politics in Georgia and Ukraine for most of the post-communist period were a large degree of volatility and the impact on party politics of a less-than-democratic political regime setting. Party assistance by virtue of its mandate was not in the position to counter two of the key enabling conditions of these outcomes - institutional arrangements and the less-than-democratic political regime setting. At the same time, assistance could in theory have worked toward countering the weak institutionalization of parties, the excessively strong position of leaders, and, by withholding assistance from 'undemocratic' parties, the impact of semi-authoritarianism on party politics. The extent of these domestic constraints on party development, however, invalidated party assistance in the form in which it was implemented. Consequently, the domestic constraints have continued to single-handedly spoil the chances of the development of stable and democratic parties. Party assistance was unable to intervene.

One can think of two ways in which party assistance could have achieved more. First, party assistance could have broken free from the standard of good practice to provide assistance to a representative, inclusive set of parties and, instead, have concentrated efforts on one or a few parties. In a similar vein, providers of assistance could have decided to work in a more limited number of countries in order to increase the amount of assistance per country. Second, party assistance may have had more effect if it would have been coupled with types of democracy assistance aimed at eliminating (some of) the domestic constraints on the development of stable and democratic parties. Specifically, it could have been attempted to convince decision-makers to adopt forms of executive-legislative relations and electoral legislation, when these were not in place, that generally go together with relatively strong party development - in particular, a political system with no or weak presidential power, and some variant of a PR electoral system.

The conclusion about the weight of domestic factors in the failure of party assistance in Georgia and Ukraine begs the question whether party assistance in its conventional form should at all be pursued in conditions of fluid party politics and a less-than-democratic political regime context. The question is particularly pertinent in relation to FSU states where one or both of these two conditions are typically present and which in addition share with Georgia and Ukraine a great degree of political and cultural legacy. Two decades after the monopoly of the Communist Party of the Soviet Union was lifted, the party 'systems' in FSU states can hardly still be thought of as 'transitional', or the parties that are available in these countries as 'proto-parties', which in time will transform into or replaced by stronger and more durable democratic forces: by now, as multi-party politics enters its third decade, the party systems in the FSU should be taken for what they are. In the FSU, donors and providers of assistance are aware of the difficulties that complicate party assistance. No assistance is provided in the closed autocracies of Turkmenistan and Uzbekistan. In Kazakhstan and Russia, party assistance to a large degree has in recent years been quietly suspended in light of adverse (political) conditions for the implementation of party assistance. Over the course of the decade during which party assistance programs were implemented in Russia, the programs 'produced no major positive effects' (Carothers 2006a: 168). As in Georgia and Ukraine, 'structural factors overwhelmed and undermined the Western party aid', with the foremost of these structural factors being 'the profoundly unfavorable context for party development' (idem: 170). Party assistance by NDI in Tajikistan was halted in

2008 after the government refused registration to NDI and harassed its staff members (NDI 2008c: 2). To avoid suppression by the government, most program components of assistance to Belarusian parties are carried out in neighboring Ukraine and Poland. Assessments of party assistance in Armenia, Georgia, and Kyrgyzstan note the absence of serious impact from assistance programs. With respect to party assistance in Armenia, it has been plainly commented that 'the political environment in Armenia is not conducive to political party building assistance' (Nelson and Katulis 2005: 27) and that '[t]he assessment found little impact from donor assistance to political parties. Parties characterized USAID-funded assistance as well-meaning but better suited for a more democratic context. The assessment team agrees and believes that more of the same type of assistance is unlikely to provide meaningful results' (idem: vii). It has been advised to scale back party assistance in Georgia primarily because 'limited interest exists within the major political parties to transform themselves into well-structured democratic organizations presenting the public with credible, differentiated policy platforms' (Black et al. 2001: iii). An evaluation of U.S. party assistance in Kyrgyzstan points out that institutional arrangements and the political context have long blocked opportunities for successful party assistance (USAID 2007: x). An earlier evaluation of party assistance by NDI in Kyrgyzstan equally saw little effect from the assistance and proposed that NDI scale back its party assistance program for two years (Roberts 2001: 30). Apparently disregarding the evaluations, party assistance in Armenia, Georgia, and Kyrgyzstan has not been suspended, while the reasons to suspend party assistance in Kazakhstan and Russia have arguably been no less applicable to these countries. The skepticism about the purpose of party assistance in Armenia particularly may with good reason have been extended to most other former Soviet republics. It is, in brief, not evident that there has been a sufficient justification to continue party assistance in the region.

When party assistance was launched in the post-communist states, an implicit assumption was that there was a genuine interest in those countries in democratization, and a genuine interest among recipient parties to transform into truly representative and democratic forces. Recipient parties were seen as constituents of a stable and democratic party system that would crystallize in the not too distant future as the transition to democracy would progress into consolidation. In much of the post-communist world as well as in many other countries outside the post-communist world where party assistance is still carried out, however, regimes are not in a state of transition toward democracy, and it is doubtful that most parties which receive assistance are really interested in internal

155

reform. As the third wave of democratization has ground to a halt, most previously third wave states are stuck in a political gray zone: they are neither liberal democracies nor closed autocracies (Diamond 2002; Howard and Roessler 2006), and most are neither becoming significantly more democratic nor are they moving backward (Carothers 2009). Whether in Africa (Basedau and Stroh 2008), South East Asia (Ufen 2007), or Latin America (Sanchez 2008b), political parties in these countries are characterized by weak institutionalization, as parties have been in Georgia and Ukraine. In the majority of 'gray zone' countries with weakly institutionalized parties, international actors are involved in providing assistance to parties.[156] They have in recent years moved out of Central and Eastern Europe, the region with most of the successful transitions to liberal democracy in the past two decades. Now that those 'easy' cases of transition have been completed, providers overwhelmingly work in countries with less sanguine prospects for democratization and stable party development. The conditions which have made party assistance in Georgia and Ukraine so difficult are therefore *mutatis mutandis* present in many other places where party assistance is carried out. The immediate prospects of political party assistance, consequently, are not bright. Confronted with adverse conditions for party assistance in so many recipient countries, the purpose and methods of assistance are due for reconsideration.

NOTES

[1] Three of which are not parties but electoral blocs, consisting of between two and ten parties each.

[2] Author's translation of: 'Politieke partijen bestaan eigenlijk nauwelijks in Georgië. Politieke bewegingen zijn feitelijk min of meer loyale clans rondom individuen.'

[3] Author's translation of: 'Die Parteien der Ukraine tragen noch immer starken Projektcharakter. Sie sind in erster Linie personenzentrierte Netzwerke, die stark mit ökonomischen Interessen ihrer Betreiber verflochten sind.'

[4] Examples include KAS (2007), NDI (2001: 26), and USAID (1999: 31)

[5] According to one estimate, political party assistance costs no less than 139 million euros per year (Catón 2007: 12).

[6] Author's interviews with political party representatives in Georgia and Ukraine, 2007-2009

[7] Notable exceptions are Elgstrom (2000) and Grigorescu (2002)

[8] In fact, most stable party systems are probably found on the two extremes of regime typologies - in liberal democracies and in political closed authoritarian states.

[9] The countries where party assistance is carried out are listed on the web sites of the main providers. See http://www.fes.de/sets/s_fes_i.htm, http://www.kas.de/wf/en/71.4782/, http://www.iri.org/, http://ndi.org/wherewework, http://nimd.org/page/nimd_programmes. Most of these countries are associated with weak party system institutionalization (Basedau and Stroh 2008; Kuenzi and Lambright 2005; Meleshevich 2007; Stockton 2001; Ufen 2007) and are characterized by a less-than-democratic political context (see http://www.freedomhouse.org/template.cfm?page=363&year=2009).

[10] Hall employs the term 'systematic process analysis' instead of 'process-tracing'.

[11] This strategy is explicitly recommended by Rivera et al. (2003), who have interviewed elites in Russia.

[12] http://dec.usaid.gov

[13] Author's calculation based on figures from Catón (2007: 12).

[14] The NIMD project in Georgia, however, is funded by OSCE/ODIHR.

[15] Relative expenditures have likely increased after 1999 due to a growth in interest in party assistance.

[16] Interview with IRI/Georgia representative, September 24, 2007

[17] Interviews with FES and KAS representatives. Berlin, May 10, 2007

[18] Interview with NIMD representative, The Hague, April 5, 2007

[19] Interview with NDI, IRI, KAS, FES, and FNS representatives in Georgia and Ukraine

[20] Interview with FES representative. Berlin, May 10, 2007

[21] Such, for example, was the selection criterion in the NIMD/ODIHR project in Georgia

[22] Interview with IRI official, April 12, 2007, Washington D.C. Also see: USAID 2003b: 10

[23] Publications and documents that have been consulted for this content analysis include: Federal Ministry for Economic Cooperation and Development (BMZ) 2005; Doherty 2002; Konrad Adenauer Stiftung (KAS) 2007a; National Democratic Institute for International Affairs (NDI) 2003; NDI 2008a; Netherlands Institute for Multiparty Democracy (NIMD) 2004; Saxer 2006a; Saxer 2006b; United States Agency for International Development (USAID) 1999b; USAID 2003b; USAID 2006d.

[24] For a similar approach to the extraction of norms from a corpus of sources, see Kratochvil (2008).

[25] E.g. interviews with Batkivshchyna representative, March 21, 2008; and with KAS/Georgia staff member, May 22, 2008

[26] Available from http://freedomhouse.org/template.cfm?page=15

[27] For an explanation of the Freedom in the World Index, see http://www.freedomhouse.org/template.cfm?page=277 (accessed January 20, 2008)

[28] On the linguistic cleavage, see Arel (1995) and Wilson (2002a). On different cultural/ideological outlooks, see Shulman (2004) and Hrytsak (2004). On regional differences in voting patterns, see Barrington and Herron (2004) and Birch (2000a).

[29] For definitions of democracy promotion and democracy assistance, see previous chapter.

[30] Areshidze (2007) carries some detail on trips to Georgia and communications by U.S. officials with Georgian politicians in 2003. On visits of U.S. officials to Ukraine in 2004, see Prystayko (2006: 129)

[31] See, for instance, USAID/Ukraine Annual Report FY 2003 and USAID/Caucasus - Georgia 2002

[32] For figures on Ukraine, see Youngs (2008: 17). For figures on Georgia, see http://www.delgeo.ec.europa.eu/en/programsactions/. Figures for 2007-2013 are at http://ec.europa.eu/world/enp/pdf/country/0703_enpi_figures_en.pdf

[33] Interview with SPU representative, March 26, 2008

[34] Interviews with Batkivshchyna representative, March 21, 2008 and KAS/Georgia staff member, May 22, 2008

[35] Interviews with SPU representative, March 26, 2008, and political scientist, Tbilisi, October 5, 2007

[36] Interviews with SPU representative, March 26, 2008

[37] Interview with Batkivshchyna representative, March 21, 2008

[38] Interview with NRU representative, November 5, 2007

[39] Interview with Our Ukraine representative, October 31, 2007

[40] Interview with PORA representative, November 9, 2007

[41] Interview with SPU representative, March 26, 2008

[42] Interview with PRU youth wing representative, March 18, 2008

[43] Interview with New Rights party youth wing, Tbilisi, October 2, 2007

[44] Interview with NDI/Ukraine representative, March 17, 2008

[45] See: http://www.aristotle.org/html/PressReleaseAAPCPollie0105.pdf

[46] Author's translation of: Політичні партії, як виявилося, позбавлені широкої социальної бази, їх ідеологія та програми неадекватно відбивають поточну ситуацію і не відповідають завданням розвитку суспільства, партії не мають у своєму розпорядженні механізмів реалізації притарманних їм функцій та завдань (Romaniuk i Shveda 2005: 239).

[47] Studies that engage in cross-national comparison include Kulik and Pshizova (2005), Meleshevich (2007), and Miller et al. (2000).

[48] Although they are formally former Soviet republics, the three Baltic republics are left out of scope here, because their post-communist political trajectory has in virtually all respects been more similar to that of Central and Eastern Europe than of the FSU.

[49] Against this, Markowski (2000) and Tóka (1997) argue that party system institutionalization is *not* crucial for democratic consolidation.

[50] See: Law of Republic of Georgia On Political Associations Of Citizens (1997) at: http://www.legislationline.org/legislation.php?tid=222&lid=1966&less=false, and Law of Ukraine on Political Parties (2001), at: http://www.legislationline.org/legislation.php?lid=3804&tid=2

[51] Sartori argued back in 1976 that studying unstructured party systems is of little value. For an argument on why and how parties can be studied even in a highly volatile environment, see Wolinetz (2006: 15)

[52] Particularly so since the path-breaking volume of Scott Mainwaring and Timothy Scully (1995) about party system institutionalization in Latin America.

[53] Andrew Wilson and Sarah Birch (2007: 61) make the point about the difficulty of calculating electoral volatility when party turnover is excessively high with reference to Ukraine.

[54] Two exceptions are found in Schedler (2004: 8) and Zimmer (2003: 10-1)

[55] Party age as an indicator of party system institutionalization is operationalized, among others, by Dix (1992) and Kuenzi and Lambright (2005). The indicator of stable roots in society is applied by Mainwaring and Scully (1995) in their study about party system institutionalization in Latin America, and in their footsteps, among many others, by Basedau and Stroh (2008).

[56] A survey by IFES (Carson 2000: 38) found that two per cent of the adult population in Ukraine are members of a political party.

[57] A notable exception is Van de Walle (2003).

[58] For a more precise definition of presidentialism, see Shugart (2006).

[59] The presence of a dual executive (Blondel 1984; Duverger 1980; Shugart 2005) is often considered the core feature of semipresidentialism.

[60] The term 'big men' is frequently applied in relation to party politics in Africa. E.g. Van de Walle (2003)

[61] Kitschelt (2000: 872) observes that 'clientelist democracy has proved durable and has commanded sufficient support to institutionalize and entrench itself for long periods in a variety of polities'. Enyedi (2006: 230) suggests that charismatic leadership in parties (at the expense of the visibility of a party program), common to party politics in Central and Eastern Europe, can strengthen party systems.

[62] E.g. Herron and Mirzashvili (2005) have documented the frequent amending of electoral legislation in Georgia.

[63] Bartolini and Mair (2001: 332) divide political party functions into representative functions and procedural functions.

[64] All election results are from the website of the Central Election Commission of Ukraine, http://www.cvk.gov.ua/

[65] Office-seeking and vote-seeking incentives in party operation, however, are not necessarily inimical to democratic party development.

[66] Interviews with political scientist, Tbilisi, September 27, 2007; and with IRI/Ukraine representative, Kyiv, May 29, 2007

[67] Examples include the Progressive Socialist Party, the Ukrainian Communist Party (o), and Yabluko (Wilson and Bitch 2007: 72-3).

[68] Interview with former NDI/Georgia representative (2000-2004), Tbilisi, October 2, 2007

[69] idem

[70] See NDI (2000c); NDI (2001c); and NDI (2002c).

[71] Interviews with former NDI/Georgia representative (2002-2004), Berlin, May 9, 2007and with former NRP representative, Washington D.C., April 21, 2007

[72] Interview with IRI/Georgia representative, Tbilisi, October 1, 2007

[73] Interview with NDI/Georgia representative, Tbilisi, October 10, 2007

[74] E.g. McGlinchey (2007), p.20

[75] Interview with IRI/Georgia representative (2003-2007), Tbilisi, September 24, 2007

[76] idem

[77] Interview with IRI/Georgia representative, Tbilisi, October 1, 2007

[78] Interviews with IRI/Georgia representative (2003-2007), Tbilisi, September 24, 2007 and with United National Movement international secretary, Tbilisi, October 11, 2007

[79] E.g. IRI (2005b); and IRI (2005c).

[80] Interview with IRI/Washington D.C. representative, Washington, D.C., April 12, 2007

[81] E.g. IRI (2005b); and IRI (2005c).

[82] Interview with NIMD representative, Tbilisi, May 14, 2008

[83] See http://www.cipdd.org/index.php?lang_id=ENG&sec_id=3&info_id=38 (accessed October 17, 2008)

[84] Interview with NIMD representative, The Hague, April 5, 2007

[85] Interview with NIMD representative, The Hague, April 5, 2007; also see ODIHR-IMD-CIPDD (2006).

[86] Telephone Interview with NIMD representative, January 14, 2009

[87] Interview with FNS/Georgia representative, Tbilisi, March 20, 2007

[88] Interview with FES representative, Berlin, May 8, 2007

[89] Interview with KAS/Georgia representative, Tbilisi, March 23, 2007

[90] Interview with KAS/Georgia representative, Tbilisi, May 22, 2008

[91] Interview with NDI/Ukraine representative, March 17, 2008

[92] Interview with former NDI/Ukraine representative (1999-2001)

[93] Interview with NDI/Ukraine representative, March 17, 2008

[94] ibid.

[95] ibid.

[96] ibid.

[97] Interview with former NDI/Ukraine representative (1999-2001)

[98] Interview with IRI/Ukraine representative, Kyiv, March 19, 2008

[99] Interview with IRI/Ukraine representative, Kyiv, May 29, 2007

[100] Interview with IRI representative, Washington, D.C., April 12, 2007

[101] Interview with IRI/Ukraine representative, Kyiv, May 29, 2007

[102] ibid.

[103] ibid.

[104] Interview with KAS/Ukraine representative, Kyiv, May 31, 2007

[105] See KAS (2008a: 31) and Interview with former KAS/Ukraine representative, Berlin, May 8, 2007

[106] See http://www.fesukraine.kiev.ua/main.php?m=6&mp=1 (accessed February 9, 2009)

[107] Interview with FES/Ukraine representative, Kyiv, October 30, 2007

[108] Interview with Interview with IRI/Ukraine representative, Kyiv, May 29, 2007; Interview with NDI/Ukraine representative, Kyiv, March 17, 2008

[109] Interview with Party of Regions representations, Kyiv, March 18, 2008

[110] Interview with former international secretary of SPU, Kyiv, March 26, 2008

[111] Telephone Interview with NIMD representative, January 14, 2009

[112] Interview with former NDI/Georgia representative, Berlin, May 9, 2007; Interview with NDI/Ukraine representative, Kyiv, March 17, 2008; and Interview with former NDI/Georgia representative, October 2, 2007

[113] Interview with IRI/Georgia representative, Tbilisi, September 24, 2007

[114] Interview with former NDI/Ukraine representative, Amsterdam, March 9, 2007, McGlinchey (2007: 19) notes that this has been the case in Bulgaria, Poland, and Romania.

[115] Interview with former NDI/Georgia representative, Tbilisi, October 2, 2007

[116] Interview with political scientist, Tbilisi, October 11, 2007

[117] Regarding the alleged bias in favor of UNM, see, e.g. Interview with international secretary of the youth wing of the New Rights Party, Tbilisi, October 2, 2007; regarding the fact that IRI allegedly plays into the hands of the ruling forces, see USAID (2007: A2/A3).

[118] Interview with IRI/Georgia representative, Tbilisi, October 1, 2007

[119] Interview with IFES representative, Washington, D.C., April 8

[120] Interview with Conservative Party of Georgia representative, Tbilisi, April 27, 2007

[121] Interview with Party of Regions representative, Kyiv, March 18, 2008

[122] Interview with NIMD representative, The Hague, April 5, 2007

[123] Interview with Batkivshchyna representative, Kyiv, March 21, 2008

[124] Interview with Republican Party of Georgia representative, Tbilisi, October 5, 2007; Interview with Party of Regions representative, Kyiv, March 18, 2008; and Interview with Socialist party of Ukraine representative, Kyiv, March 26, 2008

[125] Interview with former NDI/Georgia representative (2000-2004), Tbilisi, October 2, 2007; and Interview with former KAS/Ukraine representative, Berlin, May 8, 2007

[126] Interview with CIPDD representative, Tbilisi, September 27, 2007

[127] Interview with former KAS/Ukraine representative, Berlin, May 8, 2007

[128] Interview with Conservative Party of Georgia representative, Tbilisi, April 27, 2007; Interview with Conservative Party of Georgia representative, Batumi, October 3, 2007; and Interview with CIPDD representative, Tbilisi, September 27, 2007

[129] Interview with two Conservative Party of Georgia representatives, Tbilisi, October 10, 2007

[130] Interview with IRI/Georgia representative, Tbilisi, October 1, 2007

[131] Telephone Interview with NIMD representative, January 14, 2009

[132] Interview with CIPDD representative, Tbilisi, September 27, 2007

[133] Interview with FES/Ukraine representative, Kyiv, June 4, 2007

[134] Interview with Party of Regions representative, Kyiv, March 18, 2008

[135] Interview with IRI representative, Washington, D.C., April 12, 2007

[136] Interview with IRI/Ukraine representative, Kyiv, May 29, 2007

[137] Interview with NDI/Ukraine representative, Kyiv, March 17, 2008

[138] Interview with IRI/Georgia representative, Tbilisi, September 24, 2007

[139] Interview with NDI/Ukraine representative, Kyiv, March 17, 2008

[140] Interview with IRI/Georgia representative, Tbilisi, September 24, 2007

[141] Interview with People's Union Our Ukraine youth wing representative, Kyiv, October 30, 2007; and interview with New Rights party youth wing, Tbilisi, October 2, 2007

[142] Interview with IRI/Ukraine representative, Kyiv, May 29, 2007

[143] E.g. Interview with Georgian political scientist, Tbilisi, October 11, 2007

[144] Interviews with NDI/Ukraine representative, Kyiv, March 17, 2008 and with former KAS/Ukraine representative, Berlin, May 8, 2007

[145] Interview with Labor Party representative, Tbilisi, March 24, 2007; and interview with Conservative Party of Georgia representative, Tbilisi, September 27, 2007

[146] Interview with former NDI/Ukraine representative, Amsterdam, March 9, 2007

[147] Telephone Interview with NIMD representative, January 14, 2009

[148] E.g. Interview with SPU representative, Kyiv, March 26, 2008

[149] Translation by the author of: 'Rückblickend ist festzustellen, dass in Bezug sowohl auf die rudimentären programmatischen Konturen der Partnerparteien als auch auf die Annäherung an europäische Partner und Konzepte in dieser Phase einige Erfolge erzielt werden konnten' (KAS 2008a: 31)

[150] Interview with NDI/Ukraine representative, Kyiv, April 17, 2008

[151] Interview with ODIHR representative, Warsaw, September 6, 2007

[152] For example, a representative from NDI working on, among other countries, Georgia, in 2007 was unaware of the existence of the NIMD-ODIHR project. Interview with NDI representative, Washington, April 18, 2007

[153] The assessment concerned is USAID (2007).

[154] Interview with SPU representative, Kyiv, November 7, 2007. On the use of foreign trainers specifically, see Interview with CIPDD representative, Tbilisi, May 19, 2008

[155] E.g. Interview with CIPDD representative, Tbilisi, May 19, 2008

[156] See note 9

APPENDIX 1. POLITICAL PARTY TURNOVER IN GEORGIA

	1999	2003	2004	2008
CUG	41,9			
Union of Democratic Revival	25,7 1-Union of Democratic Revival 2-Socialist Party 3-Union of Georgian Traditionalists 4-Konstantine Gamsakhurdia Society 5-Georgian Freedom and Integrity Movement 'Chkondideli'	18,8		
IWSG	7,8 1-Industry Will Save Georgia (IWSG) 2-Movement for Georgian Statehood 3-Union of Reformers and Agrarians 4-Georgia First of All 5-Political Union 'New Georgia' 6-Sportive Georgia			
FNG		21,3 1-CUG 2- Socialist Party 3- NDP 4- Green Party of Georgia 5- Christian-Democratic Union 6- Abkhazia's Liberation Party 7- Political Union - "Strong Regions - Strong Georgia" - Political Union - "Transporters' Hall" - Georgia First of All		
National Movement		18,8 1-UNM 2- Union of National Forces 3- RPG	66.2 1-UNM 2- Union of National Forces 3-RPG	59,2 -UNM

			4- United Democrats	
LP		12,0		7,4
Burjanadze - Democrats		8,8 1-United Democrats 2-Union of Georgian Traditionalists 3- Christian-Conservators		
New Rightists		7,4 1-NRP 2-Georgian Liberal Party		
Bloc Rightist Opposition			7,6 1-NRP 2-IWSG	
Nine-Party Opposition Bloc				17,7 1-NRP 2-CP 3-Georgia's Way 4-Freedom Movement 5-On Our Own 6-People's Party 7-Movement for a United Georgia 8- Georgian Troupe 9- National Forum
Christian Democratic Movement				8,7

Sources: Wheatley (2005); Central Election Commission of Georgia at www.cec.gov.ge; (consulted on July 17, 2008); Dieset (2004); http://civil.ge/eng/category.php?id=32&result=proportional&view=regions (consulted on July 17, 2008)

Notes:
- This appendix contains election results of the four most recent parliamentary elections in Georgia, the electoral forces (whether political parties or electoral coalitions) that crossed the electoral threshold, and the composition of the electoral coalition that crossed the threshold. Parties that have competed as part of various electoral coalitions are highlighted in color.
- Only those parties are included that have crossed the electoral threshold for representation. In the 1999, 2003 and 2004, the threshold stood at 7%, in 2008 at 5%.
- All elections were conducted according to a mixed electoral system. Recorded are the results of the party list vote.
- For the 2003 elections the official results as announced by the Central Election Commission are recorded. After the Rose Revolution, these results were annulled, and repeat election were held in March 2004. Data on the annulled 2003 election have been included to demonstrate the changes between the 2003 election and the 2004 repeat elections.

APPENDIX 2. POLITICAL PARTY TURNOVER IN UKRAINE

	1998	2002	2006	2007
KPU	24,7	20,0	3,7	5,4
People's Movement of Ukraine (Rukh)	9,4			
Socialist Party of Ukraine/Peasants' Party of Ukraine bloc	8,6 1-SPU 2-Peasant's Party			
Party of Greens of Ukraine	5,4			
NDP	5,0			
Hromada	4,7			
Progressive Socialist Party of Ukraine	4,0			
SDPU (o)	4,0	6,3		
NU bloc		23,6 1-KUN 2-Liberal party of ukraine 3-Youth party of Ukraine 4-NRU 5-PRP 6-Solidarity 7-CDS 8-'Forward, Ukraine' 9-Republican Christian Party 10-Ukrainian People's Party (UNP)	14,0 1- NSNU 2-KUN 3- NRU 4-PPPU 5- CDS 6- Ukrainian Republican Party 'Sobor'	14,2 1-NSNU 2-NRU 3-Party of the Defenders of the Fatherland 4-CDS 5-European Party of Ukraine 6-'Forward, Ukraine' 7-Ukrainian Republican Party 'Sobor' 8-Ukrainian People's Party (UNP) 9-PORA 10-People's Self-Defense Movement
ZYeU bloc		11,8 1-PRU 2-People's Party 3- PPPU 4- Labor Party of Ukraine 5-NDP		
Bloc Yulia Tymoshenko (BYuT)		7,3 1-Batkivshchyna 2 Ukranian People's party 'Sobor' 3-Ukrainian Social-Democratic party (USDP)	22,3 1-Batkivshchyna 2-Ukrainian Social-Democratic party (USDP)	30,7 1-Batkivshchyna 2-Ukrainian Social-Democratic party (USDP) 3-PRP
Socialist party of		6,9	5,7	

Ukraine (SPU)				
PRU			32,1	34,3
Litvin Bloc				4,0 **1-People's Party** **2-Labor Party of Ukraine**

Source: Central Election Commission of Ukraine, http://www.cvk.gov.ua (consulted on July 17, 2008)

Notes:

- This appendix contains election results of the four most recent parliamentary elections in Ukraine, the electoral forces (whether political parties or electoral coalitions) that crossed the electoral threshold for the party list vote (4% in 1998 and 2002, 3% in 2006, 5% in 2007), and the composition of the electoral coalition that crossed the threshold. Parties that have competed as part of various electoral coalitions are highlighted in color.
- The 1998 and 2002 parliamentary election were conducted according to a mixed electoral system. For these elections, only the results of the national party list vote are recorded. In the 2006 and 2007 elections, all seats were filled from national party lists.
- Results are for parties that crossed the electoral threshold for representation.

References

Acharya, Amitav. 2004. How Ideas Spread: Whose Norms Matter? Norm
    Localization and Institutional Change in Asian Regionalism. *International*
    Organization 58 (2): 239-75.

Adesnik, David, and Michael McFaul. 2006. 'Engaging Autocratic Allies to Promote
    Democracy. *The Washington Quarterly* 29 (2): 7-26.

Almond, Gabriel A., and Sidney Verba. 1963. *The Civic Culture: Political Attitudes*
    and Democracy in Five Nations. Princeton: Princeton University Press.

Ambrosio, Thomas. 2007. Reacting to the Color Revolutions: Democratic Diffusion
    and Russian Foreign Policy toward Ukraine and Georgia. Paper presented
    at the annual conference of the International Studies Association, February
    28, in Chicago, IL.

Amundsen, Inge. 2007. *Donor Support to Political Parties: Status and Principles.*
    Bergen: Chr. Michelsen Institute.

Andrews, Josephine T., and Robert W. Jackman. 2005. Strategic fools: electoral
    rule choice under extreme uncertainty. *Electoral Studies* 24 (1): 65-84.

ARD, Inc. 2002. *Democracy and Governance Assessment of Georgia.* Washington,
    D.C.

Arel, Dominique. 1995. Language politics in Independent Ukraine: Towards one or
    two state languages? *Nationalities Papers* 23 (3): 597-622.

Areshidze, Irakly. 2007. *Democracy and Autocracy in Eurasia: Georgia in*
    Transition. East Lansing: Michigan State University Press.

Arksey, Hilary, and Peter T. Knight. 1999. *Interviewing for social scientists.* London:
    Sage Publications

Åslund, Anders. 2006. The Ancien Regime: Kuchma and the Oligarchs. in *Revolution*
    in Orange: The Origins of Ukraine's Democratic Breakthrough. ed. Anders
    Åslund and Michael McFaul, 9-28. Washington, DC: Carnegie Endowment
    for International Peace.

Bakke, Elisabeth, and Nick Sitter. 2005. Patterns of Stability: Party Competition and
    Strategy in Central Europe since 1989. *Party Politics* 11 (2): 243-263.

Barca, Peter, Elehie Natalie Skoczylas, and Jeson Ingraham. 2006. Transforming
    Elections in Ukraine. An Assessment of Progress Made in Elections
    Administration and the Challenges Ahead. Arlington. VA: Development
    Associates.

Barrington, Lowell W. 2002. Examining rival theories of demographic influences on political support: The power of regional, ethnic, and linguistic divisions in Ukraine. *European Journal of Political Research* 41 (4): 455-91.

Barrington, Lowell W., and Erik S. Herron. 2004. One Ukraine or many? Regionalism in Ukraine and its Political Consequences. *Nationalities Papers* 32 (1): 53-86.

Bartolini, Stefano, and Peter Mair. 1990. *Identity, Competition, and Electoral Stability. The Stabilisation of European Electorates 1885-1985*. Cambridge, MA: Cambridge University Press.

_____. 2001. Challenges to Contemporary Political Parties. in *Political Parties and Democracy*. ed. Larry Diamond and Richard Gunther, 327-343. Baltimore: The Johns Hopkins University Press.

Basedau, Matthias, and Alexander Stroh. 2008. Measuring Party Institutionalization in Developing Countries: A New Research Instrument Applied to 28 African Political Parties. Hamburg: GIGA German Institute of Global and Area Studies, Working Paper no. 69.

Beissinger, Mark R. 2007. Structure and Example in Modular Political Phenomena: The Diffusion of Bulldozer/Rose/Orange/Tulip Revolutions. *Perspectives on Politics* 5 (2): 259-76.

Bielasiak, Jack. 2002. The Institutionalization of Electoral and Party Systems in Postcommunist States. *Comparative Politics* 34 (2): 189-210.

_____. 2005. Party competition in emerging democracies: representation and effectiveness in post-communism and beyond. *Democratization* 12 (3): 331-56.

Binnendijk, Anika L., and Ivan Marovic. 2006. Power and persuasion: Nonviolent strategies to Influence state security forces in Serbia (2000) and Ukraine (2004). *Communist and Post-Communist Studies* 39 (3): 411-29.

Birch, Sarah. 2000a. Interpreting the Regional Effect in Ukrainian Politics. *Europe-Asia Studies* 52 (6): 1017-41.

_____. 2000b. The Effects of Mixed Electoral Systems in Eastern Europe. Paper presented at the 30th Annual Conference of the University Association for Contemporary European Studies, April 7-9, in Budapest, Hungary.

_____. 2001. Electoral Systems and Party System Stability in Post-Communist Europe. Paper presented at the annual meeting of the American Political Science Association (97th), August 30- September 1, in San Francisco, CA.

_____. 2003. The parliamentary elections in Ukraine, March 2002. *Electoral Studies* 22 (3): 524-31.

_____. 2005. Single-member district electoral systems and democratic transition. *Electoral Studies* 24 (2): 281-301.

_____. 2007. Electoral Systems and Election Misconduct. *Comparative Political Studies* 40 (12): 1533-56.

Birch, Sarah, and Andrew Wilson. 1999. The Ukrainian parliamentary elections of 1998. *Electoral Studies* 18 (2):276-82.

Black, David, Susan Jay, and Michael Keshishian. 2001. Georgia Civil Society Assessment (Including NGO Development, Media & Political Process). Washington, D.C.

Blondel, Jean. 1984. Dual Leadership in the Contemporary World: A Step Towards Regime Stability? In *Comparative Government and Politics: Essays in Honor of S.E. Finer*. ed. Dennis Kavanagh and Gillian. Peele, 162-72. Boulder, Colorado: Westview Press.

Bloom, S., and M. A. Orenstein. 2005. Transnationalism and Nationalism in Postcommunist Politics. Paper presented at the conference Postcommunist States and Societies: Transnational and National Politics at the Maxwell School of Syracuse University, September 30 – October 1.

Bogaards, Matthijs. 2000. Crafting competitive party systems: Electoral laws and the opposition in Africa. *Democratization* 7 (4): 163-90.

Boyko, Oksana. 2005. *Osoblyvosti transformatsii partiinoi systemy Ukrainy za roky nezalezhnosti*. Unpublished dissertation. Summary available at http://www.lib.ua-ru.net/inode/17634.html.

Brinkerhoff, Derick W., and Arthur A. Goldsmith. 2002. Clientelism, Patrimonialism and Democratic Governance: An Overview and Framework for Assessment and Programming. Paper prepared for U.S. Agency for International Development, Office of Democracy and Governance.

Brinks, Daniel, and Michael Coppedge. 2006. Diffusion Is No Illusion: Neighbor Emulation in the Third Wave of Democracy. *Comparative Political Studies* 39 (4): 463-489.

Brownlee, Jason. 2007. *Authoritarianism in an Age of Democratization*. Cambridge, MA: Cambridge University Press.

Brucker, Matthias. 2007. Trans-national Actors in Democratizing States: The Case of German Political Foundations in Ukraine. *Journal of Communist Studies and Transition Politics* 23 (2): 296-319.

Bunce, Valerie. 2000. Comparative Democratization: Big and Bounded Generalizations. *Comparative Political Studies* 33 (6-7): 703-34.

Bunce, Valerie J., and Sharon L. Wolchik. 2006a. International diffusion and postcommunist electoral revolutions. *Communist and Post-Communist Studies* 39 (3): 283-304.

_____. 2006b. 'Youth and Electoral Revolutions in Slovakia, Serbia, and Georgia. *SAIS Review* 26 (2): 55-65.

Burnell, Peter. 2000a. Democracy Assistance: Origins and Organizations. In *Democracy Assistance: International Cooperation for Democratization*, ed. P. Burnell, 34-66. London: Frank Cass.

_____. 2000b. Democracy Assistance: The State of the Discourse. In *Democracy Assistance: International Co-operation for Democratization*, ed. P. Burnell, 3-33. London: Frank Cass.

_____. 2000c. Promoting Parties and Party Systems in New Democracies: Is There Anything the International Community Can Do? Paper presented at the 50th annual conference of the Political Studies Association, 10-13 April, in London, UK.

_____. 2006. Promoting Democracy Backwards. FRIDE Working Paper 28.

Burnham, Peter, Karin Gilland, Wyn Grant, and Zig Layton-Henry. 2004. *Research Methods in Politics*. New York, NY: Palgrave Macmillan.

Carey, John M. 2002. Getting Their Way, or Getting in the Way? Presidents and Party Unity in Legislative Voting. Paper presented at the annual meeting of the American Political Science Association, August 28, in Boston.

Carothers, Thomas. 1992. Empirical Perspectives on the Emerging Norm of Democracy in International Law. *American Society of International Law Proceedings* 86: 262-4.

_____. 1999. *Aiding Democracy Abroad: The Learning Curve*. Washington, D.C.: Carnegie Endowment for International Peace.

_____. 2002. The End of the Transition Paradigm. *Journal of Democracy* 13 (1): 5-21.

_____. 2006a. *Confronting the Weakest Link: Aiding Political Parties in New Democracies*. Washington, D.C.: Carnegie Endowment for International Peace.

_____. 2006b. Examining Political Party Aid. In *Globalising Democracy*, ed. P. Burnell, London: Routledge Publishers.

_____. 2007. *U.S. Democracy Promotion During and After Bush*. http://www.carnegieendowment.org/files/democracy_promotion_after_bush_fInal.pdf (accessed November 3, 2007)

_____. 2009. Stepping Back From Democratic Pessimism. Democracy and Rule of Law Program, Carnegie Paper nr. 99.

Carson, Thomas P. 2000. Attitudes toward Change, the Current Situation, and Civic Action in Ukraine. Paper prepared for the International Foundation for Electoral Systems, Kyiv.

Casal Bértoa, Fernando. 2008. Party (System) Institutionalization and the Quality of Democracy in New European Democracies, East and South. Paper presented at the 4th CEU Graduate Conference in Social Sciences, June 20-22, in Budapest, Hungary.

Catón, Matthias. 2007. *Effective Party Assistance. Stronger Party for Better Democracy*. Stockholm: International Institute for Democracy and Electoral Assistance.

Central European Opinion Research Group (CEORG). 2004. Trust in Fellow Citizens, Distrust in Politics Across Central and Eastern European Countries. http://www.ceorg-europe.org/research/2004-09.pdf (accessed July 21, 2008).

Checkel, Jeffrey T. 1998. The Constructivist Turn in International Relations Theory. *World Politics* 50: 324-48.

_____. 1999a. International Institutions and Socialization. ARENA Working Papers 99/5.

_____. 1999b. Norms, Institutions, and National Identity in Contemporary Europe. *International Studies Quarterly* 43 (1): 84-114.

_____. 2002. Persuasion in International Institutions. ARENA Working Papers 02/14.

Collier, David, and Steven Levitsky. 1997. Democracy with Adjectives. *World Politics* 49 (3): 430-51.

Colomer, Josep M. 2005. It's Parties That Choose Electoral Systems (or, Duverger's Laws Upside Down). *Political Studies* 53 (1): 1-21.

Cooley, Alexander, and Lincoln A. Mitchell. 2009. No Way to Treat Our Friends: Recasting Recent U.S./Georgian Relations. *The Washington Quarterly* 32 (1): 27-41

Coppedge, Michael. 1999. Thickening Thin Concepts and Theories: Combining Large N and Small in Comparative Politics. *Comparative Politics* 31 (4): 465-76.

Cortell, Andrew P., and James W. Davis Jr. 2000. Understanding the Domestic Impact of International Norms: A Research Agenda. *The International Studies Review* 2 (1): 65-87.

Croissant, Aurel. 2002. Electoral Politics in Southeast and East Asia: A Comparative Perspective. Singapore: Friedrich Ebert Stiftung.

_____. 2006. Parteienförderung als Demokratieförderung. Vortrag auf der Auslandsmitarbeiter/Innen-Fortbildung „Parteiförderung als Instrument der Demokratieförderung", July 31, in Berlin, Germany.

Croissant, Aurel. and Wolfgang Merkel. 2001. 'Political Party Formation in Presidential and Parliamentary Systems'. University of Heidelberg, Institute for Political Science (mimeo).

D'Anieri, Paul. 2007. *Understanding Ukrainian Politics. Power, Politics, and Institutional Design*. Armonk, NY: M.E. Sharpe.

Dahl, Robert A. 1998. *On Democracy*. New Haven and London: Yale University Press.

Dakowska, Dorota. 2005. German Political Foundations: Transnational Party Go-betweens in the Process of EU Enlargement. In *Transnational European Union*, ed. Wolfram Kaiser and Peter Starie, 150-169. London: Routledge Publishers.

D'Anieri, Paul. 2007. *Understanding Ukrainian Politics. Power, Politics, and Institutional Design*. Armonk, NY: M.E. Sharpe.

Dawisha, Karen, and Stephen Deets. 2006. Political Learning in Post-Communist Elections. *East European Politics and Societies* 20 (4): 691-728.

Demeš, Pavol, and Joerg Forbrig. 2007. Civic Action and Democratic Power Shifts: On Strategies and Resources. In *Reclaiming Democracy. Civil Society and Electoral Change in Central and Eastern Europe*, ed. Joerg Forbrig and Pavol Demeš, 175-91. Washington, D.C.: The German Marshall Fund of the United States.

Delsoldato, Giorgia. 2002. Eastward Enlargement by the European Union and Transnational Parties. *International Political Science Review* 23 (3): 269-89.

Devdariani, Jaba. 2004. Georgia: Rise and Fall of the Façade Democracy. *Demokratizatsiya: The Journal of Post-Soviet Democratization* 12 (1): 79-115.

Diamond, Larry. 2002. Thinking About Hybrid Regimes. *Journal of Democracy* 13 (2): 21-35.

_____. 2003. Advancing Democratic Governance: A Global Perspective on the Status of Democracy and Directions for International Assistance. Working draft. Stanford University, Hoover Institution.

Diamond, Larry, and Juan J. Linz .1989. Introduction: Politics, Society, and Democracy in Latin America, in *Democracy in Developing Countries: Latin America*, ed. Larry Diamond, Juan J. Linz, and Seymour M. Lipset, 1-32. Boulder: Lynne Reinner

Dieset, Hans. 2004. Georgia Parliamentary Election 2003. Nordem Report 07/2004.

Dix, Robert H. 1992. Democratization and the Institutionalization of Latin American Political Parties. *Comparative Political Studies* 24 (4): 488-511.

Diuk, Nadia. 2006. The Triumph of Civil Society. in *Revolution in Orange: The Origins of Ukraine's Democratic Breakthrough*, ed. Anders Åslund and Michael McFaul, 69-84. Washington, D.C.: Carnegie Endowment for International Peace.

Doherty, Ivan. 2002. Promoting Democracy in Difficult Settings. Paper presented at CEPPS Roundtable, April 29, Washington, D.C.

Dolidze, Valerian. 2005. Political Parties and Party Development in Georgia. *Central Asia and the Caucasus* 2: 49-59.

Duffy Toft, Monica. 2000. State-Building and National Disunity in Georgia. Paper presented at the annual conference of the Political Studies Association, April 10-13, London, UK.

Duverger, Maurice. 1959. *Political Parties: Their Organisation and Activity in the Modern State.* London: John Wiley.

_____. 1980. A New Political-System Model: Semi-Presidential Government. *European Journal of Political Research* 8 (2): 165-87.

Easterly, William. 2006. Planners vs. Searchers in Foreign Aid. Asian Development Bank Distinguished Speakers Program.

_____. 2008. Introduction: Can't Take It Anymore? in *Reinventing Foreign Aid*, ed. William Easterly, 1-44. Cambridge, MA: The MIT Press.

Eduardo Frei Foundation. 2004. EFF fact finding mission to Georgia 20-23 May 2004. The Hague.

Egger, Miriam. 2006. Die Auslandsarbeit der politischen Stiftungen zwischen Entiwcklungs- und Tansformationskontext: Eine Untersuchung der Tätigkeit der Friedrich-Ebert-Stiftung in Lateinamerika und Osteuropa – Eine Studie zum organisationalen Lernen. PhD diss., Humboldt Universität.

Elgie, Robert. 2005. Variations on a Theme. *Journal of Democracy* 16 (3): 98-112.

Elgstrom, Ole. 2000. Norm negotiations. The construction of new norms regarding gender and development in EU foreign aid policy. *Journal of European Public Policy* 7 (3): 457-76.

Enyedi, Zsolt. 2006. Party Politics in Post-Communist Transition. In *Handbook of Party Politics*, ed. Richard S. Katz, and William Crotty, 228-38. London: Sage Publications.

Erdmann, Gero. 2004. Party research: Western European bias and the 'African labyrinth'. *Democratization* 11 (3): 63-87.

_____. 2006. Internationale Parteienförderung – neue Agenda und ungelöste Probleme? German Institute for Global and Area Studies, GIGA Focus no. 8.

Fairbanks, Charles. H. 2004. Georgia's Rose Revolution. *Journal of Democracy* 15 (2): 110-24.

Federal Ministry for Economic Cooperation and Development. 2002. Richtlinien für die Förderung von Maßnahmen der Gesellschafts- und Strukturpolitik. Bonn/Berlin.

_____. 2005. Promoting democracy in German development policy. Supporting political reform processes and popular participation. A BMZ position paper. Berlin.

Ferrara, Federico, and Erik S. Herron. 2005. Going It Alone? Strategic Entry under Mixed Electoral Rules. *American Journal of Political Science* 49 (1): 16-31.

Fesnic, Florin. and Angelica Ghindar. 2004. Post-Communist Party Systems and the Quality of Democracy. Paper presented at the annual meeting of the American Political Science Association, September 2, in Chicago, IL.

Finkel, Steven E., Aníbal Pérez-Liñán, and Mitchell A. Seligson. 2007. The Effects of U.S. Foreign Assistance on Democracy Building, 1990-2003. *World Politics* 59 (April): 404-39.

Finkel, Steven, Aníbal Pérez-Liñán, Mitchell A. Seligson, and C. Neal Tate. 2006-2007. Democracy Assistance Project Phase II Dataset. http://www.pitt.edu/~politics/democracy/democracy.html (accessed June 18, 2008).

Finnemore, Martha, and Kathryn Sikkink. 1998. 'International Norm Dynamics and Political Change. *International Organization* 52 (4): 887-917.

Fish, M. Steven. 1998. Mongolia: Democracy without Prerequisites.' *Journal of Democracy* 9 (3): 127-41.

_____. 2005. *Democracy Derailed in Russia: The Failure of Open Politics*. Cambridge, MA: Cambridge University Press.

_____. 2006. Stronger Legislatures, Stronger Democracies. *Journal of Democracy* 17 (1): 5-20.

Florini, Ann. 1996. The Evolution of International Norms. *International Studies Quarterly* 40: 363-89.

Formisano, Ronald P. 2000. The Concept of Political Culture. *Journal of Interdisciplinary History* 31 (3): 393-426.

Foweraker, Joe, and Todd Landman. 2002. Constitutional Design and Democratic Performance. *Democratization* 9 (2): 43-66.

Fritz, Verena. 2008. Mongolia: The Rise and Travails of a Deviant Democracy. *Democratization* 15 (4): 766-88.

Frye, Timothy. 1997. A Politics of Institutional Choice: Post-Communist Presidencies. *Comparative Political Studies* 30 (5): 523-52.

Fukuyama, Francis. 1992. *The End of History and the Last Man*. New York: Free Press.

Gandhi, Jennifer, and Adam Przeworski. 2007. Authoritarian Institutions and the Survival of Autocrats. *Comparative Political Studies* 40 (11): 1279-301.

Geddes, Barbara. 1995. A Comparative Perspective on the Leninist Legacy in Eastern Europe. *Comparative Political Studies* 28 (2): 239-74

_____. 2004. Authoritarian Breakdown. Department of Political Science, UCLA, Los Angeles, CA

_____. 2005. Why Parties and Elections in Authoritarian Regimes? Paper presented at the annual meeting of the American Political Science Association, September 1, Washington D.C.

Gel'man, Vladimir. 2006. From 'feckless pluralism' to 'dominant power politics'? The transformation of Russia's party system. *Democratization* 13 (4): 545-61.

_____. 2008. Party Politics in Russia: From Competition to Hierarchy. *Europe-Asia Studies* 60 (6): 913-30.

George, Alexander L., and Andrew Bennett. 2005. *Case Studies and Theory Development in the Social Sciences*. Cambridge, MA: MIT Press

Gerring, John. 2004. 'What Is a Case Study and What Is It Good for? *American Political Science Review* 98 (2): 341-54.

_____. 2007. *Case Study Research: Principles and Practices*. Cambridge, MA: Cambridge University Press.

Gleditsch, Kristian Skrede, and Michael D. Ward. 2006. Diffusion and the International Context of Democratization. *International Organization* 60 (4): 911-33.

Golubitskii, Aleksei. Virtual'naia Dvukhpartiinost'. 2007. http://proua.com/accent/2007/04/19/174054.html (accessed September 19, 2008).

Gorobets, Alexander. 2008. An independent Ukraine: Sustainable or unsustainable development? *Communist and Post-Communist Studies* 41 (2): 93-103

Grabbe, Heather. 2006. *The EU's Transformative Power: Europeanization Through Conditionality in Central and Eastern Europe*. New York, NY: Palgrave Macmillan.

Greene, Kenneth F. 2007. Creating Competition: Patronage Politics and the PRI's Demise. The Kellogg Institute Working Papers, Working Paper no. 345.

Grigorescu, Alexandru. 2002. European Institutions and Unsuccessful Norm
      Transmission: The Case of Transparency. *International Politics* 39: 467-89.

Gunther, Richard, and Larry Diamond. 2001. Types and Functions of Parties. In
      Political Parties and Democracy, ed. Larry Diamond and Richard Gunther,
      3-39. Baltimore, MY: The Johns Hopkins University Press.

_____. 2003. Species of Political Parties: A New Typology. *Party Politics* 9 (2): 167-
      99.

Gutbrod, Hans. 2006. 2006 Data Initiative Survey for Georgia and the South
      Caucasus. Caucasus Research Resource Centers, Tbilisi, Georgia.

Hadenius, Axel, and Jan Teorell. 2007. Pathways from Authoritarianism.' *Journal of*
      Democracy 18 (1): 143-56.

Haerpfer, Christian W. 2008. Support for Democracy and Autocracy in Russia and
      the Commonwealth of Independent States, 1992--2002. *International*
      Political Science Review 29 (4): 411-32.

Hale, Henry E. 2005. *Why Not Parties in Russia?: Democracy, Federalism, and the*
      State. Cambridge, MA: Cambridge University Press.

_____. 2006. Democracy or Autocracy on the March? The Colored Revolutions as
      Normal Dynamics of Patronal Presidentialism. *Communist and Post-*
      Communist Studies 39 (3): 305-29.

_____. 2008. What Makes Dominant Parties Dominant in Hybrid Regimes? The
      Unlikely Importance of Ideas in the Case of United Russia. Paper presented
      at the 2008 Annual Meeting of the American Political Science Association,
      August 28-31, Boston, MA.

Hall, Peter A. 2003. Aligning Ontology and Methodology in Comparative Politics. In
      Comparative Historical Analysis in the Social Sciences Comparative
      Historical Analysis in the Social Sciences, ed. James Mahoney and Dietrich
      Rueschemeyer, 373-406. Cambridge: Cambridge University Press.

Hällhag, Roger. 2008. Political Party Internationals as Guardians of Democracy -
      Their Untapped Potential. *Internationale Politik und Gesellschaft* I: 100-15.

Hanson, Stephen E. 1997. The Leninist Legacy, Institutional Change, and Post-
      Soviet Russia. In *Liberalization and Leninist Legacies: Comparative*
      Perspectives on Democratic Transitions, ed. Beverly Crawford, and Arend
      Lijphart, 228-242. University of California Press/University of California
      International and Area Studies Digital Collection.

Herron, Erik S. 2002. Causes and Consequences of Fluid Faction Membership in
      Ukraine. *Europe-Asia Studies* 54 (4): 625-39.

_____. 2004. 'Political actors, preferences and election rule re-design in Russia and
      Ukraine. *Democratization* 11 (2): 41-59.

Herron, Erik S., and Irakly Mirzashvili. 2005. 'Georgians Cannot Help Being Original': the Evolution of Election Rules in the Republic of Georgia. In *The State of Law in the South Caucasus*, ed. Christopher P. M. Waters. New York: Palgrave Macmillan.

Hershey, Marjorie R. 2006. Political Parties as Mechanisms of Social Choice. In *Handbook of Party Politics.* ed. Richard S. Katz, and William Crotty, 75-88. London: Sage Publications.

Hoffman, Amanda L. 2005. Political parties, electoral systems and democracy: A cross-national analysis. *European Journal of Political Research* 44 (2): 231-42.

Hopf, Ted. 1998. The Promise of Constructivism in International Relations Theory. *International Security* 23: 171-200.

Horowitz, Donald L. 1985. *Ethnic Groups in Conflict.* Berkeley: University of California Press.

_____. 1990. Comparing Democratic Systems. *Journal of Democracy* 1 (4): 73-9.

Howard, Marc M. 2003. *The Weakness of Civil Society in Post-Communist Europe.* Cambridge, MA: Cambridge University Press.

Howard, Marc M., and Philip G. Roessler. 2006. Liberalizing Electoral Outcomes in Competitive Authoritarian Regimes. *American Journal of Political Science* 50 (2): 365-81.

Hrytsak, Yaroslav. 2004. On Relevance and Irrelevance of Nationalism in Ukraine. The Second Annual Cambridge-Stasiuk Lecture on Ukraine. http://www.ukrainiancambridge.org/Images/Hrytsak_Cambridge_English.pdf (accessed September 2, 2007)

Hyde, Susan. 2007. Catch Me if You Can: Why Leaders Invite International Election Monitors and Cheat in Front of Them. Unpublished paper, June 14.

Inglehart, Ronald. 1990. *Culture Shift in Advanced Industrial Society*. Princeton: Princeton University Press.

Inglehart, Ronald, and Christian Welzel. 2005. *Modernization, cultural change, and democracy*. Cambridge, MA: Cambridge University Press.

International Institute for Democracy and Electoral Assistance & Center for Social Studies. 2006. Georgia. Country Report based on Research and Dialogue with Political Parties. Stockholm: IDEA.

International Republican Institute [IRI]. 1998. Republic of Ukraine Program Work Plan January - December 1999. Washington, D.C.

_____. 1999. Republic of Ukraine Program Work Plan: January - December 2000. Washington, D.C.

_____. 2001. Ukraine Work Plan 2002. Washington, D.C.

_____. 2002. Ukraine Work Plan 2003. Washington, D.C.

_____. 2004. Celebrating 20 Years Advancing Democracy Worldwide. 2003 Annual
      Report. Washington, D.C.

_____. 2005a. Annual Report 2004. Washington, D.C.

_____. 2005b. CEPPS/IRI Quarterly Report: April - June 2005. Washington, D.C.

_____. 2005c. CEPPS/IRI Quarterly Report: January - March 2005. Washington,
      D.C.

_____. 2005d. Ukraine Work Plan 2006. Washington, D.C.

_____. 2006. 2005 Annual Report. Washington, D.C.

Innes, Abby. 2002. Party Competition in Postcommunist Europe: The Great
      Electoral Lottery. *Comparative Politics* 35 (1): 85-104.

IRI, USAID, Baltic Surveys / The Gallup Organization, IPM. 2007. Georgian National
      Voter Study.
      http://www.iri.org/eurasia/georgia/pdfs/2007-05-09-Georgia-Poll3.pdf
      (accessed September 3, 2008)

Ishiyama, John T. 1997. Transitional Electoral Systems in Post-Communist Eastern
      Europe. *Political Science Quarterly* 112 (1): 95-115.

Ishiyama, John T., and Ryan Kennedy. 2001. Superpresidentialism and Political
      Party Development in Russia, Ukraine, Armenia and Kyrgyzstan. *Europe-
      Asia Studies* 53 (8): 1177-91.

Jackman, Robert W., and Ross A. Miller. 1996. A Renaissance of Political Culture?
      American Journal of Political Science 40 (3): 632-59.

Jacoby, Wade. 2006. Inspiration, Coalition, and Substitution: External Influences on
      Postcommunist Transformations. *World Politics* 58 (4): 623-51.

Jacoby, Mary, and Glenn R. Simpson. 2008. McCain consultant is tied to work for
      Ukraine party. *Wall Street Journal*, May 14.

Johnson, James. 2003. Conceptual Problems as Obstacles to Progress in Political
      Science: Four Decades of Political Culture Research. *Journal of Theoretical
      Politics* 15 (1): 87-115.

Johnston, Alastair Iain. 2001. Treating International Institutions as Social
      Environments. *International Studies Quarterly* 45 (4): 487-515.

Jones, Stephen F. 2006. The Rose Revolution: A Revolution without
      Revolutionaries? *Cambridge Review of International Affairs* 19 (1): 33-48.

Jowitt, Ken. 1991. The New World Disorder, *Journal of Democracy* 2 (Winter): 11-
      20.

_____. 1992 *New World Disorder: The Leninist Extinction*. Berkeley: University of
      California Press.

Katz, Richard S., and Peter. Mair. 2002. The Ascendancy of the Party in Public Office: Party Organizational Change in Twentieth-Century Democracies. In *Political Parties. Old Concepts and New Challenges,* ed. Richard Gunther, José Ramón Montero, and Juan J. Linz, 113-35. Oxford: Oxford University Press.

Kelley, Judith. 2006. New Wine in Old Wineskins: Promoting Political Reforms through the New European Neighbourhood Policy. *JCMS: Journal of Common Market Studies* 44 (1): 29-55.

_____. 2008. Assessing the Complex Evolution of Norms: The Rise of International Election Monitoring. *International Organization* 62 (Spring): 221-55.

Key, V. O. 1964. *Politics, Parties and Pressure Groups.* 5th edn. New York: Crowell.

Khmara, Irina. 2007. Million dollarov za Manaforta. Na Ukraine rossiiskikh polittehknologov zamenili amerikantsami. *Nezavisimaia Gazeta*, August 22

King, Charles. 2001. Potemkin Democracy: Four Myths about Post-Soviet Georgia. *The National Interest* (Summer): 93-104.

Kitschelt, H. 1995. Party Systems in East Central Europe: Consolidation Or Fluidity? Studies in Public Policy. Glasgow: Center for the Study of Public Policy, University of Strathclyde, no. 241.

_____. 2000. Linkages between Citizens and Politicians in Democratic Polities. *Comparative Political Studies* 33 (6-7): 845-79.

_____. 2001. Divergent Paths of Postcommunist Democracies. In *Political Parties and Democracy,* ed. Larry Diamond and Richard Gunther, 299-326. Baltimore, MY: The Johns Hopkins University Press.

Kitschelt, Herbert, Zdenka Mansfeldová, Radoslaw Markowski and Gábor Tóka. 1999. *Post-Communist Party Systems: Competition, Representation, and Inter-Party Cooperation*. Cambridge, MA: Cambridge University Press.

Kitschelt, Herbert, and Regina Smyth. 2002. Programmatic Party Cohesion in Emerging Postcommunist Democracies: Russia in Comparative Context. *Comparative Political Studies* 35 (10): 1228-56.

Knack, Stephen. 2004. Does Foreign Aid Promote Democracy? *International Studies Quarterly* 48 (1): 251-66.

Konrad Adenauer Stiftung [KAS]. 2007a. KAS Democracy Report 2007. Berlin.

_____. 2007b. Zusammenarbeit der Konrad Adenauer Stiftung mit Organisationen im Umfeld der christlich-demokratischen Partei Chiles. http://www.kas.de/wf/doc/kas_12240-544-4-30.pdf (accessed September 29, 2008).

_____. 2008a. International Parteienzusammenarbeit der KAS. Globales Engagement für Frieden und Demokratie. Berlin.

179

_____. 2008b. Parteien und Parteienkooperation der KAS in Lateinamerika. Berlin

Korasteleva, Elena A. 2000. Electoral Volatility in Postcommunist Belarus: Explaining the Paradox. *Party Politics* 6 (3): 343-58.

Kratochvil, Petr. 2008. The Discursive Resistance to EU-Enticement: The Russian Elite and (the Lack of) Europeanisation. *Europe-Asia Studies* 60 (3): 397-422.

Kubicek, Paul. 1999. End of the Line for the Commonwealth of Independent States. *Problems of Post-Communism* 46 (2):15-24.

_____. 2001. The Limits of Electoral Democracy in Ukraine. *Democratization* 8 (2): 117-39.

Kuenzi, Michelle, and Gina Lambright. 2005. Party Systems and Democratic Consolidation in Africa's Electoral Regimes. *Party Politics* 11 (4): 423-46.

Kulik, Anatoly, and Susanna Pshizova. 2005. *Political Parties in Post-Soviet Space: Russia, Belarus, Ukraine, Moldova, and the Baltics.* Westport CT: Greenwood Publishing Group.

Kumar, Krishna. 2005. Reflections on International Political Party Assistance. *Democratization* 12 (4): 505-27.

Kuzio, Taras. 2001. Transition in Post-Communist States: Triple or Quadruple? *Politics* 21 (3): 168-77.

_____. 2003. The 2002 parliamentary elections in Ukraine: Democratization or authoritarianism? *Journal of Communist Studies and Transition Politics* 19 (2): 24-54.

_____. 2006. Civil society, youth and societal mobilization in democratic revolutions. *Communist and Post-Communist Studies* 39 (3): 365-86.

Laakso, Markku, and Rein Taagepera. 1979. Effective Number of Parties: A Measure with Application to West Europe. *Comparative Political Studies* 12 (1): 3-27.

Ladrech, Robert. 2002. Europeanization and Political Parties: Towards a Framework for Analysis. *Party Politics* 8 (4): 389-403.

Lane, Jan E., and Svante Ersson. 2007. Party System Instability in Europe: Persistent Differences in Volatility between West and East? *Democratization* 14 (1): 92-110.

Lanskoy, Miriam, and Giorgi Areshidze. 2008. Georgia's Year of Turmoil. *Journal of Democracy* 19 (4): 154-68.

Lapins, Wulf. 2007. Demokratieförderung in der Deutschen Aussenpolitik. Friedrich Ebert Stiftung, Berlin.

Law of Republic of Georgia On Political Associations Of Citizens. 1997.

http://www.legislationline.org/legislation.php?tid=222&lid=1966&less=fals e (accessed December 18, 2006).

Law of Ukraine on Political Parties. 2001. http://www.legislationline.org/legislation.php?lid=3804&tid=2 (accessed December 18, 2006).

Legro, Jeffrey W. 1997. Which norms matter? Revisiting the failure of Internationalism. *International Organization* 51 (1): 31-63.

Levitsky, Steven, and Lucan Way. 2002. The Rise of Competitive Authoritarianism. *Journal of Democracy* 13 (2): 51-65.

_____. (forthcoming). *Competitive Authoritarianism: The Emergence and Dynamics of Hybrid Regimes in the Cold-War Era.*

Levy, Jack S. 2007. Qualitative Methods and Cross-Method Dialogue in Political Science. *Comparative Political Studies* 40 (2): 196-214.

Lewis, Paul G. 2006. Party systems in post-communist Central Europe: Patterns of stability and consolidation. *Democratization* 13 (4): 562-83.

Lewis, Paul G., and Zdenka Mansfeldová, ed. 2007. *European Union and Party Politics in Central and Eastern Europe.* New York, NY: Palgrave Macmillan.

Lieven, Anatol. 2001. Georgia: A Failing State? *Eurasia Insight*, January 30. http://www.eurasianet.org/departments/Insight/articles/eav013001.shtml (accessed November 7, 2006)

Lijphart, Arend. 1971. Comparative Politics and the Comparative Method. *American Political Science Review* 65 (3): 682-93.

_____. 1995. *Electoral Systems and Party Systems: A Study of Twenty-seven Democracies, 1945-1990.* Oxford: Oxford University Press.

Linz, Juan J. 1990. The Perils of Presidentialism. *Journal of Democracy* 1 (1): 51-69.

Lipset, Seymour M. 2000. The Indispensability of Political Parties. *Journal of Democracy* 11 (1): 48-55.

Lipset, Seymour M., and Stein Rokkan. 1967. Cleavage Structures, Party Systems, and Voter Alignments: An Introduction. In *Party Systems and Voter Alignments: Cross-National Perspectives*, ed. Seymour M. Lipset and Stein Rokkan, 1-33. New York: Free Press.

Lynch, Tammy. 2007. The Campaign that Could Change Voting Patterns. *The ISCIP Analyst, an Analytical Review* XIV (1)

Magen, Amichai. 2006. Shadow of Enlargement: Can the European Neighbourhood Policy Achieve Compliance? *The Columbia Journal of European Law* 12.

_____. 2009. Evaluating External Influence on Democratic Development: Transition. CDDRL Working Paper no. 111.

Mahoney, James, and Gary Goertz. 2004. The Possibility Principle: Choosing Negative Cases in Comparative Research. *American Political Science Review* 98 (4): 653-69.

Mainwaring, Scott. 1998. Party Systems in the Third Wave. *Journal of Democracy* 9 (3): 67-81.

Mainwaring, Scott, and Timothy R. Scully. 1995. Introduction: Party Systems in Latin America. In *Building Democratic Institutions: Party Systems in Latin America*, ed. S. Mainwaring and T.R. Scully, 1-35. Stanford, CA: Stanford University Press.

Mainwaring, Scott, and Timothy Scully, ed.. 1995. *Building Democratic Institutions: Party Systems in Latin America*. Stanford, CA: Stanford University Press.

Mainwaring, Scott, and Matthew S. Shugart. 1997. Juan Linz, Presidentialism, and Democracy: A Critical Appraisal. *Comparative Politics* 29 (4): 449-71.

Mainwaring, Scott, and Edurne Zoco. 2007. Political Sequences and the Stabilization of Interparty Competition: Electoral Volatility in Old and New Democracies. *Party Politics* 13 (2): 155-178.

Mair, Peter. 2006. Cleavages. In *Handbook of Party Politics.* ed. Richard S. Katz, and William Crotty, 371-5. London: Sage Publications.

Mair, Peter, and Ingrid van Biezen. 2001. Party Membership in Twenty European Democracies, 1980-2000. *Party Politics* 7 (1): 5-21.

March, Luke. 2006. Power and Opposition in the Former Soviet Union: The Communist Parties of Moldova and Russia. *Party Politics* 12 (3): 341-65.

March, James G., and Johan P. Olsen. 1989. *Rediscovering Institutions: The Organizational Basis of Politics*. New York: Free Press.

Markowski, Radoslaw. (2000): Party System Institutionalization and Democratic Consolidation: On the Idiosyncracies of the Polish Case. in *The Second Generation of Democratic Elites in Central and Eastern Europe*. ed. J. Frentzel-Zagórska and J. Wasilewski. Warsaw: Institute of Political Studies, Polish Academy of Sciences.

Massicotte, Louis, and André Blais. 1999. Mixed electoral systems: a conceptual and empirical survey. *Electoral Studies* 18 (3): 341-66.

Matveeva, Anna. 2003. Minorities in the South Caucasus. http://www.unhchr.ch/huridocda/huridoca.nsf/e06a5300f90fa0238025668 700518ca4/070076b3751631cfc1256d250047d982/$FILE/G0314151.pdf (accessed January 19, 2009)

McAllister, Ian, and Stephen White. 2007. Political Parties and Democratic Consolidation in Post-Communist Societies. *Party Politics* 13 (2): 197-216.

McDonagh, Ecaterina. 2008. Is Democracy Promotion Effective in Moldova? The

Impact of European Institutions on Development of Civil and Political Rights in Moldova. *Democratization* 15 (1): 142-161

McFaul, Michael. 2001. Explaining Party Formation and Nonformation in Russia: Actors, Institutions, and Chance. *Comparative Political Studies* 34 (10): 1159-87.

_____. 2004. Democracy Promotion as a World Value. *The Washington Quarterly* 28 (1): 147-63.

_____. 2005. Transitions from Postcommunism. *Journal of Democracy* 16 (3): 5-19.

_____. 2006. Conclusion: The Orange Revolution in a Comparative Perspective in *Revolution in Orange: The Origins of Ukraine's Democratic Breakthrough*, ed. A. Åslund, and M. McFaul, 165-95. Washington, D.C.: Carnegie Endowment for International Peace.

_____. 2007. Ukraine Imports Democracy: External Influences on the Orange Revolution. *International Security* 32 (2): 45-83.

McFaul, Michael, Amichai Magen, and Kathryn Stoner-Weiss. 2007. Evaluating International Influences on Democratic Transitions: Concept Paper. http://iis-db.stanford.edu/res/2278/Evaluating_International_Influences_-_Transitions_-_Concept_Paper.pdf (accessed November 1, 2008).

McGlinchey, Eric. 2007. Aiding Political Parties in Central Asia and the Caucasus. Paper presented at the 48th Annual Convention of the International Studies Association, February 28 - March 3, in Chicago, IL.

McKenna, Ted. 2007. Foreign Political Figures Taking Outreach to US. *PR Week*, March 16.

Meleshevich, Andrey A. 2007. *Party Systems in Post-Soviet Countries. A Comparative Study of Political Institutionalization in the Baltic States, Russia, and Ukraine*. New York: Palgrave Macmillan.

Melia, Thomas O. 2005. The Democracy Bureaucracy. The Infrastructure of American Democracy Promotion. A discussion paper prepared for the Princeton Project on National Security Working Group on Global Institutions and Foreign Policy Infrastructure, September, Georgetown University

Merkel, Wolfgang. 2004. Embedded and defective democracies. *Democratization* 11 (5): 33-58.

Metreveli, Ekaterine, and Ester Hakobyan. 2001. The Political Underpinnings of U.S. Bilateral Aid to the Countries of Transcaucasus. *Demokratizatsiya: The Journal of Post-Soviet Democratization* 9 (3): 367-81.

Miller, Arthur. H., Gwyn Erb, William M. Reisinger, and Vicki L. Hesli. 2000. Emerging Party Systems in Post-Soviet Societies: Fact or Fiction? *Journal of Politics* 62 (2): 455-90.

Miller, Arthur H., and Thomas F. Klobucar. 2003. Partisan Development in Post-Soviet Ukraine. *Journal of Political Marketing* 2 (1): 33-54.

Mitchell, Lincoln A. 2008. *Uncertain Democracy. U.S. Foreign Policy and Georgia's Rose Revolution*. Philadelphia, PA: University of Pennsylvania Press.

Moser, Robert G. 1999. Electoral Systems and the Number of Parties in Postcommunist States. *World Politics* 51 (3): 359-84.

Muller, Edward N., and Mitchell A. Seligson. 1994. Civic culture and democracy: the question of causal relationships. *American political science review* 88 (3): 635-52.

National Democratic Institute for International Affairs [NDI]. 1998. USAID Workplan Georgia January 1 - December 31, 1999. Washington, D.C.

_____. 1999. USAID Final Report. Ukraine Cooperative Agreement No EE-A-97-00016-00 July 1,1997 -June 6, 1999. Washington, D.C.

_____. 2000a. Final Report Georgia. USAID Cooperative Agreement No. EE-A-97-00016-00, July 1, 1997 to July 31, 2000. Washington D.C.

_____. 2000b. USAID Semiannual Report Ukraine January 1 – June 6, 2000. Washington, D.C.

_____. 2000c. USAID Workplan Georgia August 1, 2000 - July 31, 2001. Washington, D.C.

_____. 2001a. A Guide to Political Party Development. Washington, D.C.

_____. 2001b. Political Parties and the Transition to Democracy: a Primer in Democratic Party-Building for Leaders, Organizers and Activists. Washington D.C.

_____. 2001c. USAID Workplan Georgia August 1, 2001 - July 31, 2002. Washington, D.C.

_____. 2002a. CEPPS/NDI Ukraine Quarterly Report October 1-December 31, 2001. Washington, D.C.

_____. 2002b. NDI Quarterly Report: October 1 to December 31, 2001 Georgia. Washington, D.C.

_____. 2002c. Workplan for Georgia USAID Cooperative Agreement No. 114-A-00-00-00081-00, August 1, 2002 - May 31, 2003. Washington D.C.

_____. 2003. Best Practices of Effective Parties: Three Training modules for political parties. Washington, D.C.

_____. 2008a. A Guide to Political Party Development. Washington, D.C.

_____. 2008b. Minimum Standards for the Democratic Functioning of Political
Parties. Washington, D.C.

_____. 2008c. Strengthening Political Parties in Tajikistan. Washington, D.C.

Nayem, Mastafa. 2007. Ukrainskaia Pravda: American Spin Doctors at Rinat
Ahmetov's Service. *Ukrainskaia Pravda*, September 29

Neff Powell, Eleanor, and Joshua A. Tucker. 2008. New Approaches to Electoral
Volatility: Evidence from Postcommunist Countries. Paper presented at the
2008 Annual Meeting of the Midwest Political Science Association, April 3-
6, Chicago, IL.

Nelson, Sue, and Brian Katulis. 2005. Armenia Political Party Assessment.
Washington,
D.C.: United States Agency for International Development

Netherlands Institute for Multiparty Democracy. 2004. A Framework for Democratic
Party-Building. The Hague

Nix, Steven B. 2005. Remarks by Steven B. Nix, Regional Program Director Eurasia,
International Republican Institute At The Heritage Foundation's Helping
Ukraine to Reach the Safe Shore, January 27.
http://www.iri.org/eurasia/ukraine/pdfs/2005-01-27-
Steve%20Remarks.pdf (accessed February 12, 2009)

Nodia, Ghia. 2003. Political Parties in Georgia. in *Building Democracy in Georgia.
Developing a Democratic Community in Georgia*. Discussion Paper 7.
Stockholm: IDEA

_____. 2009. Georgian President's Record Mixed When Judged Against Ambitious
Goals. RFE/RL Commentary.
http://www.rferl.org/Content/Georgian_Presidents_Record_Mixed_When_J
udged_Against_Ambitious_Goals/1374287.html (accessed February 19,
2009)

Nodia, Ghia, and Álvaro Pinto Scholtbach. 2006. *The Political Landscape of Georgia*.
Delft: Eburon Academic Publishers.

Norris, Pippa. 2008. *Driving Democracy: Do Power-Sharing Regimes Work?*
Cambridge, MA: Cambridge University Press.

ODIHR-IMD-CIPDD. 2006. ODIHR-IMD-CIPDD Programme 2006-2008 Political
Institutions in Georgia. Description of the Programme for 2006/2007.
http://partiebi.ge/?l=1&i=19 (accessed February 8, 2009)

O'Donnell, Guillermo. 1994. Delegative Democracy. *Journal of Democracy* 5 (1):
55-69.

Offe, Claus. 2004. Capitalism by Democratic Design? Democratic Theory Facing the Triple Transition in East Central Europe. *Social Research: An International Quarterly of Social Sciences* 71 (3): 501-28.

OSCE Office for Democratic Institutions and Human Rights. 2006. Annual Report 2005. Warsaw

_____. 2007. Annual Report 2006. Warsaw

Owen, John M. 1994. How Liberalism Produces Democratic Peace. *International Security* 19 (2): 87-125.

Page, Jeremy. 2006. Revolution is reversed with a little Spin from the West. *The Times*, March 26.

Panina, Natalya. 2005. *Ukrainian Society 1994-2005: Sociological Monitoring*. Kyiv: Institute of Sociology, National Academy of Sciences of Ukraine, Democratic Initiatives Foundation.

Papava, Vladimer, and Michael Tokmazishvili. 2006. Becoming European. Georgia's Strategy for Joining the EU. *Problems of Post-Communism* 53 (1): 26–32.

Pedersen, Mogens N. 1983. Changing patterns of electoral volatility in European party systems, 1948-1977: Explorations in explanation. In *Western European party systems: Continuity and change*, ed. Hans Daalder & Peter Mair, 29-66. London: SAGE Publications.

Perlin, George. 2003. International Assistance to Democratic Development: A Review. IRPP Working Paper Series no.2003-04.

Peterson, M. J. 1992. Whales, Cetologists, Environmentalists, and the International Management of Whaling. *International Organization* 46 (1): 147-86.

Petrov, Nikolai, and Andrei Ryabov. 2006. Russia's Role in the Orange Revolution. In *Revolution in Orange: The Origins of Ukraine's Democratic Breakthrough*, ed. Anders Åslund and Michael McFaul, 145-164. Washington: Carnegie Endowment for International Peace.

Pickering, Jeffrey, and Mark Peceny. 2006. Forging Democracy at Gunpoint. *International Studies Quarterly* 50 (3): 539-60.

Pifer, Steven. 2007. European Mediators and Ukraine's Orange Revolution. *Problems of Post-Communism* 54 (6): 28-42.

Pleines, Heiko. 2008. Manipulating Politics: Domestic Investors in Ukrainian Privatisation Auctions 2000-2004. *Europe-Asia Studies* 60 (7): 1177-97

Pogorelskaja, Swetlana W. 2002. Die parteinahen Stiftungen als Akteure und Instrumente der deutschen Aussenpolitik. *Aus Politik und Zeitgeschichte* B 6-7: 29-38.

Pop-Eleches, Grigore. 2007. Historical Legacies and Post-Communist Regime Change. *The Journal of Politics* 69 (4): 908-26.

Powell, Bingham. 1982. *Contemporary democracies: Participation, stability, and violence*. Cambridge, MA: Harvard University Press.

Power, Greg. 2008. Donor support to parliaments and political parties: An analysis prepared for DANIDA.

Price, Richard. 1998. Reversing the Gunsights: Transnational Civil Society Targets Landmines. *International Organization* 52: 613-644.

Price, Richard, and Christian Reus-Smit. 1998. Dangerous Liaisons?: Critical International Theory and Constructivism. *European Journal of International Relations* 4 (3): 259-294.

Pridham, Geoffrey. 1991. International Influences and Democratic Transition: Problems of Theory and Practice in Linkage Politics. In *Encouraging Democracy: The International Context of Regime Transition in Southern Europe*, ed. Geoffrey Pridham. New York: St. Martin Press

Prizel, Ilya. 2002. Ukraine's Hollow Decade. *East European Politics and Societies* 16 (2): 363-85.

Protsyk, Oleh. 2002. Campaign and Party Finance in Ukraine: Dilemmas of Regulation in the Context of Weakly Institutionalized Political and Legal Systems. International Foundation for Election Systems (IFES) Report, Washington, DC.

_____. 2003. Troubled Semi-Presidentialism: Stability of the Constitutional System and Cabinet in Ukraine. *Europe-Asia Studies* 55 (7): 1077-95.

Puddington, Arch. 2009. Freedom in the World 2009. Setbacks and Resilience. http://www.freedomhouse.org/uploads/fiw09/FIW09_OverviewEssay_Final .pdf (accessed February 19, 2009)

Puglisi, Rosaria. 2003. The rise of the Ukrainian oligarchs. *Democratization* 10 (3): 99-123.

Putnam, Robert D. 1993. *Making Democracy Work: Civic Traditions in Modern Italy*. Princeton: Princeton University Press.

Randall, Vicky. 2007. Political Parties and Democratic Developmental States. *Development Policy Review* 25 (5): 633-52.

Remmer, Karen L. 2008. The Politics of Institutional Change. Electoral Reform in Latin America 1978-2002. *Party Politics* 14 (1): 5-30.

Resende, Madalena, and Hendrik Kraetzschmar. 2005. Parties of Power as Roadblocks to Democracy: The Cases of Ukraine and Egypt. In *Democratisation in the European Neighbourhood*, ed. Michael Emerson, 153-67. Brussels: Centre for European Policy Studies.

Riabchuk, Mykola. 2008. Ukraine: Lessons Learned from Other Postcommunist Transitions. *Orbis* (Winter 2008): 41-64.

187

Richards, David. 1996. Elite Interviewing: Approaches and Pitfalls. *Politics* 16 (3): 199-204.

Risse, Thomas. 1999. International Norms and Domestic Change: Arguing and Communicative Behavior in the Human Rights Area. *Politics and Society* 27: 529-60.

_____. 2003. Let's Argue!: Communicative Action in World Politics. *International Organization* 54 (01): 1-39.

Risse-Kappen, Thomas, Stephen C. Ropp, and Kathryn Sikkink. 1999. *The Power of Human Rights: International Norms and Domestic Change*. Cambridge, MA: Cambridge University Press.

Rivera, S. W., P. M. Kozyreva, and E. G. Sarovskii. 2003. Interviewing Political Elites: Lessons from Russia. *PS: Political Science and Politics* 35 (4): 683-8.

Roberts, Sean R. 2001. Evaluation of the National Democratic Institute (NDI) in Kyrgyzstan, February 23- March 10, 2001. Washington, D.C.

Roeder, Philip G. 1999. Peoples and States after 1989: The Political Costs of Incomplete National Revolutions. *Slavic Review* 58 (4): 854-82.

Roessler, Philip G., and Marc M. Howard. 2007. Measuring and Analyzing Post-Cold War Political Regimes. Paper presented at the 2007 Annual Meeting of the American Political Science Association, August 30-September 2, in Chicago, IL.

Romaniuk, Anatolii, and Yurii Shveda. 2005. *Partii ta Elektoralna Politika*. Lviv: Astrolyabiya.

Rustow, Dankwart. 1970. Transitions to Democracy. *Comparative Politics* 2 (3): 337-63.

Samuels, David J. 2002. Presidentialized Parties: The Separation of Powers and Party Organization and Behavior. *Comparative Political Studies* 35 (4): 461-83.

Sanchez, Omar. 2008a. Party Non-Systems: A Conceptual Innovation. Paper presented at the annual meeting of the MPSA Annual National Conference, April 3, Chicago, IL.

_____. 2008b. Transformation and Decay: the De-Institutionalisation of Party Systems in South America. *Third World Quarterly* 29 (2): 315-37.

Sapsford, Roger, and Pamela Abbott. 2006. Trust, confidence and social environment in post-communist societies. *Communist and Post-Communist Studies* 39 (1): 59-71.

Sartori, Giovanni. 1976. *Parties and party systems*. New York: Cambridge University Press.

_____. 1991. Comparing and Miscomparing. *Journal of Theoretical Politics* 3 (3): 243-57.

_____. 1997. *Comparative Constitutional Engineering: An Inquiry Into Structures, Incentives, and Outcomes.* New York: NYU Press.

Sasse, Gwendolyn. 2001. 'The New Ukraine: A State of Regions', *Regional and Federal Studies* 11 (3): 69-100

Saxer, Marc. 2006a. Die Förderung politischer Parteien in der internationalen Demokratieförderung der Friedrich-Ebert-Stiftung. Mimeo, Berlin.

_____. 2006b. Parteiförderung als Element der Demokratieförderung. Mimeo, Berlin.

Scarrow, Susan E., Paul Webb, and David M. Farrell. 2000. From Social Integration to Electoral Contestation: The Changing Distribution of Power within Political Parties. In *Parties without Partisans: Political Change in Advanced Industrial Democracies.* ed. Russell J. Dalton and Martin P. Wattenberg, 102-28. Oxford: Oxford University Press.

Schattschneider, Elmer Eric. 1942. *Political Parties.* New York: Holt, Riehart, and Winston.

Schedler, Andreas. 2002. The Nested Game of Democratization by Elections. *International Political Science Review* 23 (1): 103-22.

_____. 2004. Degrees and Patterns of Party Competition in Electoral Autocracies. Paper presented at the annual meeting of the American Political Science Association, September 2, in Chicago, IL.

Schedler, Andreas, ed. 2006. *Electoral Authoritarianism: The Dynamics of Unfree Competition.* Boulder: Lynne Rienner.

Schimmelfennig, Frank. 2005. The International Promotion of Political Norms in Eastern Europe: a Qualitative Comparative Analysis. Working Paper available at: http://www.ces.fas.harvard.edu/publications/docs/pdfs/Schimmelfennig.pd f (accessed 17 March 2008)

_____. 2007. European Regional Organizations, Political Conditionality, and Democratic Transformation in Eastern Europe. *East European Politics and Societies* 21 (1): 126-141.

Schimmelfennig, Frank, and Ulrich Sedelmeier. 2004. Governance by conditionality: EU rule transfer to the candidate countries of Central and Eastern Europe. *Journal of European Public Policy* 11 (4): 661-79.

Schmitter, Phillipe. 1986. An Introduction to Southern European Transitions from Authoritarian Rule: Italy, Greece, Portugal, Spain, and Turkey. In *Transitions from Authoritarian Rule: Southern Europe,* ed. Guillermo

O'Donnell, Philippe Schmitter, and Laurence Whitehead, 3-10. Baltimore, MD: Johns Hopkins University Press.

Schmitter, Philippe C., and Imco Brouwer. 1999. Conceptualizing, Researching and Evaluating Democracy Promotion and Protection. EUI Working Paper SPS No. 99/9.

Schmitz, Hans Peter. 2004. Domestic and Transnational Perspectives on Democratization. *International Studies Review* 6 (3): 403-26.

Schraeder, Peter J. 2003. The State of the Art in International Democracy Promotion: Results of a Joint European-North American Research Network. *Democratization* 10 (2): 21-44.

Shabad, Goldie, and Kazimierz M. Slomczynski. 2004. Inter-Party Mobility among Parliamentary Candidates in Post-Communist East Central Europe. *Party Politics* 10 (2): 151-76.

Shugart, Matthew S. 1998. The Inverse Relationship Between Party Strength and Executive Strength: A Theory of Politicians' Constitutional Choices. *British Journal of Political Science* 28 (1): 1-29.

_____. 2005. Semi-Presidential Systems: Dual Executive and Mixed Authority Patterns. Graduate School of International Relations and Pacific Studies, University of California, San Diego. Working Papers

_____. 2006. Comparative Executive-Legislative Relations. In *The Oxford Handbook of Political Institutions*. ed. R.A.W. Rhodes, Sarah B. Binder, and Bert A. Rockman, 344-65. Oxford: Oxford University Press.

Shugart, Matthew S., and John M. Carey. 1992. *Presidents and Assemblies: Constitutional Design and Electoral Dynamics.* Cambridge, MA: Cambridge University Press.

Shugart, Matthew S., and Martin P. Wattenberg. 2001. *Mixed-Member Electoral Systems: The Best of Both Worlds?* Oxford: Oxford University Press.

Shulman, Stephen. 2004. The contours of civic and ethnic national identification in Ukraine. *Europe-Asia Studies* 56 (1): 35-56.

Siaroff, Alan. 2005. *Comparing Political Regimes: A Thematic Introduction To Comparative Politics.* Toronto: Broadview Press.

Siegle, Joseph T., Michael M. Weinstein, and Morton H. Halperin. 2004. Why Democracies Excel. *Foreign Affairs* 83 (5): 57-71.

Silitski, Vitali. 2004. Preempting Democracy: The Case of Belarus. *Journal of Democracy* 16 (4): 83-97.

_____. 2007. Belarus and Russia: Comradeship-In-Arms in Preempting Democracy. http://www.strategicstudiesInstitute.army.mil/pdffiles/PUB781.pdf (accessed November 29, 2008)

Slomczynski, Kazimierz M., Goldie Shabad, and Jakub Zielinski. 2008. Fluid Party Systems, Electoral Rules and Accountability of Legislators in Emerging Democracies: The Case of Ukraine. *Party Politics* 14 (1): 91-112.

Smyth, Regina, Anna Lowry, and Brandon Wilkening. 2007. Engineering Victory: Institutional Reform, Informal Institutions, and the Formation of a Hegemonic Party Regime in the Russian Federation. *Post Soviet Affairs* 23 (2): 118-37.

Stepan, Alfred. 2005. Ukraine: Improbable Democratic Nation-State But Possible Democratic State-Nation? *Post Soviet Affairs* 21 (4): 279-308.

Stockton, Hans. 2001. Political Parties, Party Systems, and Democracy in East Asia: Lessons From Latin America. *Comparative Political Studies* 34 (1): 94-119.

Strom, Kaare. 1990. A Behavioral Theory of Competitive Political Parties. *American Journal of Political Science* 34 (2): 565-98.

Sushko, Oleksandr. 2002. The 2002 Parliamentary Elections as an Indicator of the Sociopolitical Development of Ukraine *Demokratizatsiya: The Journal of Post-Soviet Democratization* 10 (4): 568-76.

Sushko, Oleksandr, and Olena Prystayko. 2006. Western Influence. In *Revolution in Orange: The Origins of Ukraine's Democratic Breakthrough*, ed. Anders Åslund and Michael McFaul, 125-44. Washington, D.C.: Carnegie Endowment for International Peace.

Szporluk, Roman. 2000. *Russia, Ukraine, and the Breakup of the Soviet Union.* Stanford: Hoover Institution Press.

Tansey, Oisín. 2007. Process Tracing and Elite Interviewing: A Case for Non-probability Sampling. *PS: Political Science and Politics* 40 (4): 765-72.

Tarkhan-Mouravi, Giorgi. 2006. Politicheskie Partii v Gruzii. Zatiunuvsheesia Stanovlenie. *Political Science Quarterly* 1: 243-267

Tarnoff, Curt. 2003. The Former Soviet Union and U.S. Foreign Assistance. CRS Issue Brief for Congress

_____. 2007. U.S. Assistance to the Former Soviet Union. CRS Report for Congress

Tavits, Margit. 2005. The Development of Stable Party Support: Electoral Dynamics in Post-Communist Europe. *American Journal of Political Science* 49 (2): 283-98.

____. 2008a. On the linkage between electoral volatility and party system instability in Central and Eastern Europe. *European Journal of Political Research* 47 (5): 537-55.

_____. 2008b. Policy Positions, Issue Importance, and Party Competition in New Democracies. *Comparative Political Studies* 41 (1): 48-72.

191

Thames, Frank C. 2007. Discipline and Party Institutionalization in Post-Soviet
Legislatures. *Party Politics* 13 (4): 456-77.

Thames, Frank C., and Joseph W. Robbins. 2007. Party System Institutionalization
and the Level of Democracy. Paper Presented at the Annual Meeting of the
American Political Science Association, August 29 - September 1, 2007, in
Chicago, IL.

Tóka, Gábor. 1997. Political parties and democratic consolidation in East Central
Europe. Glasgow: University of Strathclyde, Working Paper no. 279.

Toole, James. 2003. Straddling the East-West Divide: Party Organisation and
Communist Legacies in East Central Europe. *Europe-Asia Studies* 55 (1):
101-18.

_____. 2007. The historical foundations of party politics in post-communist East
Central Europe. *Europe-Asia Studies* 59 (4): 541-66.

Topolianskyi, Aleksandr. 2009. Nukonets. Partiia Yushchenko tikho umiraet.
http://www.intv-inter.net/ru/news/article/?id=57761747 (accessed March
3, 2009)

Ufen, Andreas. 2007. Political Party and Party System Institutionalisation in
Southeast Asia: A Comparison of Indonesia, the Philippines, and Thailand.
German Institute of Global and Area Studies, GIGA Working Papers no. 44.

United States Agency for International Development [USAID]. 1996. United States
Strategic Development Plan for Georgia FY 1996-2000. Washington, D.C.

_____. 1999a. Georgia. Strategic Plan 2000-2003. Washington, D.C.

_____. 1999b. Political Party Development Assistance. Technical Publication Series.
Washington, D.C.

_____. 2000. Managing Assistance in Support of Political and Electoral Processes.
Washington, D.C.

_____. 2002. Results Review and Resource Request. Washington, D.C.

_____. 2003a. Annual Report FY 2003 Ukraine. Washington, D.C.

_____. 2003b. USAID Political Party Assistance Policy. Washington, D.C.

_____. 2005. Democracy Rising. Grassroot Revolutions. Washington, D.C.

_____. 2006a. Final Project Report. Support to the new Government of Georgia.
Washington, D.C.

_____. 2006b. OECD/DAC Peer Review of the United States. Washington, D.C.

_____. 2006c. Operational Plan FY 2006. Washington, D.C.

_____. 2006d. User's Guide to DG Programming. Washington, D.C.

_____. 2007. A Study of Political Party Assistance in Eastern Europe and Eurasia.
Washington, D.C.

Usupashvili, David. 2004. An Analysis of the Presidential and Parliamentary Elections in Georgia: A Case Study, November 2003–March 2004. In *Election Assessment in the South Caucasus*, 75-100. Stockholm: IDEA.

Vachudova, Milada. 2002. The Leverage of the European Union on Reform in Postcommunist Europe. Paper presented at Workshop 4 Enlargement and European Governance of ECPR Joint Session Workshops, March 22-27, in Turin, Italy.

Van Biezen, Ingrid. 2004. How Political Parties Shape Democracy. Center for the Study of Democracy, Working Paper 04-16, University of California, Irvine.

_____. 2005. On the theory and practice of party formation and adaptation in new democracies. *European Journal of Political Research* 44 (1): 147-74.

Van Evera, Stephen. 1997. *Guide to Methods for Students of Political Science.* Cornell: Cornell University Press.

Van de Walle, Nicolas. 2003. Presidentialism and clientelism in Africa's emerging party systems. *The Journal of Modern African Studies* 41 (2): 297-321.

Van Zon, Hans. 2001. Neo-Patrimonialism as an Impediment to Economic Development: The Case of Ukraine. *The Journal of Communist Studies and Transition Politics* 17 (3): 71-95.

Verheije, Marga, André Krouwel, Dessy Gavrilova, and Theo van Koolwijk. 2006. Van partij naar partij: Nederlandse ondersteuning van politieke partijen in Europese landen in transitie. Evaluatie Matra Politieke Partijen Programma 2000-2005. Wormerveer.

Voitsekhovskii, Sergei. 2006. Amerikanskie polittekhnologi na sluzhbe u SDPU(o), Regionov i Pory? http://glavred.info/archive/2006/01/18/181126-6.html (accessed October 18, 2008)

Wachsmuth, Ralf. 2006. Ukraine. In *Parteienzusammenarbeit der KAS in Mittel-, Ost- und Südosteuropa*. ed. Peter Fischer-Bollin, 66-9. Berlin: Konrad-Adenauer-Stiftung e.V.

Walecki, Marcin, and Oleh Protsyk. 2007 Party Funding in Ukraine. In *Political finance and corruption in Eastern Europe. The transition period*, ed. Daniel Smilov and Jurij Toplak, 189-208. Aldershot: Ashgate.

Ware, Alan. 1996. *Political parties and party systems.* New York: Oxford University Press.

Way, Lucan. 2005. Kuchma's Failed Authoritarianism. *Journal of Democracy* 16 (2): 131-45.

_____. 2008. The Real Causes of the Color Revolutions. *Journal of Democracy* 19 (3): 55-69.

Webb, Paul, and Stephen White. 2007. Political Parties in New Democracies: Trajectories of Development and Implications for Democracy. In *Party Politics in New Democracies*, ed. Paul Webb and Stephen White, 1-20. Oxford: Oxford University Press.

Wejnert, Barbara. 2005. Diffusion, Development, and Democracy, 1800-1999. *American Sociological Review* 70 (1): 53-81.

Wheatley, Jonathan. 2005. *Georgia from National Awakening to Rose Revolution: Delayed Transition in the Former Soviet Union.* Aldershot: Ashgate Publishing, Ltd.

Whitefield, Stephen. 2002. Political Cleavages and Post-Communist Politics. *Annual Review of Political Science* 5 (1): 181-200.

Whitehead, Laurence. 1996. 'Concerning International Support for Democracy in the South'. In *Democratization in the South. The Jagged Wave*, ed. Robin Luckham and Gordon White, 243-73. Manchester: Manchester University Press

Wilson, Andrew. 2001. Ukraine's New Virtual Politics. *East European Constitutional Review* 10 (2/3).

_____. 2002a. Elements of a theory of Ukrainian ethno-national identities. *Nations and Nationalism* 8 (1): 31-54.

_____. 2002b. Ukraine's 2002 Elections: Less Fraud, More Virtuality. *East European Constitutional Review* 11 (3): 91-8.

_____. 2006. Ukraine's Orange Revolution, NGOs and the Role of the West. *Cambridge Review of International Affairs* 19 (1): 21-32.

Wilson, Andrew, and Artur Bilous. 1993. Political Parties in Ukraine. *Europe-Asia Studies* 45 (4): 693-703.

Wilson, Andrew, and Sarah Birch. 2007. Political Parties in Ukraine. Virtual and Representational. In *Political Parties in New Democracies. Trajectories of Development and Implications for Democracy*, ed. Paul Webb and Stephen White, 53-84. Oxford: Oxford University Press.

Wolinetz, Steven B. 2002. Beyond the Catch-All Party: Approaches to the Study of Parties and Party Organization in Contemporary Democracies. In *Political Parties. Old Concepts and New Challenges*, ed. Richard Gunther, José Ramón Montero, and Juan J. Linz, 136-65. Oxford: Oxford University Press.

_____. 2006. Party System Institutionalization: Bringing the System Back In. Paper presented at the Annual Meeting of the Canadian Political Science Association, May 29-June 1, in Saskatoon.

World Bank. 2004. World Development Report 2004: Making Services Work For

Poor People. Washington, D.C.

Yakimenko, Yurii, and Igor Zhdanov. 2003. Novye gorizonty ukrainskoy
        mnogopartiynosti. *Zerkalo Nedeli* 24

Youngs, Richard. 2006. Ukraine. In *Strategies for Democratic Change. Assessing
        the Global Response* ed. Ted Piccone and Richard Youngs, 97-121.
        Washington D.C.: Democracy Coalition Project

_____. 2008. A Door Neither Closed Nor Open: Europe's Inconsistent Support for
        Democratic Reform in Ukraine. http://www.ucd.ie/dei/wp/WP_08-
        5_Richard_Youngs.pdf (accessed December 12, 2008)

Zimmer, Kerstin. 2003. Khozyaistvenniki and Political Machines in Donetsk:
        Economic and Political Regionalism in Ukraine. ECPR Conference 2003,
        Marburg, Germany, September 18-21.

ABSTRACT

International assistance to political parties has been continuously carried out in Georgia and Ukraine for almost all of the post-communist period, as in most other post-communist states, and as part of a broader policy of democracy promotion. Despite this sustained effort, parties in Georgia and Ukraine have remained far removed from the type of stable, democratic, and representative organization that is commonly aimed for by party assistance. This thesis asks why party assistance during the second decade of multi-party politics in Georgia and Ukraine has failed to exert a bigger positive impact on parties. In search of an answer, the thesis looks at both the input of the assistance (the international dimension) and domestic constraints on the development of stable and democratic parties (the domestic dimension). In relation to the input of assistance the thesis identifies a 'party assistance norm' that is shared between the main providers of assistance, and accordingly conceptualizes party assistance as a type of norm promotion. It is then argued that there are inherent qualities to the 'party assistance norm' which contribute to limit its impact, including a lack of determinacy and moral urgency, a cognitive and ideational distance between providers and recipients of assistance, and incompatibility with the incentives to which parties are often exposed. Regarding the domestic dimension, two constraints on stable and democratic party development which in particular have undercut the effectiveness of party assistance are highlighted: first, a high degree of volatility in party politics, resulting in large part from institutional arrangements and the 'elite ownership' of parties; and second, the impact on party development of a (often) less-than-democratic political context, reflected mainly in the existence of regime-initiated parties which distort the electoral playing field. As a consequence of these constraints on party development, most relevant parties that were eligible to receive party assistance were in fact unsuitable recipients: they were either unlikely to survive long, or their operation was driven by incentives which were incompatible with the values that party assistance sought to infuse into party politics, or both. The practice of party assistance in Georgia and Ukraine moreover reveals that providers of assistance were generally powerless against the domestic constraints on party development, due in large part to standards of party selection to which assistance has to adhere. Only if party assistance had adopted a highly unconventional approach that would have violated the prevalent standards of party selection, would party assistance perhaps have generated more effect. The existence of the domestic constraints on party development therefore has practically presented a sufficient condition for the failure of party assistance. Given that these constraints on party development are also found in many other recipient countries, it appears plausible that the account offered in this thesis can be extended to other cases.

Samenvatting

Internationale hulp aan politieke partijen is in Georgië en Oekraïne gedurende bijna de gehele postcommunistisch periode onafgebroken aangeboden, zoals in de meeste voormalige communistische staten, en als onderdeel van een breder democratiebevorderingsbeleid. Ondanks deze aanhoudende inspanning staan partijen in Georgië en Oekraïne als voorheen ver af van het type stabiele, democratische, en representatieve organisatie waaraan hulp aan politieke partijen probeert bij te dragen. In dit proefschrift wordt de vraag gesteld waarom hulp aan partijen gedurende het tweede decennium van de ontwikkeling van een meerpartijenstelsel in Georgië en Oekraïne niet een grotere impact heeft gehad op partijen. Om deze vraag te beantwoorden neemt het proefschrift zowel de input van de hulp aan partijen (de internationale dimensie) als binnenlandse beperkingen aan partijenontwikkeling (de binnenlandse dimensie) in ogenschouw. In relatie tot de input van de hulp aan partijen stelt het proefschrift het bestaan vast van een 'norm' in de hulp aan partijen die wordt gedeeld door de voornaamste aanbieders ervan, en in aansluiting stelt het hulp aan partijen voor als een vorm van normbevordering. Vervolgens wordt bepleit dat de norm in de hulp aan partijen gekenmerkt wordt door een aantal inherente eigenschappen die de impact van de norm beperken. Deze eigenschappen zijn onder andere een gebrek aan duidelijkheid en morele urgentie, cognitieve en ideële distantie tussen de aanbieders en ontvangers van de hulp, en onverenigbaarheid met de prikkels waaraan partijen dikwijls blootstaan. Met betrekking tot de binnenlandse dimensie wordt de nadruk gelegd op twee beperkingen op de ontwikkeling van stabiele en democratische partijen die in het bijzonder de effectiviteit van de hulp aan partijen hebben ondergraven: ten eerste, een hoge mate van volatiliteit, die voor een groot deel het resultaat is van institutionele schikkingen en van het gegeven dat partijen in de regel worden beheerst door hun leiders; ten tweede, de impact op partijenontwikkeling van een (vaak) minder-dan-democratische politieke context, weerspiegeld in het bestaan van door het regime geïnitieerde partijen die het electorale speelveld verstoren. Als gevolg van deze beperkingen op partijenontwikkeling waren de meeste relevante partijen die ervoor in aanmerking kwamen hulp te ontvangen in feite als zodanig ongeschikt: óf deze partijen zouden waarschijnlijk niet lang bestaan, óf hun activiteit werd gedreven door prikkels die onverenigbaar zijn met de waarden die de aanbieders van hulp aan partijen in de partijpolitiek probeerden te brengen, óf allebei. De praktijk van hulp aan partijen in Georgië en Oekraïne laat bovendien zien dat de aanbieders van de hulp over het algemeen geen antwoord hadden op de beperkingen op partijenontwikkeling, voor een groot deel als het gevolg van het bestaan van standaarden bij de selectie van partijen (in de hulp aan partijen) waaraan de aanbieders moeten voldoen. Alleen als de hulp aan partijen voor een zeer onconventionele benadering had gekozen waarbij men zich niet zou hebben gehouden aan de standaarden van selectie van partijen, zou hulp aan partijen mogelijk meer effect hebben gehad. Het bestaan van de beperkingen op partijenontwikkeling is derhalve in praktische zin een toereikende voorwaarde geweest voor het falen van de hulp aan partijen. Aangezien deze beperkingen op partijenontwikkeling ook aanwezig zijn in veel andere landen waar hulp aan partijen wordt aangeboden, lijkt het aannemelijk dat de bevindingen van dit proefschrift ook elders toepasbaar zijn.

For Product Safety Concerns and Information please contact our EU
representative GPSR@taylorandfrancis.com
Taylor & Francis Verlag GmbH, Kaufingerstraße 24, 80331 München, Germany

9 789056 296315